Human Relations
and
Police Work
Second Edition

Larry S. Miller
Michael C. Braswell
East Tennessee State University

WAVELAND
PRESS, INC.

Prospect Heights, Illinois

For information about this book, write or call:

Waveland Press, Inc.
P.O. Box 400
Prospect Heights, Illinois 60070
(708) 634-0081

Copyright © 1988, 1983 by Waveland Press, Inc.

ISBN 0-88133-292-5

Printed in the United States of America

8   7   6   5

Acknowledgements

Many students and professional colleagues in academic and agency settings provided valuable input regarding the development of this book. Of special mention are James S. Fann and J. Méchelle Roach for their research efforts.

We are especially indebted to the following professors who responded to our survey for input on this second edition: Geoff Alpert, Kay Barchas, Paul DeLauder, Martin S. Devers, Mary Green, Paul Lahance, Sam Latimore, Raymond E. Lloyd, II, D.A. Miller, Leonard S. Moore, James J. Nees, Laura Otten, John P. Sargent, Pat Sullivan, Jonathan White.

Contents

Section II
Family and Crisis Intervention

Section III
The Police and Juveniles

Contents

Section IV
The Police and the Emotionally Disturbed 75

Section VII
Police Administration and Supervision.............................. 155

A newly appointed Chief finds himself having to be an
administrator rather than just one of the officers.
An older Chief of Police nearing retirement is faced with
taking an easy way out or fighting to straighten out his
problem-laden department.
A city council complains to the Chief of Police that his
officers are overweight and out-of-shape.

Introduction

The intention of this book is to provide persons with the opportunity to identify with the various roles of a law enforcement officer. The reader is placed in common law enforcement and police situations and is expected to make a decision based on his or her best judgement. The roles range from police patrol officer to Chief; from small-town police departments to metropolitan police agencies. The reader should try to remember that police rank, department type, and State law may influence the situations presented. In cases where State law may have a bearing on the outcome of a given situation, the reader should attempt to apply his or her own State law.

The book attempts to emphasize the learning aspects of both role playing and identification, and problem solving. No answers are necessarily wrong or right. It is hoped that each case will provide the impetus for open discussion concerning the situations presented as well as other similar situations encountered daily in the police and law enforcement profession.

It is the authors' hope that this book will be viewed as a collection of examples of common and not so common occurences in police work which require an action or response by the individual officer. In this way, the reader can become the decision maker and can rely on his or her own personality, experience, knowledge, and common sense in order to alleviate the problems presented. The reader will be asked to make decisions regarding case situations by responding to several questions located at the end of each case. The reader will also have the opportunity to discuss how the police officer handled the situation and if the situation could have been treated differently by the officer. It should be noted that a procedure followed by an individual officer in one of the case situations may have presented a problem in itself.

The book is divided into seven sections. Each section deals with a particular area of concern to law enforcement officers. The reader should note that there may be some overlapping of section topics. For instance, the section dealing with Police-Community Relations may also contain problems which concern the topics of the section dealing with Police and Juveniles, and so on.

At the end of each section is a Selected Bibliography of publications directly relating to the section topic. It is suggested that the reader complete each section by reading, answering, and discussing the questions presented for the cases and then review the literature from the Selected Bibliography or other related publications. The reader may then determine if his or her solutions and decisions represent the preferred course of action for a given case.

Finally, it is the intention of this book to show that there are no two situations alike in police work. Each situation calls for a fresh and creative approach. In short, law enforcement and police work is not a simple black and white process, but consists of an endless variety of shades of gray.

There have been several revisions made for this second edition. A number of cases have been replaced and others revised. Text material for each section has been updated to reflect new legal procedures and more current research. These changes reflect the suggestions the authors have received from colleagues, practitioners and students. Responses from other professors and students as well as empirical research on the experiential model has indicated that the learning process can be enhanced using an experiential case study approach. Changes in the current edition of this text attempt to build upon and expand the positive applications of using this approach to acquaint the reader with the many facets of the criminal justice experience.

Section I

The Police and
Community Relations

Introduction

Police-community relations in the United States has been a growing concern of criminal justice practitioners for decades. Sociologists, psychologists, and a host of other professionals have offered theories, ideas, and potential solutions for poor police-community relations. There are several reasons why police-community relations are of vital concern to criminal justice practitioners. Elected law enforcement officials may view police-community relations as a means of re-election; the patrol officer may view police-community relations as a means of gaining respect; criminal investigators may utilize police-community relations as a means for obtaining information; and, police administrators maintain police-community relations as a means of obtaining funding for department programs. Perhaps, the most significant aspect of police-community relations remains as the context in which the police and the community can work together in an effort to reduce criminal activity and insure the safety of citizens.

During the previous decades of policing, the community has become separated from those persons that police. The police are expected by society and by members of their own profession to transcend the individuals they are sworn to protect and serve. Such a separation often creates an aura of mystique concerning the police profession from the community's view point and a cautious attitude of police officers toward society. This separation of police and community may have been the result of technological innovations or the historically political and corruptive influences concerning the police role; or changing social values and structures. Regardless of the reason, the fact remains that the police are at times, not only combating the criminal element in a community, but, in a sense, the community as well.

The Public's View of the Police

After decades of public neglect of the police officer's role in society, the onset of the late 1960's and early 1970's accented public visibility of the police. During this era of social unrest and political protest and confrontation, the police were conceived as members and enforcers of the "system." During this time, police-community relations became vitally important for the stability of communities confronted with social conflicts. The increasing visibility of the police in the community which was reflected in the nation's press and media, prompted a wide variety of misconceptions regarding the police role. Many Americans began to view the police as being solely responsible for controlling crime; a view that still exists in some segments of the public.

Our basic law enforcement ideals and organizational structures were imported from England. The British police system has always maintained that the police are the public and the public are the police (More, 1985). The British police system contends that it is every citizen's obligation to help police his or her society, but certain citizens are set aside to do the job on a full-time basis. The police, in this way, assists all citizens in their job. Our police system has not adequately related the reality that the public are, in fact, the police. When crime rates are high in a community, it is because the police are not doing their job, rather than society has failed, to some extent, in their responsibilities.

The President's Commission on Law Enforcement recognized in the late 1960's that law enforcement as an occupation, demanded a great degree of skill and intelligence (National Advisory Commission on Criminal Justice Standards and Goals, 1973). For decades the public has often been inclined to perceive the police as low-paid job holders with limited intelligence (Hodge, 1964). The fact that the public often seems to believe that the police are corruptable and influenced by political forces, nurtures the suspicious and cynical attitudes of the community toward police officers (Fosdick, 1920). In order to alleviate those attitudes, the President's Commission on Law Enforcement helped establish the Law Enforcement Assistance Administration (LEAA) whose duty was to provide federal funding for police agencies in the United States. This agency increased the potential for professionalism regarding the police role. Increased training, education, salaries, and equipment for police officers and agencies were believed to give the police not only the tools required to combat crime, but a means to gain increased community support and respect for the police. Although the LEAA was somewhat successful in providing the police with tools to combat crime, they did not gain the community support and respect for the police that they had aspired to.

Public attitudes toward police are embellished with fear and cynicism. American and many other western societies seem to have always feared a strong police force. Fear and distrust of government authority, as symbolized by the police, is reinforced by the American culture of individual freedom. Police authority is criticized by many and praised by few. When a police officer risks his or her life to stop a criminal act, there is seldom substantial public recognition by the community. After all, the police were simply performing their duty. When a police officer utilizes authority to regulate behavior such as speeding, they are often condemned by many in the community. When a police officer abuses his or her authority, they are chastised by the media and community. Unfortunately, the community remains uninformed concerning positive police activities although the situation is improving with police-community crime prevention and other relevant programs.

The Police View of the Public

Police officers have traditionally been trained to be suspicious of all persons for the practical purpose of self-preservation. Such a suspicious attitude, reinforced by the public's attitude toward the police can enhance the separation between the police and the community. Skolnick (1975) indicates that police officers possess personality traits unlike that of other professions. The combination of authority with danger as inherent elements of the police profession can isolate the police from the community. Such isolation allows the police to come together as a fraternal group with an "us against them" attitude. This type of solidarity creates a fraternal brother-sisterhood among police officers.

Because the police officer is continually occupied with anticipating potential violence, he or she develops a perception of those who are potentially dangerous. Police officers tend to stereotype certain individuals in society as symbolically dangerous based on their appearance. The tough-looking gang of youths on a street corner are scrutinized more closely by police officers on patrol than the clean-cut group of boy scouts in the church-yard. However, the clarity of these situational perceptions is generally not as evident as depicted in the above example. Many police training films use scare-tactics to illustrate to police officers that anyone can be dangerous. Many police firearms training films illustrate that even the most innocent in appearance may be a potential assailant. While the police wear uniforms for recognition, the criminal is not as easily identified. Therefore, police officers may view suspiciously all persons unfamiliar to them, since their well-being may depend on such evaluation. Even off-duty police officers tend to socialize more readily with those in their respective or related profession.

Degrees of suspiciousness exist regarding the police view of the community. Police officers are inclined to view members of the higher social classes with less suspicion than those in the lower social strata. Members of the higher social classes generally possess a greater portion of money, power, political ties and may appear more law-abiding. Because most police officers are generally derived from the middle class, they often tend to view those of the upperclass with more respect. Upperclass sections of the community are not as apt to portray violent crimes as the lower class areas. As a result, police officers may be more concerned with prevention of crimes such as burglary in these neighborhoods and less concerned regarding robberies, rapes, or assaults. Many police officers view the upperclass commission of crimes as those of social distinction such as murder, embezzlement, insurance fraud and the like. However, police officers on patrol in the lower class sections of the community may anticipate crimes of violence and maybe much more cautious of the people living there.

Police Use of Discretionary Decision-Making

Wilson (1968) has identified three styles of police behavior in America: 1) legalistic style of policing; 2) watchman style of policing; and, 3) service style of policing. The legalistic style of police behavior is concerned with those police officers who believe they are representatives of the law that they are sworn to uphold. Legalistic police officers refrain from judgment on the basis of the spirit of the law, trying to judge only whether a law is broken or followed. The legalistic style of policing could be equated with the "police officer who would give his own mother a ticket for speeding" philosophy. The watchman style of policing produces the opposite type of police officer. The watchman police style "overlooks" or ignores many violations of the law. These police officers, when not acting on a violation, are inclined to issue more warnings than tickets, and make fewer arrests. The service style of policing makes the greatest use of discretion. These police officers judge each situation on its own merits and base their decision to arrest on the well being of the community. The service style of policing is a balance between the legalistic and the watchman styles of policing and has been suggested as providing one of the better forms of police-community relations (Wilson, 1968).

Police discretion has been defined as "the power to consider all circumstances and then determine whether any legal action is to be taken. And, if so taken, of what kind and degree, and to what conclusion (Breitel, 1960)." Many citizens as well as police officers feel police should not have the authority of discretion. These individuals feel such judgment should be left to the court's discretion whether to inflict punishment upon a law-breaker or ultimately to decide whether an offense has been committed. The conception of police officers as non-judges is a misnomer. Police officers must utilize judgment on their job performance. Police discretion is used as an arrest or not-to-arrest judgment in the same manner a prosecuting attorney uses discretion in the plea-bargaining process. However, the prosecuting attorney and the judge usually do not have the power of discretion until the police officer makes the decision to arrest. The police officer's decision to arrest is the first step in the criminal justice process and is, perhaps, one of the most important steps. How the police officer utilizes his or her discretionary powers will affect the community view of the police and, to a large extent, the crime rates of the community (Price, 1979; Broderick, 1987).

In a general sense, when the police take a legalistic approach to the control of crime and enforcement of the law, crime rates will rise because of increased arrests. When the police take a watchman approach to law enforcement, crime rates may decline because of decreased arrests. When the police take a service approach to law enforcement, there may be less arrests but the conviction rates should be higher and the types of crimes solved more serious in nature. The public is not inclined to report crime or cooperate with the police when they feel that the police are incompetent or more concerned with writing tickets than investigating crimes. When the police make visible efforts to cooperate with the public by using a service style of policing, the public becomes more cooperative. As a result, wise use of police discretion can enhance the police image and provide for better police-community relations.

Community Crime Prevention

The American police profession has traditionally been one of crime — apprehension — prosecution, rather than prevention. Although the 1970's and 80's have brought increased attention to crime prevention, the concept is not new. The British police have, for decades, been concerned with the concept of investigating potential crime scenes before the fact.

Most people realize that the police cannot combat crime totally by themselves. The old British concept that the "police are the public and the public are the police" has brought new meaning to crime prevention programs developing in the United States. Economic situations and increasing rates of violent and property crimes, have encouraged public outcry toward crime. Liberal views toward the offender of the 1960's have been replaced by more conservative views of crime control in the 1980's.

Crime prevention concepts with goals to improve police-community relations, have emerged in such forms as neighborhood watch programs, Citizen's Band radio patrols, Operation Identification, fleet watch programs, and reserve police forces. These types of programs allow the public to become more involved in the control of crime. Crime prevention programs can be effective in reducing crime while at the same time, provide better police-community relations. Of course, such programs require that police agencies educate the public and gain community support.

Summary

In the past, the public has often viewed the police as inept, uneducated and corrupt political puppets, or as straight-laced tough guys with little compassion for their fellow-citizens. Such views have, to some extent, been encouraged by the media, reinforced by social unrest, and promoted by police treatment of the general public. Police officers were expected to be a combination of lawyer, psychologist, soldier, and social worker. The police profession has, on many occasions, promoted mistrust, fear, and cynicism. In the same context, police officers have been trained to be suspicious of all, but to assume a role of objectivity and authority over those they serve. This has led to an unfortunate separation between the police and the community with the police officer in the middle fighting criminal elements as well as community elements that criticize their actions.

With use of police discretion in enforcement of the law and encouragement of the community to help the police combat a common enemy has increased community support for police. Crime prevention and education programs by police agencies have provided better police-community relations. Such programs can only be effective in creating better police-community relations when every police officer realizes that he or she must take the first step in showing the public that they too are citizens who wish to assist the public in policing the community.

References

Breitel, C.D. (1960). "Controls in Criminal Law Enforcement," *The University of Chicago Law Review*, 27 (Spring).

Broderick, J.J. (1987). *Police in a Time of Change*, 2d ed. Prospect Heights, IL: Waveland Press.

Fosdick, R.B. (1920). *American Police Systems*. New York: The Century Co.

Hodge, R.W., et al. (1964). "Occupational Prestige in the United States, 1925-1963," *American Journal of Sociology*, 70 (November).

More, H.W. (1985). *Critical Issues in Law Enforcement*, 4th ed. Cincinnati: Anderson Pub. Co.

National Advisory Commission on Criminal Justice Standards and Goals. (1973). *Police*. Washington, D.C.: U.S. Government Printing Office.

Price, R.P. (1979). "Integrated Professionalism: A Model for Controlling Police Practices," *Journal of Police Science and Administration*, (March).

Skolnick, J., and T.C. Gray (1975). *Police in America*. Boston: Little, Brown and Co., Inc.

Wilson, J.Q. (1968). *Varieties of Police Behavior*. Cambridge, MA: Harvard University Press.

Cases in the Police and Community Relations

The following seven cases are designed to enable you to understand the impact police have upon the general public. A police officer's main responsibility is to protect the public. This responsibility often causes the police officer to become socially isolated. Social isolation may cause numerous conflicts between the police and the community. Earning community respect and support is always a difficult task for the police. How the police perform their duties in the public eye reflects positively or negatively upon the entire police profession.

As you react to the next seven cases and try to develop solutions to the problems presented, you should be aware of the impact your solutions may have upon the community.

Case number one, "Public Duty or Brotherhood," deals with a police officer who has received a family disturbance call at another police officer's home. Upon arriving, the officer finds a group of community members gathered outside the home waiting to see how the situation is handled. The officer realizes that he should perform his duty in order to maintain a working relationship with the community. The officer is also aware of the problems associated with arresting a fellow police officer.

Case number two, "Fraternity Party," involves a common parking problem at a fraternity house during a party. The responding police officer seems to have mishandled the situation and has created an explosive situation between the police and the students. The shift Lieutenant must try to resolve the conflict quickly and quietly before the situation gets out of hand.

Case number three, "Case Load," centers upon a veteran detective Sergeant who has become disillusioned with burglary-larceny investigations. The Sergeant believes that there is little he can do to solve such crimes and becomes calloused in his attitude regarding investigations. When the Sergeant becomes a candidate for promotion, he must decide how to respond to the questions the promotion board puts before him.

Case number four, "Officer Friendly—Unfriendly Neighborhood," deals with a police-community relations officer describing "neighborhood watch" programs for an older neighborhood. The officer is faced with trying to explain the police position to a group of angry senior citizens.

7

Case number five, "Liberty and Justice for All," is concerned with the profound social and cultural problem within the inner city. A police patrolman is transferred from a higher socio-economic class neighborhood patrol zone to an inner city patrol zone. The officer finds that different people are handled in different ways by the police. The officer finds himself making more arrests and becoming increasingly aggressive with individuals.

Case number six, "Hot Dog," involves a rookie police officer who has become a problem for a veteran officer attempting to "break him in." The rookie abuses his police authority by deliberately provoking citizens and handling situations in an aggressive manner. The veteran officer is faced with the responsibility of teaching the rookie the correct way of handling and interacting with people.

Case number seven, "To Protect and Serve," explores the social isolation police have with the community. A rookie police officer finds that former "close friends" are now becoming more distant and are treating him differently because he is now a police officer.

Public Duty or Brotherhood

You are a young police officer in a small town. You have worked for the police department for almost nine months. In four weeks you will be off probationary status and will be eligible for a salary increase.

You grew up in the town you work for. Both yourself and your family are well liked and respected by most members of the community. You know many families in your town and feel you have a good relationship with most of them.

One night on patrol you receive a domestic disturbance call. From the dispatcher's remarks, you realize it is apparently a family fight complaint which was turned in by a neighbor.

Upon arriving at the scene, you notice that several of the neighbors have gathered in the front yard of the house. As you get out of your vehicle you can hear loud arguing coming from inside the house.

As you walk toward the house you advise the people in the yard that they should return to their homes. A couple of people voice objections and demand to know how you are going to handle the call. One man states, "He won't do anything to a fellow cop!"

You did not recognize the address as being a police officer's home but you do recognize the car in the carport being in the police parking lot. You now realize that a police officer does live here. You do not know the officer very well because he works a different shift than you do. However, you do know his name is Jason and that he has been on the force for about five years.

As you knock on the door of the house you glance behind you at the people still standing in the front yard. They are wondering and waiting to see how you will handle the situation. After the third knock, Jason opens the door. You smell beer and can see Jason has been drinking heavily.

Jason belligerently asks what you want. You explain that a neighbor has complained about the argument he is having with his wife. Jason's wife suddenly runs to the door and demands that you take Jason out of the house. Jason turns around, slaps her hard on the face, and then pushes her back into the house. You start inside and Jason turns to you and tells you to keep out of his and his wife's business. "I don't need no rookie to tell me how to run my private life," Jason yells at you. Jason sees the people standing in the front yard and screams for them to go away or he will throw them all in jail.

You are thinking to yourself that if Jason was not a police officer, you would not be as hesitant regarding your next move. Had he been any other person, you would already have put him in the back of your cruiser heading to jail. But, Jason is a fellow police officer. You have never had to handle a call involving another police officer before. You have heard from the other officers in the department how police officers have to take care of themselves, like a fraternity. You have previously let other officers off for minor speeding violations and such because they were fellow police officers. You have even gotten out of a few tickets yourself for the same reason. But this is a different situation. Private citizens are watching how you are going to handle this particular call.

You quickly step inside the house and close the door. Jason shouts, "I told you to get away from here." You see Jason's wife, sitting on the floor, sobbing. She has obviously been beaten.

You ask Jason for an explanation. Jason tells you there is nothing you can do except leave him alone. Jason's wife then shouts at you to take Jason to jail because she is afraid of him. Jason tells her to shut up, that nobody is going to put another police officer in jail.

You get Jason into the living room and have him sit on the couch. Using as much tact as you can, you explain the problem to Jason and urge him to calm down. After talking with Jason a few minutes, he becomes more subdued. Jason's wife is still upset and wants you to arrest Jason.

You look out the living room window and see even more people gathered outside. You know that some type of action must be taken. If you arrest Jason, you will defuse the crowd outside as well as temporarily protect Jason's wife from futher abuse. If you do not arrest Jason, you may contribute to a serious problem between the community, yourself, and the police department. You may also lose your job. Jason will more than likely lose his job if he is arrested.

You are still looking out the window at the crowd of people waiting for you to take action. They want you to arrest a fellow police officer. Either way you go, you are going to have some problems.

Based on what you have read, answer the following questions:

1. What steps should the young officer take to alleviate the problems with a) the crowd outside, b) Jason, and c) Jason's wife? Explain what impact your solutions will have on police-community relations.

2. How will the community view their local police if a) Jason is arrested by the officer and, b) Jason is not arrested by the officer?

3. How will the other members of the police department view this encounter? How would they react if Jason were arrested? If Jason were a police officer with another law enforcement agency, would there be a difference?

1) Tell Jason that your going to take him to your house to let him sober up. Let the community think that you arrested him. When he sobers, tell him that you'll get him family counseling.

2) That their doing their jobs and not just busting citizens. Just the opposite.

3) good, hate me, no & yes

NO - cops are cops

yes - people from other department would hate me
some people from my depart. would be mad some not.

Fraternity Party

You are a lieutenant on the four p.m. to twelve p.m. shift. You are in charge of six patrolmen. Tonight has been typically quiet and you have only one hour to go before you are off-duty. The only call your shift has received has been a parking problem on a street where a fraternity house is located. The fraternity house is apparently having a party, and there have been some complaints from the residents of the neighborhood about cars blocking the street. One of your officers, Ted Bates, responded to the call. Ted is a good officer although he is a little hot headed at times. He is young and inexperienced, but should eventually overcome those limitations. "He should be able to handle a simple parking problem," you think to yourself.

Your cup of coffee is interrupted by Ted shouting on the radio, "Officer needs help, officer needs help!" Ted is obviously shaken. You try to call him back, but he does not answer. The other five officers are now on the radio advising headquarters they are enroute to back Ted up. You also respond because you are in command.

It takes you several minutes to drive to the other side of town. Upon your arrival on the scene, you see all six patrol cars, with blue lights flashing, parked in the street. There are also two university police cars at the scene. The university is located only several blocks away. As you get out of your car, you see fifty to sixty students crowded in the street in front of the fraternity house. Some of your officers have already seized and arrested several students. People in the community are beginning to gather and watch what is happening.

Ted runs up to you. Ted's uniform is torn and he reeks of beer. He has his gun drawn. He is very upset explaining that he went inside the fraternity house to tell the students to move their cars at which time they attacked and threw beer on him. As you look around, you hear students shouting obscenities at the officers and see beer bottles being thrown. Realizing that Ted is very distraught and may "blow his cool," you tell Ted to holster his gun and to go sit down in your patrol car. It is humiliating to both Ted and you having to order him to sit in the patrol car. However, you would rather be humiliated than have Ted shoot one of the students.

You ask one of the students who has been arrested what happened. The student informs you that Officer Bates came into the fraternity house and yelled for the owners to get the cars off the street or be placed in jail. The student informed you that everyone had been drinking and they were angered by Bates' threats as well as his generally intimidating manner. He states that one of the students threw a cup of beer on Bates, then everything seemed to go "crazy."

Students are scattered everywhere. Some are scuffling with your officers, some are shouting, some are running for their cars, and others are simply watching. The street is completely blocked by now and traffic cannot get through. More residents are coming down the street to observe the disturbance. Several onlookers are shouting for your officers to place the students in jail. You are in command, what are you going to do?

Based on what you have read, answer the following questions:

1. How should Officer Bates have handled the situation to begin with?
2. There are university police officers on the scene. How would you, as the Lieutenant, utilize them to help you with the problem?
3. Do you feel that the students should be arrested? Why? How should the Lieutenant handle the situation as it is presented?

Case 3

Case Load

You are a detective Sergeant in a metropolitan police department. You have been working in the Burglary and Larceny Bureau for almost three years. You generally work ten to twelve burglary and larceny cases a week. There is little time to make a thorough investigation with such a large case load and your other supervisory duties as Sergeant. With property crimes becoming increasingly difficult to investigate and prosecute, you have decided to concentrate on solving what you feel are the bigger and more significant cases.

It is now one o'clock in the morning and you are on your way home. You were supposed to get off duty at eleven, but you had to work a drug store break in. The alarm had been tripped and you were advised to back up the patrol officer who responded because you were near the scene. You are upset because you had to waste so much time to answer an alarm that turned out to be false. Lately it seems that most burglar alarms you have answered have turned out to be false ones.

The dispatcher is calling you on the radio. He advises that a residential burglary complaint has just come in and a detective is requested.

"Where's the guys on the night shift?", you ask the dispatcher, growing more irritated.

The dispatcher informs you that the other detectives are all out on calls. You mumble a few obscenities to yourself and begin heading toward the address the dispatcher gave you. You could have simply checked out of service and gone home, but it always looks good to the supervisor to see that you work so hard.

When you arrive, you notice a patrol car is sitting in front of the house. You cannot understand why the patrol officer did not take the preliminary report instead of calling you.

You knock on the front door and a middle aged man answers. The patrolman is standing inside and he introduces you to the victims, Mr. and Mrs. Johnson.

"They're pretty upset and they demanded to see a detective," the patrolman explains.

The officer looks very young and is probably inexperienced in routine investigative matters. You advise the patrolman that he can return to his beat now that you are on the scene. You turn to Mr. Johnson and ask what happened. Mr. Johnson tells you that he and his wife had just come home from a party and found that the house had been broken into.

As you survey the house, you find that the back door has been kicked open and every room of the house has been ransacked. Mr. Johnson informs you what is missing in each room. From what Mr. Johnson reports is missing, you suggest that the burglary was probably committed by juveniles. Mr. Johnson is new in the neighborhood and knows very few of his neighbors, much less any potential suspects.

Mr. Johnson points to several items that were disturbed by the burglar and wants you to take fingerprints. From your experience you know that searching for fingerprints will probably not produce any identifiable prints. You reluctantly tell the Johnsons that you will look for fingerprints while thinking to yourself what a waste of time it is. You go through the motions of dusting for fingerprints then advise the Johnsons all you found were unidentifiable smudges. You then advise them that you will write out a report for their insurance company.

The Johnsons seem to be getting impatient and ask if that is all you can do. You reply that you will check with the Juvenile Bureau for leads, but that you do not know whether or not the stolen property will be recovered. You add that you will advise the Crime Prevention Bureau to come out and explain what the Johnsons can do to prevent future burglaries.

The Johnsons are becoming increasingly upset and ask why you are unable to find out who committed the burglary. You explain to them the same reasons that you have told many other burglary victims. There are just too many cases to work and the chances of arresting a suspect are small. All the Johnsons' can do is report the theft to their insurance company and make a claim.

It has been several weeks and several more cases since the Johnson burglary. You are waiting to be called in for an interview by the Police Promotion Board. The Lieutenant's position in command of Burglary and Larceny Bureau is open and you feel you have a good chance of acquiring the position.

The interview is going smoothly. You seem to have answered most of the questions correctly judging by the Board's feedback. One civilian member of the promotion board, Mr. Woods, begins to ask you some questions regarding burglary and larceny offenses.

"Sergeant, I've talked with several people in the community and they feel the police are unable or unwilling to solve burglaries and larcenies in this city. I've known a few people who did not report these crimes to the police knowing the police could do nothing about the crime except write out a report. This isn't good for police-community relations. If you were the Lieutenant in command of the Burglary and Larceny Bureau, what steps would you take to alleviate this problem?

Mr. Wood's question caught you somewhat by surprise. You know that Mr. Woods' comments are correct, but you cannot truthfully say that the Bureau needs more men to handle the case load. The Board has probably heard man-power related excuses many times before from every Bureau and Division head in the police department. The Board is now waiting to see what solutions you may have to the problem. What are you going to say?

Based on what you have read, answer the following questions:

1. Why do you think the detective Sergeant has such a calloused attitude toward burglary-larceny investigations? Do you think the Sergeant, if promoted, would change his attitudes?
2. How do you think the Sergeant's attitudes are affecting community opinions about the police? How should the Sergeant answer Mr. Wood's questions?
3. What resources are available to increase public awareness of burglary and larceny prevention?

Case 4
Officer Friendly - Unfriendly Neighborhood

You are a police-community relations officer in a police department serving a city of 250,000 people. Your primary duties are concerned with community crime prevention programs and providing educational seminars to schools and civic groups. You enjoy your job and feel you are making a contribution in the efforts to decrease criminal activity in your city. Just last year your seven-man Police Community Relations (PCR) unit was cited by the mayor as being largely responsible for the continuing decrease in burglaries in your city over the past three years. The mayor's recognition also resulted in a positive special feature article in the local newspaper complete with a picture of you and your unit.

The PCR unit was your first assignment after graduating from the academy five years ago. Since then, you have helped organize numerous neighborhood watch programs, a fleet watch program with telephone and utility workers, a police scout program with teenagers and an operation identification program.

While preparing for tomorrow's speaking engagement at a junior high school on a "Just Say No" anti-drug program, your Sergeant enters your office.

"Jim, sorry to interrupt you but I need to speak with you for a moment."

"Sure, Sarge, let me find a place for you to sit down," you state clearing away some pamphlets from a chair.

"Jim, as you know, Officer Adams' wife is ready to have her baby at any time now so I'm trying to keep his schedule as flexible as I can in case he has to go to the hospital."

"I know. Adams has been a nervous wreck all week," you respond with a grin.

The Sergeant continues, "Adams is scheduled for a neighborhood watch meeting tonight at the Pinecrest Community and I'd like to have you go instead. I'll give you some time off today to compensate."

"Sure thing, I'll be glad to help. After all, Adams helped me the time I had those night classes at the university," you state.

"Good," the Sergeant replies. "Let me fill you in on Pinecrest Community. As you know it's an older neighborhood, mainly retired and senior citizens, lower middle-class, blue-collar families. Criminal Investigation has informed us that burglaries and larcenies are on an increase there. Also, there's been some increase in violent crime, muggings, assaults and so on. Seems like some of the younger thugs have moved over there for some easy targets. We've gotten several complaints from the residents on gang activity and crime. A lot of those people are angry."

"I take it that this is the community's first neighborhood watch meeting?" you ask.

"Yes. Adams set it up a couple of days ago with John Webster the pastor at the church there on the corner of Oak and Dale. Webster scheduled a meeting with the residents at his church tonight at 7."

"I'll go through the usual routine on starting a watch program then tonight and try to set up monthly meetings with them," you respond.

"OK Jim. Thanks a lot," your Sergeant replies, leaving your office.

There never seems to be enough hours in the day. After hurrying through supper at a local fast-food restaurant, you arrive for the meeting a few minutes late. As you hand out pamphlets to the residents in the meeting hall at the church, you notice that most of the people seem apprehensive and, in some cases, unfriendly.

"Probably the uniform," you think to yourself.

You walk to the podium and begin: "Ladies and gentlemen, may I have your attention. I'm certainly glad you were able to make it here tonight for our first Neighborhood Watch meeting. I'm Officer Jim Mabry."

"You should all have some pamphlets that I passed around. We can go over these later after the video-tape presentation," you state while preparing the video-tape machine.

"Officer Mabry," one of the citizens states raising his hand near the back of the room.

"Uh, yes Sir, we'll have time for questions and discussions after the video-tape," you interrupt.

"Well, all I wanted to know is what are you boys doing about the crime problem in Pinecrest?" the man states anyway with several of the people around him voicing their support for his question.

"That's what I'm here for,...." you respond.

Looking around and gaining confidence, the man continues, "Look, I haven't seen as many as one cop do a damn thing around here. Why don't you boys go out here and arrest these hoodlums. You all make it sound as if it's our fault we're being robbed and mugged. I know several of my neighbors who didn't come here tonight 'cause they were afraid to go out after dark. We don't need no slide shows and pamphlets—we need action." Several of the citizens angrily shout their support for his words.

"Young man, young man...." A frail-looking older woman in the front row tries to get your attention by waving her pamphlets at you.

"Yes ma'am?" you respond.

"Are you a real policeman?" she asks.

Based on what you have read, answer the following questions:

1. How should the officer respond to the crowd? Can the officer gain their respect and adequately address the problems they have with crime in their community?

2. What resources could the officer use to help him deal with the angry residents?

3. What are some advantages and disadvantages in establishing neighborhood watch programs and police-community relations approaches in general?

Liberty and Justice for All

You are a police officer in a large metropolitan city. For the past eight months you worked in a middle and upper class suburban patrol zone. Most of the people you came in contact with were respectable members of the community. You had good rapport with most of the community and they were generally quite cooperative with the police. Now you are being transferred to another patrol zone which is in a lower class area near the inner city.

The first week you are in the new zone, you are assigned to work with Mike, a veteran officer who has been working this zone for almost four years. Mike drives you around pointing out informants, drunks, thieves, and places where they hang out. You immediately notice that Mike has a somewhat harsh, even punitive attitude regarding the people he comes in contact with on his beat.

"You have to treat these people tough, intimidation is the only way to communicate with them," Mike explains to you.

After one week in your new zone, you become aware of a great difference in police work with different types of people. You rarely made arrests in your old zone. Most problems there could be worked out by talking rationally with the people you came in contact with. In this zone, however, you have made more arrests and have had to use more force with people. It becomes apparent to you that there are even more drunks and criminals living in the new zone than you had ever expected. People living in the slums seem to be more apathetic as well.

Mike told you that if you needed information on criminal activity, just pick somebody up and threaten to arrest them if they did not tell you what you needed to know. This method worked as your new partner seemed to demonstrate frequently. Mike would "plant" drugs or a gun on somebody then threaten to arrest them if they did not give him information or become an informant for him. Mike has occasionally beat confessions out of suspects then threaten to "get them" if they did not plead guilty to offenses.

You become aware of more violent crimes in your new zone. There are more murders, assaults, and rapes here than would happen in the middle and upper class neighborhoods. Mike defined rape "victims" as those persons who did not get paid for their services. "Not even worth writing a report on," Mike told you. Murder investigations are routinely handled by the investigators in this zone. The detectives seldom perform a comprehensive investigation on any offense here. In the middle and upper class zone, all offenses were investigated thoroughly and the victims were given excellent attention by investigating officers.

You find that more police officers are assaulted in the lower class zone than in your old zone. The people living in the lower class zone do not appear to respect the police. It seems they only respect force.

"Don't ever turn your back on these people," Mike advised you. Mike also advised you to have your gun ready at all times.

"Shotgun's the best, they're really scared of 'em," Mike told you.

You also notice that more officers in this zone use deadly force than officers in other zones of the city. The police shot five people here last year.

"And probably a few more they didn't count," Mike chuckles.

After working in the new zone for two months and seeing what kind of people live in the area, you find yourself agreeing more and more with Mike's attitude and methods.

You and Mike receive a radio call to back up another unit a couple of blocks away. As you pull up beside the other cruiser, you see two police officers beating up a young man in the alley.

"C'mon Mike, you want a piece of this?" one of the officers shout.

Mike takes out his slapjack and moves in with the other two officers beating the youth.

"What did he do?" you ask.

"He made the mistake of calling us names," one of the officers responds. "We're going to let this one be an example."

The young man could not be over seventeen years old and appears to be badly hurt. You know the officers will leave him in the alley when they are finished beating him. Of course, there will be no arrest.

You begin to think about how you have changed. Mike always says "fight fire with fire." Right now you are wondering who the criminals are. What should you do?

Based on what you have read, answer the following questions:

1. How would Mike respond to the community if the situation were reversed (i.e., if Mike was transfered to a higher income neighborhood zone)?

2. What would happen if you, as the new officer in the zone, reported the incidents to your superiors?

3. How do police affect community relations in inner city areas? What can the police do to help promote police-community relations in lower socio-economic neighborhoods?

Case 6
Hot Dog

You are a veteran police officer with twelve years of experience. You hold the rank of Sergeant in the Patrol Division. Your Lieutenant has asked you to help "break-in" a rookie police officer who has just graduated from the police academy.

Your new partners' name is Eddie. Eddie is 22 years old and tells you he has a Bachelor's degree in criminal justice. You always wanted to get a degree in law enforcement or criminal justice but you have a son in college which puts quite a strain on your family budget. Eddie tries to impress you with his education by referring to studies and theoretical aspects of modern law enforcement during the shift. You take Eddie's remarks in stride and tell him that knowing law enforcement is one thing and performing it is another.

During the first week, you notice that on several calls, Eddie has acted harshly with people. He has also taken his nightstick out, slapped it in his hand, and toyed with it while talking to people. You mention it to him and he does not seem to listen. On one occasion, in a semi-serious way, Eddie threatened a restaurant waitress with a parking citation if she did not give him a police discount on his lunch. Eddie explained to you that he was only kidding the waitress. You try to explain that sometimes people take "kidding" the wrong way.

Eddie is always wanting you to stop vehicles on the highway for speeding. You tell Eddie that a police officer cannot arrest everyone for exceeding the speed limit or everyone would be in jail. You allowed Eddie to handle one speeder on his own in order for him to learn the procedure.   While you were sitting in your cruiser, it became obvious that Eddie and the speeder were shouting at each other. You got out of the cruiser and had to tell Eddie to get back to the cruiser and sit down before the situation deteriorated even further. The speeder had his children in the car and appeared to be angry. The speeder told you that Eddie chewed him out in front of his children and even used curse words. You apologized to the speeder and issued him a warning ticket. When you got back to your cruiser, Eddie was very angry. Eddie told you that you should have let him write the speeder up as much for his disrespect as for his speeding. You tried to explain to Eddie that police officers must earn respect and not demand it from the public. You also explained that an officer must always try to treat the public with respect if he expects respect from the public. Eddie did not seem to listen.

Eddie is off today and you are thankful you only have to ride with him a couple of days a week. The Lieutenant calls you in to talk about Eddie. The Lieutenant asks you to go over to Eddie's house and talk with him. The Lieutenant explains that there have been several complaints from Eddie's neighborhood about his behavior. It appears that Eddie has been "playing policeman" around the neighborhood while he has been off-duty.

As your cruiser comes to a stop in front of Eddie's house, you take a deep breath as you try to find the right words to say to Eddie.

Based on what you have read, answer the following questions:

1. Do you think Eddie is typical of most rookie police officers?
2. Do you think Eddie will "outgrow" his attitudes and manners?
3. What should the Sergeant say to Eddie after the last incident? Would you, as the Sergeant, report Eddie's conduct to the Lieutenant and recommend that Eddie be terminated?

To Protect and Serve

You are a rookie police officer preparing for your first tour of duty. You have just finished an intensive ten week training that is supposed to prepare you for every aspect of police work. You have a lot to remember and, just to be sure, you have brought along your academy notebook for reference.

It is getting close to roll call time and you grab your gunbelt from your locker and run toward the roll call room. You wonder which of the officers at roll call will be your partner as you look around at their faces. You were almost late and decided to sit at the back of the room so as not to attract attention to yourself.

"Patrolman Shipley, Unit 17-Baker, your new partner is a rookie named Wallace, William C., good luck," the Sergeant announces with a laugh.

You strain to see what Officer Shipley looks like but cannot because of your seat position.

The roll call Sergeant finishes his announcements and dismisses the shift. You notice that you forgot and left your academy notebook back in the locker room. You run back to the locker room then out to the police parking lot.

Opening the passenger door of Unit 17-Baker, you see that Officer Shipley is already sitting on the passenger side. Shipley is a big man in his late fifties and appears friendly as he looks up at you and smiles.

"Get on the other side, kid; I don't feel like driving today," Shipley says as he closes his door.

You introduce yourself to your new partner as you start the cruiser toward your assigned beat. Shipley begins to explain the beat to you, the people, the places, and what to watch out for. Shipley has very definite opinions about police work and does not hesitate telling you what they are. He talks about how persons in the community you serve do not respect the police.

"They don't think we're human, all they see is the uniform," Shipley explains to you.

Shipley goes on to say that the community often complains about police action. You remember the psychology and sociology topics at the police academy and the discussions about handling verbal abuse from community members.

"Everybody gets upset when they get speeding or parking tickets, they have to take it out on somebody and we're just handy," you explain to Shipley.

"It's not just speeding and parking tickets, kid; most people don't appreciate what we're trying to do."

You look at Shipley with a puzzled expression and decide to change the subject.

"When did you go to the police academy, Tom?"

"Didn't have an academy when I started. They just pinned a badge on you, gave you a gun and told you to go out and enforce the law. The streets were our training academy."

After an hour and a half of listening to Shipley talk about the old days and the complete history of the police department, you again decide to try and change the subject.

"My wife and I are going to a party next Friday night with some old friends of mine, you want to come with us?" You ask Shipley, really hoping that he will refuse.

"No thanks, kid; the only parties I go to are the F.O.P. parties. I also go out once in awhile with some old police buddies. You ought to join the F.O.P., they have some good get-togethers. I'll bring you an application if you want."

You smile at Shipley, thinking how it would be to spend your free time with the same people you had to work with. You are not sure you would like it.

"Don't you have any friends that aren't cops?" you ask Shipley.

"Sure, but not many. I don't feel as comfortable around them as I do fellow cops. Anyways, regular people don't want cops as friends, unless they want tickets fixed or something. You'll find that out soon enough."

Shipley's words really begin to bother you. It seems evident that Shipley does not care about anyone except fellow cops. You always believed that the police were supposed to protect and serve the public. Surely that does not mean that the police are supposed to avoid the public socially. You start remembering all those general orders the police department made you memorize at the academy. "Officers should not frequent bars, become intoxicated in public, and must act in a responsible and official manner at all times." In other words, you are a police officer twenty-four hours a day. But, these orders do not mean that you cannot have fun and be sociable with people.

It is now Friday afternoon and you are getting off duty. You have learned a lot during the past week riding with Shipley. He may be old fashioned in his ways of dealing with people, but he has a lot of experience that you can learn from. You think of how much more you have learned in the past week than the entire ten weeks at the academy. As you head for home, you remember the party you are going to tonight and begin to think how nice it will be to see your old friends again.

That evening, as you and your wife pull in front of your friend's house, you see that the party has already started. It is always good to be fashionably late, you think to yourself as you knock on the door. Your friend has a nice home and makes a good living as an automobile salesman. You have not seen him or any of your other friends since you joined the police force. The door opens and your friend and his wife greet you and ask you in. Your friend goes to the kitchen to fix you and your wife a drink as you go around saying hello to all your other friends at the party.

"Putting any crooks in jail these days?", your friend asks you while handing you a drink.

You start to tell him about the drunk you arrested the other day but decide not to after seeing several of your friends at the party well on their way to intoxication.

"No, not yet. But give me time, I'm sure to catch a murderer or two," you jokingly respond.

After a couple of hours, you notice that several of your friends have already asked you to fix parking tickets, asked your opinion on legal issues, and even asked if you mind if they smoked pot at the party. Other party goers seem more distant, even uncomfortable when they learn of your profession. Tom Shipley's words again return to your consciousness..."regular people don't want cops as friends..."

As the party continues, you become increasingly aware that things are different now that you are a police officer. Perhaps some of what Shipley said was true. The question is, how are you going to handle it? You do not intend to give up your chosen profession, but are not sure how to put your non-police relationships in an appropriate perspective.

Based on what you have read, answer the following questions:

1. Why do you think the community isolates the police?
2. Does the community stereotype police officers?
3. Would you, as the officer, attempt to "break the barrier" between you and your friends or would you seek new police friendships? If the officer found no barrier between himself and his friends at the party, do you think the friendships would last?

Section I
Selected Bibliography

Ahern, J.F. (1972). *Police in Trouble.* New York: Hawthorne Books, Inc.

Bent, A.E., and R.A. Rossum (1976). *Police, Criminal Justice and, the Community.* New York: Harper and Row.

Broderick, J.J. (1987). *Police in a Time of Change,* 2d ed. Prospect Heights, IL: Waveland Press.

Cohn, A.W., and E.C. Viano (1976). *Police-community Relations: Images, Roles, Realities.* Philadelphia: J.B. Lippincott Co.

Cox, S.M., and J.D. Fitzgerald (1983). *Police in Community Relations.* Dubuque, IA: Wm. C. Brown Publishers.

Drodge, E.F. (1973). *The Patrolman: A Cop's Story.* New York: New American Library.

Farmer, R.W., and V.A. Kowalewski (1976). *Law Enforcement and Community Relations.* Reston, VA: Reston Publishing.

Manning, P.K., and J.V. Maanen (1978).·*Policing: A View from the Street.* Santa Monica, CA: Goodyear Publishing Co.

McDowell, C.P. (1984). *Criminal Justice: A Community Relations Approach,* 2d ed. Cincinnati: Anderson Publishing Co.

McEvoy, D.W. (1976). *The Police and Their Many Publics.* Metuchen, NJ: The Scarecrow Press.

Morris, D.F. (1973). *Police-community Relations: A Program That Failed.* Lexington, MA: Heath and Co.

Mueller, W. (1983). "Crime Prevention: Why Officer Friendly Eats Lunch Alone," *Police Magazine,* 6(2).

New Jersey Department of Community Affairs (1985). *Crime Prevention Guide for Senior Citizens.* Trenton, NJ: Department of Community Affairs.

Persico, J.E., and G. Sunderland (1985). *Keeping Out of Crime's Way: The Practical Guide for People over 50.* Glenview, IL: Scott, Foresman and Co.

Roberg, R. (1976). *The Changing Police Role: New Dimensions and New Issues.* San Jose, CA: Justice Systems Development, Inc.

Trojanowicz, R.C., and S.L. Dixon (1974). *Criminal Justice and the Community.* Englewood Cliffs, NJ: Prentice-Hall, Inc.

U.S. Department of Justice (1985). *Community Crime Prevention.* Washington, D.C.: Bureau of Justice Assistance.

Walker, S. (1983). *The Police in America.* New York: McGraw-Hill Book Co.

Section II

Family and Crisis Intervention

Introduction

A major part of the police service role deals with a variety of interpersonal crises. Quarreling family members, street disturbances, neighborhood disputes, landlord-tenant disputes, child abuse, alcoholism, drug crisis, and mental disorders are but a few of the crises a police officer is faced with. The primary objective of the police regarding crisis intervention calls is to restore and preserve the peace and safety of individuals involved in the disturbance, as well as to the community. Crisis intervention calls represent the most frequent requests for police services. Although many of these calls are related to criminal offenses, some are of a civil nature and not within the area of police jurisdiction.

The average citizen exhibits little knowledge regarding the limits of police authority. His or her only concern is that a grievance or dispute must be settled. In their anger or frustration, citizens turn often to the police for assistance. Even though the source of the citizen's concern may be of a civil nature, the police have the responsibility to restore order and preserve the peace. The manner in which this task is undertaken may be instrumental in the prevention of a civil matter from becoming a criminal one.

The lethal nature of police crisis intervention is grimly registered in police statistics. Over twenty percent of the total number of police officers killed in the line of duty meet their deaths while intervening in such crisis situations as family fights and street disturbance calls (U.S. Department of Justice, 1986). Whenever a police officer responds to a crisis intervention call he or she must be prepared for anything. A lax attitude in responding to a call may contribute to the seriousness of the circumstances. In order to perform his or her responsibility effectively, the police officer must maintain constant vigilance, critically survey and analyze the situation, use interpersonal communication and anticipate the unexpected.

Family Disputes

There are few assignments considered more distasteful to a police officer than a family dispute. In these tension-packed moments, emotions are inclined to escalate. The individuals involved may say and do things they would normally refrain from doing. In many cases, family members re-direct their anger toward the intervening police officer.

In comparison to middle and upper class individuals, persons from lower class neighborhoods are more likely to call the police during family disputes. While the reasons might vary, they seem to include: 1) the prohibitive expense of professional helping services; 2) lack of awareness of free or inexpensive community mental health services; 3) perceived stigma of going to a professional mental health practitioner; and, 4) familiarity with police presence and intervention in such matters (McDowell, 1984). The opposite seems true concerning persons from upper and middle classes involved in family disputes. They seem more likely to utilize alternative professional helping services rather than call the police.

The police officer, upon entering a home involving a family dispute, should remember that not all family disputes involve the commission of a crime. Police officers should be aware that families who have requested police services are in need of outside intervention for problems which may have progressed beyond the point of self-mediation or control. Therefore, it is important that the officer avoid creating an impression of disinterest, cynicism, or belittlement of the problems for which the officer has been summoned.

When intervening in a dispute of a violent nature involving physical contact, immediate police action must be initiated. Physical intervention on the part of the police officers may be necessary in this type of disturbance. Officers responding to such calls should place themselves in a position which will limit the possibility of personal injury. The intervening officers should separate the persons involved and make a wide visual survey of the area for objects which could be used as weapons. Once this has been accomplished, the officers may assess the situation further in order to determine if formal police action is in order.

It is very common for alcohol to be involved in family disputes. It is difficult to gather the facts accurately in a dispute if one of the persons involved has been drinking. Some intoxicated persons are violent in disputes. Intervening police officers should remain professionally objective when dealing with an intoxicated individual and indicate that they want to help, but should not demonstrate too much sympathy for his or her intoxicated condition.

When intervening in any family dispute, the police should utilize tact, sensitivity, and interpersonal communication skills. There has been substantial documentation regarding the need for police officers to possess and demonstrate such skills in domestic crisis situations (Braswell and Meeks, 1982). These findings are of particular significance for interpersonal intervention in lieu of the amount of time an officer spends answering such calls and the number of officers injured or killed while attempting to resolve such problem situations (Cumming, 1965; Bard, 1970; Goldstein, 1977).

Neubauer (1974), in his study of a midwestern city of 900,000, reported the attitudes of the local police toward family disputes. Police officers had little training to rely on short of common sense. Police powers of arrest were limited on private property. The complainant often (usually the wife) was hesitant to file charges but wanted the police to do something to quiet the husband. If the police did make an arrest, the other spouse frequently became belligerent with the officers. Generally, police officers saw little point in making arrests on such calls anyway since it would …"probably end up taking the food money for the kids to pay the fine (Neubauer, 1974)."

If family dispute calls are being processed by officers who are untrained or unsure of their abilities to manage the crisis intervention successfully, two things are likely to occur, and in fact, frequently do occur. Either the police are viewed as incompetent professionals or as heavy-handed intruders in a private situation (Farmer and Kowalewski, 1976). However, with careful training, motivation, and aptitude on the part of police officers, such views of the police can be avoided and police injuries can be decreased.

Reiser (1973) has suggested a three-phase approach to police intervention in family disputes. The first phase is the initial intervention; the second consists of a combination of defusing and assessment; and, the third phase involves resolution and/or referral. The initial intervention is the most critical phase and involves six ground rules: 1) stay calm, 2) do not threaten, 3) do not take sides, 4) do not challenge a man's masculinity, 5) do not degrade a woman's femininity, and 6) give verbal escape routes to help people save face. The defusing and assessment phase involves listening to all involved parties without taking sides. The listening approach allows individuals to "blow off steam" and release the tension and hostility. This "defuses" a potentially explosive situation as well as allowing the intervening police officer the opportunity to assess the situation. The officer may be able to determine through tactful questioning, the frequency of the family disputes, how long the disputes have existed, what caused the disputes, and what the underlying motives are for the disputes. The police officer may find that one or more of the parties have emotional problems that require professional help. The third phase, resolution and/or referral, require the intervening police officer to make a judgment about the situation. The officer may allow the disputing parties to help make this judgment. If their response seems realistic and agreeable, the dispute can be resolved at that point. However, if desireable and/or necessary, a referral to a helping agency should be made.

One of the standard procedures that has been developed for police intervention in family disputes involves having two officers respond to the call together and separating the disputing parties with one officer going with each person into a separate room. The officer then allows the person to talk and explain the situation, asking questions for the purpose of clarification. The officers then switch with each other to check-out stories and obtain a better evaluation of the total situation. The couple is then brought together to tell their side to each other, but allowing only one person to talk at a time. The police officers are then able to point out discrepancies, contradictions, or common feelings, and obtain a reaction from the disputing parties after making suggestions (Reiser, 1973).

Crisis Intervention

Farmer and Kowalewski (1976) use two terms to illustrate the police officer's role in crisis intervention; crisis intervention and crisis management. Crisis management is defined as "the police response to situations when officers act primarily as law officers rather than as helping agents (Farmer and Kowalewski, 1973)." The police officers attempt to contain community conflict or prevent police contact with an individual from developing into an uncontrollable situation. Such attempts keep the peace in the community, uphold the law, and minimize the use of force. While arrests may be necessary, they are undertaken as a last, not first, resort. Police objectives should be to identify the cause of the crisis, to assist the individual in meeting the impact of the crisis and to mobilize appropriate helping agency resources. The main objective for police officers intervening in a crisis situation is to bring the case to a close as a police matter while securing the necessary help for those involved.

Spiegel (1976) describes four roles that third party intervenors play in crisis situations: 1) the advocate, 2) the conciliator, 3) the mediator, and 4) the arbitrator.

The advocate represents a person or a group entering a crisis conflict situation as an advisor or consultant to one of the disputing groups. The advocate is not neutral in the conflict. He or she contributes skills as an organizer to one of the disputing groups, helping to create a structure capable of taking action and advising the group on the formulation of demands and on sources of support. In some situations the advocate in a dispute may be seen as an outside agitator, particularly when his or her function is to escalate a conflict in order to bring the issues to a head and to achieve change. As a result of the late 1960's riots, attitudes toward advocates in community conflicts have changed. It is generally believed that the more highly organized and successfully led the protest group, the greater the opportunity to avoid irrationality and violence (Spiegel, 1976). Although the advocate contributes to conflict regulation, emotions continually escalate and are unpredictable, and the conflict may still mount to a crisis situation.

The conciliator attempts to cool down tempers by creating a physical and/or emotional distance between the conflicting groups and by making suggestions that may temporarily resolve the crisis conflict. The action of conciliators are distinguished from advocates because they represent the interests of both sides in a conflict (Spiegel, 1976).

Mediators have been defined as those third parties who are acceptable to all conflicting groups or persons in a dispute that helps them in reaching a mutually satisfactory settlement of their differences (Spiegel, 1976). In distinguishing between conciliators and mediators, one might state that conciliators produce the environment in which mediation is possible. Sometimes mediators are also called negotiators, because they offer neutral meeting locations, interpret each side's position for the other, carry messages back and forth, and by using steady, optimistic attitudes facilitate a compromise and resolution of the conflict whenever possible.

Arbitrators are similar to mediators, but have one additional function — to make a judgment for one party or all conflicting parties in order to settle the dispute. Police officers intervening in a crisis conflict are usually seen as arbitrators. Arbitrators, like mediators, must be acceptable to both sides in a conflict before making any arbitrary judgments. Police officers must often first play all roles in a conflict before being acceptable as an arbitrator.

Police officers intervening in a crisis conflict must play the role of advocate, conciliator, mediator, and arbitrator. By separating and listening to each side, officers are able to play the role of advocate, opening lines of communication and enjoining respect from the conflicting parties. As conciliator, the police officer may be able to resolve a conflict situation temporarily by suggesting that one or both of the conflicting parties follow a course of action. As a mediator, the police officer may allow both conflicting parties to resolve their crisis on their own and work their own problems out without conflict. As an arbitrator, the police officer may resolve the situation on his or her own by taking an overt or other course of action. The role of arbitrator should be the last resort. The police officer, as an arbitrator in a crisis situation, is almost always blamed by one or both of the conflicting parties because of the officers authority (Spiegel, 1976; Roberts, 1984).

Crisis Intervention Skills

Police officers should demonstrate an interest in acting in a helping role; they should possess emotional maturity in a sense that the officer can accept the responsibility for his or her actions and can live with the outcome of a crisis intervention. A non-judgmental attitude is also vital. It is important that the police officer be able to assess a crisis situation and face his or her client without imposing personal views and values. It is also essential that the police officer possess patience and a willingness to explore every possible avenue for solution to a problem before breaking off contact, making a referral, or using the power of arrest.

While one of the prime reasons for police officers to employ crisis intervention methods is to avoid arrest, the officer should not hesitate to use such authority when common-sense indicates that a particular situation may not be resolved through the use of crisis intervention techniques.

The successful police crisis intervention officer must accept a dual role: that of being primarily a helping agent but one who must also employ his or her enforcement authority when an occasion merits such a response (Braswell and Meeks, 1982).

Domestic Violence

During the early 1970's, police training in crisis intervention for domestic disturbances was inclined to stress a non-arrest approach. The police, often unsure of their legal authority in private homes, responded to domestic disturbances with a peace-keeping attitude. Some police departments even created crisis intervention units to relieve patrol officers of the burden of handling domestic disputes. The police response emphasis was on diverting family members away from the criminal justice system and into mental health, welfare, and other social service agencies. While such an emphasis is noble and directed more at helping families, the police often became increasingly reluctant to utilize what police authority they did have in crisis intervention situations. Prosecuting attorneys also became more reluctant regarding pressing charges in family dispute cases.

It should be noted that there is a difference between domestic disturbances and domestic violence. Domestic disturbances may not involve physical injuries or threats of physical violence. In such disturbances, the police may be proper in acting primarily as a helping agent.

In the late 1970's and early 1980's, concerned feminists and other civil rights groups began to criticize the police for not adequately protecting women in domestic violence situations (Bae, 1981). When domestic disputes became violent, wives were usually the victims (Bell, 1984). Battered-spouse programs and emergency shelters further accentuated the concern regarding the police response to domestic violence. In response to these and other related criticisms, many states began to pass legislation increasing and making more accountable police authority in responding to domestic violence. Many states now have spousal abuse laws which empower the police to make misdemeanor probable cause arrests in spousal assault cases even if the victim is unwilling to prosecute and even if the police did not witness the assault. Some current research tends to support a more legalistic approach, indicating that arrest of the assailant is the single-most, effective, short-term method of preventing additional violence (Sherman and Berk, 1984).

Summary

Crisis intervention calls represent the most frequent requests for police services. Although crisis intervention includes a broad range of interpersonal crises such as child abuse, drug abuse, suicide, rape, and mental disorder: family disputes calls are the most typical and frequently the most dangerous for police officers. Police intervention in such disputes places the police officers in the dual role of enforcer and helping agent. While most police officers have had training as enforcement agents, few officers have the training or skill that adequately prepare them as helping agents in family disputes. The fact that there is little training for such skills emphasize the concern of many police officers that acting as a social worker in family disputes is not a police duty. Many states have supported this view by enacting domestic violence legislation which increases the powers of the police intervening in such cases.

References

Bae, R.P. (1981). "Ineffective Crisis Intervention Techniques: The Case of the Police." *Crime and Justice*, 4:61-82.

Bard, M. (1970). *Training Police as Specialists in Family Crisis Intervention*. Washington, D.C.: LEAA, U.S. Government Printing Office.

Bell, D.J. (1984). "Police Response to Domestic Violence: An Exploratory Study." *Police Studies*, 7:23-30.

Braswell, M., and R. Meeks (1982). "The Police Officer as a Marriage and Family Therapist: A Discussion of Some Issues," *Family Therapy*, 9(12).

Cumming, E., et al. (1965). "Policeman as Philosopher, Guide, and Friend," *Social Problems*, 11(2).

Farmer, R.E., and V.A. Kowalewski (1976). *Law Enforcement and Community Relations*. Reston, VA: Reston Publishing Co.

Goldstein, A., et al. (1977). *Police Crisis Intervention*. Kalamazoo, MI: Behaviordelia.

McDowell, C. (1984). *Criminal Justice: A Community Relations Approach*, 2d ed. Cincinnati: Anderson Publishing Co.

Neubauer, D.W. (1974). *Criminal Justice in Middle America*. Morristown, NJ: General Learning Press.

Reiser, M. (1973). *Practical Psychology for Police Officers*. Springfield, IL: Charles C. Thomas.

Roberts, A.R. (1984). *Battered Women and Their Families: Intervention Strategies and Treatment Programs*. New York: Springer Publishing Co., Inc.

Sherman, L.W., and R.A. Berk (1984). "Specific Deterrent Effects of Arrest for Domestic Assault," *American Sociological Review*, 49 (April).

Spiegel, J.P. (1976). "Third Party Intervention in Community Conflicts," in J.J. Parad, et al. (eds.), *Emergency and Disaster Management*. Bowie, MD: Charles Press Publishers, Inc.

U.S. Department of Justice. (1986). "Danger to Police in Domestic Disturbances: A New Look," *Research in Brief*, November. Washington, D.C.: U.S. Government Printing Office.

Cases in Family and Crisis Intervention

One of the more difficult duties of a police officer is the handling of complaints concerning family crises. The officer must enter into a situation that he or she has little, if any, knowledge of and preserve the peace. The manner in which the officer responds to these situations is the key to what can be a peaceful, even therapeutic, resolution of the problems or tragedy. It may be wise to keep in mind that more officers are assaulted while responding to family disturbance calls than for any other single category of police work.

Case number one, "The Color of a Living Room," explores how a simple disagreement between a husband and wife can result in a serious encounter with the police. Two officers, a male and his female partner, answer a family disturbance call. The female officer finds that she must handle both her angered partner and the family in a delicate manner.

Case numer two, "Between a Rock and a Hard Place," is concerned with a dispute over child custody. Serving court orders can sometimes create dangerous and frustrating situations for an officer. In this case, a deputy sheriff must take custody of a small child and deliver the child to the rightful mother. The child's mother is obviously unfit in the eyes of the officer as well as to the child's grandmother. Regardless of the right or wrong aspects of the situation, the officer feels he must carry out his duty.

Case number three, "Christmas Eve," examines the routine approach many officers utilize in answering family disturbance calls. Although family crisis intervention calls are commonplace in police work, they pose special problems during the holiday season which cannot be routinely handled.

Case number four, "Wife Battering," deals with the legal, as well as the emotional, task of handling wife beating cases. Police officers often find it frustrating to have a victim who refuses to prosecute an offender. Wife beating cases are twice as perplexing when an officer realizes that the victim may be too terrified to prosecute her husband.

Case number five, "Domestic Violence: A View from the Law," is concerned with the legal and policy implications of police intervention in domestic violence. A police captain must design a policy that will enforce the law as well as help those families involved in domestic violence.

Case number six, "Police Officer or Social Worker," attempts to portray a family crisis situation which the police may be unprepared to resolve. Police officers are frequently cast in the role of psychologist, counselor, or social worker when dealing with family problems regardless of whether or not they have received adequate training.

Case number seven, "Feuding Families," explores the problem of two immature neighbors fighting with one another. Police officers often find these types of conflicts comical but, if not effectively resolved, can become very serious. In this case, each neighbor accuses the other of committing criminal acts and the intervening police officer realizes that such conflict could result in serious complications if the issue is not promptly resolved.

Case 1

The Color of a Living Room

You are a female police officer. You have worked for the police department a little over two years as a juvenile officer and have transferred into the patrol division only a few weeks ago. You enjoyed working in the juvenile bureau but felt you had greater career potential as a patrol officer. Some of the male patrol officers seemed apprehensive when you transferred into the patrol division. You had expected some feelings of insecurity from male officers, but you believed that you could eventually prove yourself. You currently have a male partner who still tries to assume the role as your protector when you answer calls.

You and your partner have just finished eating dinner when you receive a radio call about a family fight. As you proceed toward the address, you think about the training you received concerning how to handle family disputes.

As your patrol car comes to a stop in front of the house in question, you can hear screaming and shouting coming from inside. After quickly surveying the surrounding area your partner looks through the front porch window and observes a middle aged couple having an argument. The screaming diminishes when your partner knocks on the front door and announces your presence.

A middle aged man comes to the door and asks if he can help you. Your partner introduces you and himself and asks if it is alright to come in the house and talk.

Following the man and your partner into the living room, you see the woman sitting on a sofa. The living room is a mess. There are paint cans, paint brushes, and newspapers laying around the floor. It is obvious that they are in the process of painting the living room.

You ask the woman what the trouble is and she becomes belligerent. The woman has obviously been drinking and is becoming quite intoxicated. The woman explains to you that she wanted light blue paint in the living room and that her husband started painting the room in beige. The woman suddenly gets up from the sofa and begins to weave around the living room cursing her husband. The woman's husband apologizes to you for his wife's behavior. He tells you that he was painting the living room when his wife came home from a friend's house — apparently having had too much to drink. He further explains that he is afraid his wife may be becoming an alcoholic.

The woman seems to become even more infuriated and, picking up a paint roller, threatens him with it. You step toward the woman in an attempt to quiet her down. She unexpectedly swings the roller at you hitting you on the arm, splattering paint over your uniform.

Your partner "protector" aggressively relieves the woman of her paint roller and threatens even more violent action unless she settles down. Reacting to the sudden outburst the woman's husband begins to shout at your partner to leave his wife alone and moves toward him in a belligerent manner.

You can see the situation rapidly getting out of hand and know that you must do something.

Based on what you have read, answer the following questions:

1. What should the female officer do at this point?
2. Would the situation have been different if both officers were male?
3. What suggestions can you make that would prevent a similar occurence?

Case 2

Between a Rock and a Hard Place

You are a Deputy Sheriff in a small rural county. Your main duties are to serve court processes such as warrants, subpoenas, and court orders. The Sheriff has called you to the office to pick up and serve a court order.

As you walk inside the Sheriff's office, you notice a small-framed, dirty looking woman in her early thirties sitting in a chair. You know the woman because she has been on the arrest docket for everything from prostitution to child abuse.

The Sheriff gives you a Court Order from the Judge. The order is to be served on the woman's mother-in-law. You ask the Sheriff what the Court Order concerns and he explains that apparently the woman's small child was being treated for a minor illness at the hospital and the woman's mother-in-law came to the hospital and picked the child up without permission. The Sheriff further explained that the woman's mother-in-law refused to return the child to his mother. The Sheriff advises you to serve the court order on the mother-in-law. The Sheriff further advises that "a lady from Human Services will meet you at the scene to take custody of the child."

The Court Order sickens you. You feel that the woman may only want the child back to get back at her mother-in-law. Based on her previous behavior, you feel the woman is an unfit mother, but the court seems reluctant to remove the child from her care and supervision. The woman's husband left her when the baby was born and the mother-in-law has tried to take custody of the child on several occasions. In fact, the woman and the mother-in-law have been fighting over the child for three years.

You know that the woman is using the law and you to get the child back. The woman does not seem to have any real concern for the well-being of the child and appears to want only the extra welfare money she receives. You know the woman's mother-in-law will not give the child up easily. You even hope that the mother-in-law and child will not be at home when you arrive with the Court Order.

As you arrive at the mother-in-law's home, you can see the child peering out a window. While knocking on the front door, you glance back and notice the Human Services representative arriving with the mother.

"Why the hell did she bring the mother over here?" you mumble to yourself. The mother-in-law comes to the door and becomes increasingly angry as you try to explain that you have a court order and must take the child and return it to its mother.

The mother-in-law begins to explain the reasons she took the child. She tells you the mother had not taken proper care of the child. She tells you the child was sick and malnourished. She adds that the hospital had treated the child for a severe chest cold and that she had taken the child in order to clothe and feed it.

You know that the mother-in-law is probably right. But, you also feel that you have no choice but to pick the child up and return it to its mother.

The mother-in-law picks up an old single barrel shotgun from behind the door and points it at you. She tells you that she will kill you before letting the child go back to the mother.

The mother-in-law is getting very upset and begins to cry. Pointing the shotgun, she threatens the child's mother with violence. The child's mother begins to yell at you and her mother-in-law. The mother-in-law is becoming increasingly upset. The Human Services lady looks surprised and indecisive.

The child in question is also beginning to cry. What are you going to do?

Based on what you have read, answer the following questions:

1. What should the deputy do at this point?
2. Can the deputy legally do anything to prevent the mother from taking custody of her child?
3. What would have been the best course of action to start with?

Case 3
Christmas Eve

You are a police officer responding to a family disturbance call. It is Christmas Eve and your department has a skeleton force working the three to eleven p.m. shift, so you are alone on the call.

You recognize the address of the complaint. You have been there previously on the same type of call. The house to which you are enroute contains a man, his wife, and two young children. The husband, Charlie Adams, drinks heavily and subsequently becomes obnoxious. You assume that Charlie is drunk again. In the past, you have been able to calm Charlie down by threatening to take him to jail.

When you arrive at the scene, you notice an out-of-state car parked in the driveway and wonder if the Adams have family in for the holidays. You advise the dispatcher that you have arrived and get out of your cruiser. While walking up to the front porch, you can hear loud arguing coming from inside the house.

After knocking on the door several times, Charlie opens it. He is obviously intoxicated and becomes agitated when he sees you. He asks what you want and you explain that you received a call from the neighbors again. You add that you are becoming tired of having to quiet him so frequently. Charlie's wife is behind him in the living room and angrily suggests that you lock him up.

There are other people in the living room and Charlie indicates they are his in-laws. As you step inside the living room you notice several bottles of liquor sitting on the table. Everyone has apparently been drinking. Using a familiar play, you tell Charlie that if he does not keep quiet that you will take him to jail.

Mrs. Adams comes up to you and begins telling you that Charlie has become a nuisance and she wants him out of the house. The brother-in-law also begins to talk negatively about Charlie. Mrs. Adams continues her tirade by telling you that Charlie is an unfit father and hates the children.

The two children come into the living room to see what is happening. Mrs. Adams tells the children to go to their room because daddy is drunk again.

Suddenly, Charlie screams at his wife and grabbing her by the hair, begins to slap her. The two guests retreat in fear to the other end of the room. You quickly attempt to separate the two, primarily to keep Charlie from seriously injuring his wife. Charlie lets go of his wife and begins to struggle with you. By now Charlie has completely lost his cool and you find yourself becoming more aggressive out of necessity. You have finally pinned Charlie against the wall and are putting handcuffs on him when his wife and in-laws begin threatening to attack you. Although you have temporarily subdued Charlie you realize a new threat exists as his wife and in-laws become increasingly agitated.

You are alone and the situation is rapidly deteriorating. What are you going to do?

Based on what you have read, answer the following questions:

1. What options does the officer have in handling the situation? Which option will be the most effective?

2. If the officer had a partner, could the situation be handled differently?
3. What can the police do in "repeat calls" to help prevent them from occuring over and over again?

Case 4

Wife Battering

You are a police officer assigned to an inner city beat comprised of mostly poor minority families. You and your partner have been assigned to this beat for only a few weeks and are both uncomfortable with relations between the police and the community.

You receive a call to proceed to a nearby housing project regarding a domestic disturbance. Upon your arrival, you hear shouting and banging noises coming from within the house. When your partner knocks on the door and announces your presence, the noise inside the house subsides. After a few moments of silence, the door is opened by a seven or eight year old boy.

The young boy is obviously frightened. The boy tells you that his mother is sick and cannot come to the door. The boy also tells you that his father is not at home. You explain to the young boy that it is necessary that you see his mother. The boy runs back inside the house and down the hallway. You and your partner step inside the doorway.

You hear a man's voice coming from the dark hallway. The man is cursing as he walks down the hallway toward you and your partner. The man belligerently orders you to leave his house. He adds that he did not call you and that he does not want or need you on his premises.

Remembering that the radio dispatcher advised you to see a woman complainant, you ask to see the man's wife. The man tells you that his wife is in the bathtub and cannot come out. You explain to the man that you will wait for his wife to finish her bath so you can talk with her. The man curses again and shouts for his wife to come out.

As the woman comes out of a bedroom down the hallway, you can see that she is in pain. Her face is bruised and swollen and she is holding her left arm as if it were broken. You ask the woman if there is any problem. Although her lips are swollen badly, she tells you everything is alright. The woman will not answer any additional questions. Each time you ask her a question you notice that she glances at her husband in a terrified manner. The husband again orders you and your partner to leave his house.

It is obvious to you that the woman is in need of medical care. Her arm appears as though it may be broken and her face has been badly beaten. She refuses to talk to you and her husband has ordered you out of the house. What are you going to do?

Based on what you have read, answer the following questions:

1. What are the legal implications in this situation? What can the police do legally?
2. Would the situation have been different if the child had been the one beaten?
3. What community resources are available to assist the police and families in these problem situations?

Case 5

Domestic Violence: A View from the Law

You are a Captain in charge of training and special programs for your police department of 468 sworn officers. Ten years ago you were instrumental in organizing a special crisis intervention response team for domestic disturbance calls. Your special unit was a model for other police departments in your state. The team was designed around the current research at the time on police intervention with family violence. Your unit was trained in counseling techniques, defusing violent situations, referrals and other helping responses to family disturbances. You were proud of the team's capability in handling these types of cases without having to use regular patrol officers. As a result, patrol officers found more time to devote to other serious crime prevention and investigation efforts.

During the past several years, budget cuts in your department have compromised many specialized units including the Domestic Disturbance Response Team (DDT). The administration cut your unit by 50 percent in manpower and budget allocations. The officer in charge of the current five-person detail has relied on volunteers and other community service agencies to help fill the gaps. You regret that the unit you had started was being reduced but you are also aware of the budget problems in your department. Because of the "cuts," most domestic disturbance calls are now answered by regular patrol officers with little training in crisis intervention techniques.

The news media have increasingly begun to focus on a number of family violence issues in and around your city. In fact, last month there were two deaths resulting from a domestic squabble in your city. There have been five instances of death and/or serious bodily injuries in family violence cases in your immediate metropolitan area over the past three months. The news media seems to be providing high exposure for these cases due to the public's increased awareness of family violence situations. You personally feel that it is not so much an increase in family violence as it is an increase in awareness of the problem.

The state legislature recently passed a new law in response to the increasing awareness of family violence problems. The new law provides more police authority in dealing with family violence. Basically, the new law gives police officers the discretion to make an arrest with probable cause in family assault cases even if the victim does not wish to press charges. In response to the new law, your Chief of Police added some "muscle" to the procedure by issuing a mandatory arrest policy in such cases. The new procedure has opened the door to possibly eliminating the Domestic Disturbance Response Team.

The new procedure has also increased the number of arrests in your city for domestic assaults. However, there seems to be a decrease in the number of overall calls for police intervention regarding family disturbances and the calls that are received seem to be the more serious cases.

Feedback from patrol officers in training sessions concerning the new procedure indicate they support the policy for the most part. Prosecuting attorneys also appear to support the new procedure, but they also seem to be pressing for convictions rather than solving family problems.

Several leaders of community and religious organizations have begun to call the Chief to complain that the new procedure detracts from actually helping families caught in domestic disturbance situations. The Chief has called you into his office.

"Ed, you've been good at getting to the root of problems regarding our response to family violence and coming up with innovative solutions. I've got a new one for you to work on. This new domestic violence law has some good points to it but I believe it's just a band-aid solution. I've got these community organizations on my back wanting us to provide more helping tactics rather than just arresting people in domestic disturbance situations. I've got this new law to enforce. I must keep us out of civil liability. I've got an increase in the number of husbands in our jail population. They've got hungry kids and wives to support and they're also on my back. I've got a budget that's already in the red. And if that's not enough, I'm out of Alka-Seltzer. Ed, I'm putting you in charge of figuring a way to resolve these problems. I need an answer yesterday, but I'll give you to the end of the week."

"Well, Chief, I may be able to solve one of your problems right away. It looks as though I'm going to need some Alka-Seltzer too," you respond.

Based on what you have read, answer the following questions:

1. What options and resources does the Captain have to help solve these problems? Briefly outline a plan of action you would take to solve some of these problems. Include ways of dealing with the budget, the community, the legal system and officers in your department.

2. What are the advantages and disadvantages of police intervention with arrest in domestic violence cases? If the Captain persuaded the Chief to rescind the mandatory arrest order and follow the discretionary arrest law as written, would this alone solve the problem?

3. What are your state laws on police intervention in domestic violence cases?

Case 6
Police Officer or Social Worker?

Jack and Ann Smith are a married couple with three children ranging in age from five months to six years. Jack is unemployed and is sixty percent disabled from a wound he received in Vietnam. Ann has to provide primary care for the children and also has a part-time job at a nearby grocery store. Jack and Ann live in a housing project where the rent is based on the government welfare checks they receive.

It is near the end of the month and the food stamps have almost been depleted. Jack spent what little money they had left on beer for himself and his friends. Over the years, Jack has continued to feel bitter about his disability and apparently tries to drown his problems with alcohol.

Jack and Ann had an argument earlier in the day over the amount of money Jack spends on beer and wine. Ann was also becoming increasingly upset over Jack frequenting bars and not trying to help with household responsibilities and chores. Ann even accused Jack of feeling sorry for himself and of being a failure in general. Jack responded by slapping Ann several times and leaving the house in a fit of temper.

While Jack was gone, the two eldest children began fighting with each other which resulted in the youngest child crying. Although Ann had carefully cleaned the apartment the day before, the children had again made a mess of the house. Her patience wearing thin, Ann rocked the youngest child in a rocking chair in an effort to stop his crying. After substantial threats from their mother, the two oldest children started playing in the kitchen and eventually broke several dishes that were on the table. That was the last straw! Ann began whipping the oldest child for breaking the dishes. Full of anger and frustration, she whipped the child so hard that he fainted and was apparently unconscious.

Jack came back to the apartment a short time later, intoxicated and still upset over the argument he and Ann had engaged in earlier. He found the younger children crying, the oldest child badly beaten, and Ann sitting in a kitchen chair sobbing. In a fit of rage, Jack began beating Ann.

The next-door-neighbor, aware of what was happening, called the police and explained the situation.

You are a patrol officer assigned to the call. Your partner is a female officer with little police experience. Not knowing for sure what the situation is, you do not call for a back up car. In your opinion, at this point, it is a routine family disturbance call.

Standing outside the Smith's apartment door, you hear children sobbing. No one answers the door or speaks to you when you knock. You think to yourself, "These people need a social worker, not a police officer." Your partner looks at you, uncertain and waiting for instructions. You take a deep breath and try to decide what the best course of action will be.

Based on what you have read, answer the following questions:

1. What can the officers legally do?
2. What other agencies other than the police could help in this situation?
3. Should the police become involved in these types of situations?

Case 7
Feuding Families

You are a police officer working in a middle class residential neighborhood. You are currently on your way to answer a domestic disturbance call. You are aware of the problem because this is the third time in a month you have answered such a call at the Wallace residence.

The problem apparently exists between the Wallaces and their next-door neighbors, the Murrays. At one time, the Murray family were close friends with the Wallaces. Both husbands worked in the same factory until a strike occurred. After several weeks of being on strike, Mr. Wallace crossed the picket line and returned to work. He did not really want to go against his union, but felt that he had to in order to meet his family's needs. Wallace and several of the strike-breakers felt the strike benefits were too meager to feed and maintain their families.

Mr. Murray has been a staunch union member for years and deeply resented Mr. Wallace returning to work. The Murray's broke off all relations with the Wallaces which made Mr. Wallace upset. Several weeks later someone broke out the windshield of Mr. Wallace's car and poisoned his dog. Mr. Wallace felt that Mr. Murray was responsible and called the police. Being on duty, you had answered the call.

The second time you answered a call at the Wallace residence, Mr. Wallace had reported that someone had tried to set fire to his house. He immediately accused Mr. Murray of attempted arson and almost became involved in a fist fight with his neighbor on the sidewalk in front of the house. You had to break up the confrontation before they began hitting one another. Although angry, Mr. Murray refused to press charges but did repeatedly threaten Mr. Wallace in front of you.

The vandalism, dog poisoning and attempted arson were investigated by yourself and the detectives. There was no evidence which indicated Mr. Murray was the perpetrator. However, Mr. Wallace continued to accuse the Murray's for all the offenses even though there was no evidence or other grounds for arresting Mr. Murray.

Mr. Murray is the complainant on the call you are now responding to. Apparently on this occasion there has been a fire at the Murray residence.

As you stop your cruiser behind the fire truck in front of the Murray house, you notice that the garage has been on fire. There seems to be little damage to the structure and the firemen are preparing to leave. After questioning the fire marshal you find that the fire was started by gasoline stored in the garage.

Mr. Murray comes up to you and angrily demands that you arrest Mr. Wallace. In your conversation Mr. Murray admits that he did not see anyone setting the fire in his garage. Nevertheless, he is convinced Mr. Wallace is trying to get even with him.

You question Mr. Wallace and he denies having anything to do with the fire. In fact, Mr. Wallace contends that Mr. Murray started the fire himself just so he could accuse Mr. Wallace.

You realize there are no grounds for an arrest based on such speculations. You are also now concerned that if no action is taken soon, the situation will become worse and may even result in serious injury to one or both of the neighbors. This is the third call you have had to answer and it is obvious that a family feud is quickly developing. What are you going to do?

Based on what you have read, answer the following questions:

1. What should the officer do or say to Mr. Wallace and Mr. Murray? How will this resolve the conflict?
2. Should the officer arrest Mr. Murray for verbally threatening Mr. Wallace?
3. If another neighbor had seen Mr. Murray setting the fire on his own property, what would you do?

Section II
Selected Bibliography

Bard, M., and J. Zacker (1976). *Police and Interpersonal Conflict: Third-party Intervention Approaches.* Washington, D.C.: The Police Foundation.

Bell, D.J. (1985). "Police Response to Domestic Violence: A Multiyear Study," *Police Studies,* 8(1).

Campbell, J., and J. Humphreys (1984). *Nursing Care of Victims of Family Violence.* Stanford, CA: Hoover Institution Press.

Coffey, A.R. (1974). *Police Intervention into Family Crisis: The Role of Law Enforcement in Family Problems.* Santa Cruz, CA: Davis Publishing Co.

Columbus Police Department (1974). *Developing Skills for Family Crisis Intervention.* Columbus, GA: Columbus Police Department.

Delaware Commission for Women (1984). *Domestic Violence Task Force Report.* Wilmington, DE: Delaware Commission for Women.

Faragher, T. (1985). "Police Response to Violence against Women in the Home," in J. Pahl (ed.), *Private Violence and Public Policy.* Boston: Routledge and Kegan Pauls, Ltd.

Goldstein, A.P., et al. (1977). *Police Crisis Intervention.* Kalamazoo, MI: Behaviordelia, Inc.

Goolkasian, G.A. (1986). *Confronting Domestic Violence: A Guide for Criminal Justice Agencies.* Washington, D.C.: Government Printing Office.

Green, E.J. (1976). *Psychology for Law Enforcement.* New York: John Wiley and Sons.

International Association of Chiefs of Police (1974). *Crisis Intervention - Training Key.* Gaithersburg, MD: IACP.

Jolin, A. (1983). "Domestic Violence Legislation: An Impact Assessment," *Journal of Police Science and Administration,* 11(4).

Kobetz, R.W. (1974). *Crisis Intervention and the Police: Selected Readings.* Gaithersburg, MD: International Association of Chiefs of Police.

Phelps, L.G., and J.A. Schwartz (1971). "Training an Entire Patrol Division in Domestic Crisis Intervention Techniques," *The Police Chief,* 38(July).

Roberts, A.R. (1984). *Battered Women and Their Families.* New York: Springer Publishing Co.

U.S. Department of Justice (1970). *Training Police as Specialists in Family Crisis Intervention.* Washington, D.C.: Government Printing Office.

U.S. Department of Justice (1976). *To Keep the Peace: Crisis Management in Law Enforcement.* Washington, D.C.: Government Printing Office.

U.S. Department of Justice (1985). *All They Can Do: Police Response to Battered Women's Complaints.* Washington, D.C.: National Institute of Justice.

Section III

The Police and Juveniles

Introduction

The majority of police contact with juveniles comes after they get involved in some antisocial or delinquent behavior. Because of this limited contact, police officers may perceive many juveniles as either delinquent or potentially delinquent. Therefore, it is easy for an officer to develop negative attitudes toward juveniles in general. Most police officers realize that a large number of adult offenders have juvenile offense records. This factor also increases the negative attitudes of police officers toward juvenile offenders.

The juvenile justice system is a separate and distinct system from the adult criminal justice system. Juvenile offenders do not commit crimes, they commit delinquent acts. Therefore, police officers must handle juveniles much differently than adults. Many police officers are apprehensive about the juvenile justice system. Officers often view juvenile justice in the same light as criminal justice. The philosophy of juvenile justice maintains that it is different from criminal justice. Nevertheless, police officers frequently become irritated and frustrated when they see a juvenile "get off easy" for a crime which would send an adult to prison.

Police officers are also directly or indirectly involved in the assistance, aid, and counseling of juveniles. Police officers are expected in many cases to counsel potentially delinquent juveniles. Many police agencies and juvenile court agencies utilize off-duty police officers on a voluntary basis as "guidance counselors" for misguided youth. This follows the same philosophy as the juvenile courts in that juvenile offenders need help or guidance rather than punishment.

The Philosophy of the Juvenile Justice System

Courts and law have been inclined to take a special attitude toward juveniles who commit offenses. Under the English Common Law, a child under seven could not be convicted of a crime. The child was regarded as not responsible and not chargeable with the offense. For children between the ages of seven and fourteen, the common law presumed that a child was not responsible for an offense, but was open to

49

review by the court to determine if the child had enough intelligence to realize the act was wrong. Because many of these children could pass the test, it was not uncommon for them to be sentenced to long penitentiary terms or to death.

During the nineteenth century, public opinion changed and turned against imprisoning young children with hardened adult criminals. Reformatories and training schools were developed for the detention, education, and rehabilitation of young offenders. Special courts were established along with procedures for dealing with delinquent youth. To carry out the court philosophy of care and protection rather than punishment, these courts were given jurisdiction over dependent and neglected children as well.

In most states the Juvenile Court handles cases involving juveniles below the age of eighteen. If the juvenile offender has committed a serious offense, such as murder, the Juvenile Court may waive jurisdiction and send the child to an adult criminal court providing the child meets age requirements. Theoretically, a juvenile offender is not prosecuted and there is no conviction. The state is not trying to punish the offender, but is trying to find out what is wrong and how to deal with it in a way that is both beneficial for the child as well as the public (Miller, 1976). As a result, the Juvenile Court is usually informal and private, although more recently appellate and supreme court decisions have made the procedure more formalized in order to protect the child's due process rights.

The Police Officer's View of Juvenile Offenders

It is often difficult for police officers to accept the Juvenile Court's point of view regarding juvenile offenders. The Juvenile Court is committed to the viewpoint of aiding a juvenile offender, even those who are serious and repeat offenders. The laws applying to juvenile offenders are designed to help the youth as much as possible without subjecting the community to threat of danger or disruption. Many police officers are often frustrated by, what appears to them, the Juvenile Court letting juvenile criminals go free and unpunished. As a result, police officers are inclined to feel uncomfortable in dealing with juvenile offenders because of the philosophy of the juvenile justice system.

There is a fine line that exists between delinquent behavior and delinquent criminal behavior which is not always clear and often confusing for police officers. Many offenses for which a juvenile may be arrested are not offenses for adults. Possession of alcoholic beverages, running away from home, and violation of curfew are offenses for juveniles and are, thus, status offenses. Delinquent criminal acts are offenses for which an adult could also be arrested. Therefore, many police officers become apprehensive toward making arrests of juveniles committing status offenses. Police officers may feel that such juvenile offenders would be "better off" when punished by their parents or a referral agency rather than bringing formal charges in Juvenile Court. In this respect, police officers have a great deal of discretionary flexibility when dealing with juveniles. The appropriate use of this flexibility may not only prevent the stigma of labeling a juvenile a delinquent, but may also prevent the juvenile's behavior from progressing to adult criminal offenses.

The Juvenile's View of Police Officers

The police officer has one important negative barrier to overcome even before contact is made with a juvenile: to most juveniles, a police officer is the symbol of bad experiences with other authority figures including fathers, mothers, and teachers. As a result, the police officer may become a victim of displacement, where the negative attitudes juveniles have toward other authority figures becomes focused on the officer.

When a juvenile is in the presence of his or her peer group approached by a police officer, he/she may react in a disrespectful "tough" manner. Norms of a juvenile's peer group can create a view of the police as foes and disrespect may be demonstrated by refusing to be "shoved around" or "clamming up" when police officers ask questions. Therefore, it is important that police officers recognize that any relationship formed with a juvenile will, to a large extent, be dependent upon the officer's manner of approach, the officer's ability to communicate, and the impact of peers present at the interaction.

Police officers who approach a juvenile in a negative manner immediately decreases the possibility for any positive relationship or communication with the juvenile. Police officers who use excessive authority and adopt overbearing attitudes are communicating disrespect to a juvenile and will find it very difficult to gain the trust or confidence of the youth in question. Juvenile mistrust of police officers may even continue into their adulthood. Juveniles are often very sensitive to the insecurities and attitudes of adults in general and may be able to detect even the slightest amount of deception.

Juveniles often interpret events quite differently than adults. For instance, an adult who receives a speeding citation may dismiss it as bad luck being caught whereas a juvenile who receives a ticket may experience substantial fear of being cited including significant dread of any punitive consequences. The juvenile may also perceive the officer's speeding citation as a form of harassment. In addition, some police officers refuse to give the same consideration as they do to adults. When this occurs, juveniles often perceive such differential treatment as discrimination.

Policing Juvenile Offenders

When police officers detect an offense by a juvenile, a discretionary judgement is usually made. The juvenile offender may either be diverted from the juvenile justice process or taken into custody. Two-thirds of the juveniles who come into contact with the police are handled informally (Klein, 1976). Informal handling may include verbal reprimands, counseling with the youth and his/her parents, or referral to a community agency for treatment. Formal handling involves official arrest, detention, and court appearances.

Diversion is a commonly used approach when dealing with juvenile offenders. Diversion usually consists of an agreement between the juvenile, the parents, and the police which includes referral to a community helping agency and informal probation. With such arrangements the juvenile typically reports to a probation officer on a scheduled basis.

Generally, the legal standards for juvenile offenders are broader than those for adult arrests. Whereas the probable cause standard is used in adult arrest, police officers have more discretion in determining if juvenile offenders fall under the jurisdiction of the Juvenile Court (Senna and Siegel, 1981). Discretion of arrest in juvenile cases has both positive and negative aspects. The flexibility given police officers in decision making can be beneficial, but this flexibility can be misused and indiscriminately applied to an individual juvenile.

Studies of police arrest patterns indicate that several factors are important in determining whether a juvenile offender is handled formally or informally. The most influential factor in the arrest decision process seems to be the severity of the offense (Piliavin and Briar, 1964). Serious offenses are generally handled formally by the police. The number of prior contacts a juvenile offender has had with the police, the social status of the juvenile, the race of the juvenile, the age of the juvenile, and the juvenile offender's general attitude and demeanor are all additional factors influencing whether the police handle the juvenile offender formally or informally (Murrell and Lester, 1981).

When police officers handle juvenile offenders in a formal manner, the practice follows procedures similar to those for adults. Court decisions have established due process guidelines for juvenile offenders along the same general lines as due process rights of adults (Fox, 1984).

The Police and Child Abuse

The police and the juvenile justice system plays a very critical role in the problem of child abuse. Child abuse not only includes the physical battering and mistreatment of children but also neglect. A wide range of behavior may be defined as child abuse. Abuse may include physical, emotional, medical, educational, and moral forms of neglect (Johnson, 1975). Physical neglect relates to environmental conditions in which a child may be confined. The physical condition of the child's home where dirt and a lack of sanitation exists is considered physical neglect. In addition, improper care for a child such as inadequate clothing or lack of food constitutes physical neglect. Emotional neglect involves the failure of parents to provide adequate emotional support for a child. Medical neglect are those instances where the parents do not provide necessary medical treatment to correct a condition from which a child suffers. Educational neglect may occur when the parent fails to make a child available for school as required by state statutes. Moral neglect occurs when the child is subjected to immoral influences which may be corruptive.

Even with increased legal authority for police officers, teachers, and physicians to act on behalf of abused children, the courts have often been reluctant to remove children from such environments (Dyke, 1980; Smith and Meyer, 1984). One of the major problems is the definition of child abuse and neglect. Although one can label the types of abuse and neglect as moral, physical, emotional, educational, and medical, it is sometimes difficult to determine where to draw the line. What is considered physical abuse by one person may be considered proper control by another (Gelles, 1978). The courts are reluctant to break apart families by removing children unless the abuse is very serious or if charges of abuse have been brought before the court previously. By the same token, police officers are reluctant to interfere with the parents' control of their children. The difference in perception of child abuse by juvenile court judges and vague laws regarding child abusive parents, creates a sense of apprehensiveness for police officers acting on suspected child abuse cases.

There is concern over the increasing reports of child sexual exploitation and molestation. Child sexual abuse, incest and exploitation cases are often difficult for police to discover. Many child sexual molesters are non-violent, respected members of the community. In most cases, the exploiting adult, the child victim and, often, the parents of the victim conspire in silence for mutual protection from the police and criminal justice system (Caplan, 1982). The discovery and/or reporting of child sexual abuse is typically by accident and often not due to any rigorous investigative efforts. For example, it appears that in father-daughter incest cases, the mother may often be aware of the problem and may even support the practice (Ward, 1985).

Summary

Police officers have a unique impact on juveniles' attitudes. How a police officer relates to a juvenile has a significant impact on the type of attitude the youth will have toward law enforcement in general for years to come. It is important for police officers to realize that they are usually the first contact a juvenile has with "the system." The difference between the juvenile justice system and the criminal justice system provides an avenue of discretion for police officers dealing with juvenile offenders.

Because the philosophy of the juvenile justice system is focused on the care and protection of the child, the police are allowed to utilize the same philosophy in their dealings with juveniles. This philosophy not only provides broader discretion for police officers, but also allows for broader action by police officers in trying to help correct problem juveniles. Police officers and other officials have broad authority under the law to act on suspected cases of child abuse and neglect. Therefore, police officers are not only acting as representatives of the law with juveniles, but also can provide a social service or helping function when interacting with youth.

References

Caplan, G. (1982). "Sexual Exploitation of Children," *Police Magazine*, January.

Dyke, E.V. (1980). "Child abuse," *New York Teacher*, May 18.

Fox, S. (1984). *The Law of Juvenile Courts in a Nutshell*. 3rd ed. St. Paul, MN: West Publishing Co.

Johnson, T.A. (1975). *Introduction to the Juvenile Justice System*. St. Paul, MN: West Publishing Co.

Klein, M. (1976). "Issues in Police Diversion of Juvenile Offenders," in R. Carter and M. Klein, (eds.), *Back on the Street*. Englewood Cliffs, NJ: Prentice-Hall.

Miller, F., et al. (1976). *The Juvenile Justice Process*. Mineola, NY: The Foundation Press.

Murrell, M., and D. Lester (1981). *Introduction to Juvenile Delinquency*. New York: MacMillan Publishing Co.

Piliavin, I., and S. Briar (1964). "Police Encounters with Juveniles," *American Journal of Sociology*, September.

Senna, J., and L. Siegel (1981). *Juvenile Delinquency: Theory, Practice and Law*. St. Paul, MN: West Publishing Co.

Smith, S.R., and R.G. Meyer (1984). "Child Abuse Reporting Laws and Psychotherapy: A Time for Reconsideration," *International Journal of Law and Psychiatry*, 7(3-4): 351-366.

Ward, E. (1985). *Father-daughter Rape*. New York: Grove Press.

Cases in the Police and Juveniles

The impact the police have on juveniles is largely determined by the attitudes and personal conduct of the individual officer. Every police officer must bear in mind that he or she is not only a representative of the law, but may also have to fulfill social service functions when interacting with juveniles.

In dealing with a younger child or older juvenile who has violated the law, the police officer is often the system's first official contact. Many times he or she takes on the additional responsibilities of being prosecutor, judge, and correctional representative as well. There are thousands of cases each year in which youths are unofficially counseled and worked with by police officers. These officers exert considerable influence, for better or worse, in the lives of juveniles with which they come in contact.

Case number one, "Right Side of the Tracks, Wrong Side of the Law," deals with a group of upper middle-class teenagers involved in drug dealing and vandalism. A deputy sheriff must decide what he will recommend to the judge. The Sheriff wants the case dismissed; the D.A. wants blood.

Case number two, "I Sorry Officer," explores a situation common among lower socio-economic class juveniles. A police officer is faced with not only a law enforcement matter, but one that brings the officer to a face-to-face reality with the problems of the poor.

Case number three, "The System," portrays a situation where a police officer has stereotyped all juveniles as delinquents. Police officers sometimes become cynical and view the majority of juveniles negatively which creates a barrier between the police and younger citizens.

Case number four, "A Loving Father?" examines the problem of father-daughter incest. A police officer and social worker must investigate two young girls' accusations of incest by their father.

Case number five, "The Bust," focuses on a common occurence in police work. What should a police officer do when faced with a juvenile in possession of marijuana? Aware of the decreasing penalties for marijuana possession, the police officer in this case attempts to find an approach that will benefit the juvenile offender in the most effective manner.

Case number six, "Neighborhood Brat," examines a police officer interacting with the parents of a juvenile offender. It is sometimes difficult for parents to understand that their children are not always what they view them to be. In this case, the parents of a young boy refuse to believe that their son can commit delinquent acts.

Case number seven, "The Hitchhikers," involves the legal and emotional concerns of a police officer dealing with run-aways." The officer finds that while locating and returning juvenile run-aways to their parents is a police responsibility, the circumstances surrounding the run-away act may be more important.

Case 1

Right Side of the Tracks—
Wrong Side of the Law

You are a criminal investigator for a medium-sized sheriff's department serving a county population of nearly 1 million people. The Sheriff, an elected official, usually keeps out of the business of law enforcement and would rather seek public attention and political recognition. The Sheriff has indicated that he would like to seek a higher public office such as state representative in the near future. The Chief Deputy, Hal Owens, takes care of the daily business of running the Sheriff's Department.

You have received a call from the principal at one of the county's high schools regarding possible drug dealing, vandalism and larcenies occurring in and around the school. You are scheduled to meet with Mr. Jaynes, the school principal this morning.

"Good morning Mr. Jaynes. I'm Detective Bill Anderson," you state walking into the principal's office.

"Yes, good morning. May I get you a cup of coffee?" Mr. Jaynes asks as he reaches for the coffee pot.

"That would be great, thanks. I take it black," you respond while sitting down next to the desk.

"I know you're busy so I'll get right to it. We've had some problems with vandalism and larcenies here at the school. I've also been suspicious of some of the students involved in drug dealing here on school grounds," Mr. Jaynes explains.

"Do you know who they are?" you ask fumbling for your pen.

"Well, I don't have any proof but I've made a list of those students I suspect. They hang out together," Mr. Jaynes states handing you the list.

I'm not too familiar with these names, except...is this Guy Edwards, Jr. the state senator's son?" you ask, pointing to the list. "Yes, it is. I know you must be surprised because of his father's position, but he's no angel here at the school. Those other kids are all from good families too. Bobby's father is a physician, Andy's is an attorney and Gary's is president of the oil company here," Mr. Jaynes continues.

"Well, I am surprised these kids would get into anything as serious as drug dealing," you respond.

Later that day you decide to visit the District Attorney to determine the best tactic in investigating the case.

"Yes, Bill, I see why you are concerned after reading this list of names," the D.A. states.

"I wanted to check with you to see how I should go about investigating these allegations," you respond.

"I'm not too concerned with the vandalism and petit larcenies at this time but I am concerned about their involvement in selling drugs. I would suggest you stake out the school where they've been known to deal and get the usual evidence, photographs, and so on," the D.A. states.

Two weeks later, one of your undercover surveillance officers calls you to report that three of the boys had been arrested at the stake out. One of the boys is the state senator's son, Gary Edwards, Jr.

"Caught them red-handed Bill. Had 'coke,' 'crack,' and a bunch of Dilaudids they were selling like candy," the detective tells you while handing you the arrest reports.

"This is their first offense according to Juvenile Hall. They'll probably get off with probation and some community service work," you state.

The next day, Chief Deputy Owens calls you into his office.

"Bill, we've got a little problem with these kids on the dope charges. You know one of them is Senator Edwards' son. Senator Edwards and the Sheriff are of the same political party and are good friends. The Senator has been supporting the Sheriff to run for state representative. You also may know that the D.A. is seeking the same office and is in a different party. Now, the D.A. wants to press this for all he can get politically. If he can get some bad publicity for Senator Edwards and the Sheriff, it may help him during his campaign. The Sheriff wants to know if you can help get these kids off as easy and as quickly as possible without a lot of media attention. Now I'm not talking about doing something unethical here. If those boys are truly guilty, the Sheriff says to throw the book at them. He can't afford a scandal either with something that looks like a cover-up," the Chief explains.

"I understand. I'll see what I can do," you reply.

You have a meeting scheduled with Ralph Davis, a juvenile probation officer at Juvenile Hall.

"Ralph, what about these kids? Are they really rotten or do they have some hope?" you ask, referring to the arrest reports.

"I've never seen such a bunch of cry babies in my life. These kids are scared to death. You know I've been in this business a long time and I know when I'm being conned. These kids have just gotten in with the wrong guy. They've all admitted to dealing drugs for this adult guy named Scooter Johnson and they said they'd testify against him. All they were looking for was some excitement and I guess some attention," Ralph advises.

"So, they're willing to testify against their supplier, huh?" you acknowledge.

"I'll tell you something, Bill. That D.A. doesn't care about getting Johnson. All he's interested in is convicting these boys. He told me he's going for incarceration for these kids at Afton State Youth Center," Ralph advises.

"The kiddie prison?" you ask in a surprised manner.

That's right. These kids don't need to go to Afton. I could handle them on probation and you could get their supplier on adult charges. If you will go to the Judge with me, I believe we can convince him of that," Ralph explains.

You know that Ralph may be correct in his judgment. The boys would have a better chance on probation than incarceration. You could satisfy the Sheriff and get the adult supplier as well. However, you need a good working relation with the D.A.'s office. The D.A., even if his priorities are different, may be correct in pressing for incarceration. After all, the boys were dealing with some hard drugs and may even be involved in other illegal activities. They may have even conned Ralph into believing their story. You remember when you were their age. You came up the hard way with no special privileges. Your father was a steelworker who believed in his country and the law. Besides, you never have cared much for cry babies. Still, this is their first offense even if it is a rather serious one. What are you going to do?

Based on what you have read, answer the following questions:

1. Should the detective go along with the juvenile probation officer and recommend probation? Explain the pros and cons of your decision.

2. If the boys were allowed on probation, what might result in terms of the boys future? What if they were incarcerated?

3. How do you think your decision will affect your relations with the Sheriff? The D.A.?

Case 2
I Sorry Officer

You are a police officer assigned to patrol in an urban residential area. Your beat is a lower socio-economic area comprised of housing projects, small stores, and warehouses. You are currently working the day shift.

While cruising through Elm Street, you routinely pull into a grocery store parking lot. Sometimes you are able to find stolen automobiles that have been abandoned in various public parking lots. As you begin to check a car with no license plates, you notice a small boy running between the parked cars. The boy appears to be attempting to hide from you. You get out of your patrol car and walk over to where the boy is hiding. You find the boy squatting behind one of the cars. He could be no more than seven or eight years old and is carefully guarding a large shopping bag he has in his possession.

You ask the boy where his mother is, thinking that a parent would not be far from such a small child. He quickly informs you that his mother is working at a factory two blocks away. The boy further explains that his father does not live with him and his mother anymore. He goes on to explain that his name is David and that he lives alone with his mother in a project several blocks away.

You look into the shopping bag and find that it contains C.B. radios, tape players, and other items found in automobiles. You ask David where he got the contents of the bag and he tells you he found them. David is unable to explain to you where he found the items. You pick up the shopping bag and take David by the hand and walk through the parking lot with him. You notice several cars with doors partially open and windows broken. Upon closer inspection, you find that they were apparently burglarized. Again, you ask David where he got the items in the shopping bag. David begins to cry and tells you he stole them from the cars in the parking lot.

You take David back to your patrol car and have him sit down in the front seat. By the way David is dressed you know he is poor. Sitting next to David in the car, you ask him what he was going to do with the stolen items. Still crying, he tells you about how he takes the stolen merchandise to a nearby high school and sells them to a teenage student. Apparently this is not the first time David has stolen things. David only knows the teenage fence by his first name, Willie. He tells you that Willie usually gives him a couple of dollars for the stolen items. It is obvious that Willie has a good racket going by buying several hundred dollars worth of goods for only a couple of dollars. Willie probably re-sells the items for three or four times the money he gives the small teary-eyed boy sitting in your cruiser. Seven year olds and teenagers! Your gut starts to ache as you wonder for a moment where it will stop, or if it, in fact, ever will.

David goes on to tell you that he only began stealing things a couple of weeks ago. He continues to explain that he only wanted enough money to buy a birthday present for his mother next week. David says that his mother has not received a birthday present since his father left. He wants to buy his mother a new dress.

A lot of kids have lied to you before, but this time you believe what David is telling you. You feel sorry for him. Knowing that what action you take will have a lasting impression on the child makes you uncomfortable and frustrated. Generally, all you would have to do would be to turn David over to the juvenile authorities and let them handle the case. It sickens you to think about treating the child in a formal police manner. You could wait until the owners of the property returned to their cars, give the items back to them and take David home. But, David needs to learn right from wrong. He needs so many things. You wonder how many other Davids are stealing for Willie. You buy David a coke to buy yourself some time, you need to think. He looks up at you for an answer. Your cruiser's radio breaks the silence, "DWI on Elm Street...".

Based on what you have read, answer the following questions:

1. What should the officer do?
2. Could the officer effectively handle the situation by himself? What options does the officer have?
3. The young boy could be an effective link into a serious burglary-larceny problem. What is the problem and how could it be handled by the police?

Case 3
The System

You are a young patrol officer with the traffic division of the police department. You recently graduated from the police academy and have been riding with a veteran officer for about a week. Your partner is, Jim Duncan, in his mid-forties and has eighteen years of experience with the department. Jim is up for a promotion to sergeant in a few weeks.

Your partner has been very helpful to you in explaining the "ins" and "outs" of working with the police department. Jim is also very likeable and you enjoy working with him. Although he has few negative qualities, one of them concerns his attitude toward juvenile drivers.

Jim seems to treat juvenile traffic offenders rather harshly. He seldom gives warning citations to juvenile traffic offenders regardless of the circumstances, and usually charges them with the maximum allowable offenses. Through your talks with Jim, you learn that his attitude may to a large extent be attributed to an accident his daughter was in several years ago. Jim has told you that his teenage daughter was on a date when her boyfriend wrecked the car killing her and only experiencing minor injuries himself. The boyfriend had been drinking and had run off the road into some trees. The boyfriend not only survived the accident, but was also able to beat the charges that were brought against him.

On one occasion, while working radar with Jim, you saw a red mustang come through the speed trap. The mustang was not speeding yet Jim chose to pursue the car. When you asked Jim why he was stopping the mustang, he replied that a "kid" was driving the car. Although confused, you noticed the unmistakable look of anger on your partner's face and decided not to ask any more questions.

After stopping the mustang, Jim got out of the patrol car and approached the driver. The driver was young, probably sixteen or seventeen years old. Jim took the teenager's drivers license and began to berate him for driving too fast. Still confused, you got out of the patrol car to see what your partner was doing. Jim continued to verbally abuse the teenager, cursing him and the type of car he was driving. The teenager began to get irritated and demanded to know why he was stopped. Jim wrote out a speeding citation and then checked the car closely in an effort to find additional code violations. It is becoming increasingly clear to you that Jim is not being very rational regarding the car and its passenger. You wonder why? Perhaps the car reminded him of his daughter's death. Again you decided to keep quiet.

A couple of weeks passed after the red mustang incident. You are unexpectedly called into the station to see your shift commander, he indicates that he has received several complaints from parents about your partner stopping teenagers for no cause and harrassing them. The commander asks you if you know of any such incident. Knowing that what you say may have a detrimental effect on Jim's promotion, and even his career, you hesitate in answering.

You know that Jim's behavior is creating a bad impression in the community. You are also becoming convinced that he probably needs some type of personal counseling to help him deal with his grief over his daughter's death and his current attitude problem. Should you share your feelings with the shift commander? On the other hand, what about Jim's promotion? He *is* your partner. The commander is waiting for an answer.

Based on what you have read, answer the following questions:

1. What seems to be Officer Jim Duncan's problem?
2. What would you say to the shift commander?
3. What should the shift commander do if he discovered Officer Duncan's problem? Would this decision affect Officer Duncan's career?

Case 4

A Loving Father?

You are a criminal investigator for a small police department serving a city of 78,000 people. You have worked as a criminal investigator for seven of your twelve years in the police department. Although crime in your city is not as serious as it would be in larger cities, you find there is plenty of work to do for a three-man detective division.

June Wilson, an attractive Human Services social worker has given you a telephone call.

"Pete, we need to get together and talk," June states.

"I'll chat with you anytime, anywhere," you state in a flirting manner.

"Now be nice Pete. I'm serious. I've got a case you need to be involved in. I've got a 15-year-old girl and her 10-year-old sister in my office and they're accusing their father of rape," June explains.

"Who did he rape, their mother?" you ask.

"Afraid not. He allegedly raped them," June responds.

"I'll be over in a few minutes," you advise.

Walking into June's office you notice the two girls sitting on a couch in the reception area.

Exchanging hellos, June continues, "Hi Pete. Just got off the phone with the Juvenile Court Judge. She's sending over a court order to place the girls into protective custody at the Emergency Youth Shelter until this investigation is over."

"How did you find out about this rape thing?" you ask.

"The older girl told her school nurse what had happened and the nurse called me. I went over to the school and interviewed the girl briefly. Then we picked up her sister," June explains.

"When did they say their father raped them?" you ask.

"It wasn't a single act. Evidently this has been going on for some time with the older girl, Alice. Alice said her father began having intercourse with her when she was 11. Now she says her father is having intercourse on a regular basis with both her and her 10-year-old sister," June replies.

"This is sick. Do you think they're telling the truth?" you ask.

"I've talked with both of them together and separately and I believe they're sincere. We'll have to go through the routine of taking their statements and video-taping their responses," June advises.

"Who's their father?" you ask.

"Name's Freddie Allen, resides at 1010 Elm Street with wife Eleanor," June states reading from her notes.

"Is that the same Freddie Allen who teaches at the junior high school?"

"One and the same. He also is the choir leader at school and teaches Sunday school and is the youth advisor at church," June responds.

"I'll need to talk with Mr. and Mrs. Allen," you advise.

"They're on their way here now," June replies.

A few minutes later the Allens arrive at June's office.

"What's going on here? Why are my kids down here?" Mr. Allen states angrily pushing his way into June's office, his wife following a few feet behind him.

"Sit down Mr. Allen, Mrs. Allen. I'm Detective Rogers and this is Ms. Wilson. We need to ask you a few questions," you advise them in a calm, yet assertive voice.

"Look, all I want to know from you is why my kids are here and not in school," Mr. Allen repeats with his wife looking scared behind him.

You notice Mr. Allen is sweating profusely and appears to be on the verge of an emotional outburst.

"Mr. Allen, I must advise you of your constitutional rights,...." you explain, verbally reading the Miranda warnings from your notebook.

"What's this all about? What am I supposed to have done?" Mr. Allen questions, getting more agitated and red-faced.

"Your daughters have accused you of having sexual intercourse with them on several occasions. A violation of state penal code number 245-23-454b," June explains reading from her notes.

"Wait a minute. That's a lie. I've never touched them. Ask my wife; she'll tell you I've never touched them. I'll take a lie detector test. Bring them in here and let them say it to my face. They must be on drugs or something," Mr. Allen angrily interjects.

"Mr. Allen, I would suggest you contact your lawyer about this. The Judge has issued a court order to place your daughters into protective custody until this is resolved. I personally haven't taken any statements from them yet. I'm not ready to ask you any specific questions until after I've interviewed your daughters," you explain.

"Freddie would never do anything like this. He's a good father and a good husband. He's a good provider. I don't know what we would do without him. My daughters are mistaken," Mrs. Allen adds with a shaky voice.

"I assure you, Mr. Allen, we will get to the bottom of this. We just needed to inform you of the current situation," you advise.

"Where are they? I'll get to the bottom of this. Let me talk with them," Mr. Allen demands.

"I can't let you do that at this time Mr. Allen. You and your attorney will have a chance to cross-examine them later," you advise.

You proceed to make an appointment for Mr. Allen to come to your office tomorrow and he leaves in a belligerent and frustrated manner. After talking with the two girls you learn that the 15-year-old reported her father because he started having intercourse with her sister. She always felt protective of her younger sister and felt she had to report her father before it was too late. You believe the girls are telling the truth but find there is little physical evidence to back up their story. It is basically their word against the word of their father and mother.

You have been aware in past experiences where juveniles have lied about having sex with adults. Just last year you investigated a coach at the local high school for allegedly having molested some of the cheerleaders. He was acquitted. A terrible joke was played on him by some of the girls, but his career was ruined. No one ever believed he was really innocent after the accusations. You are aware that if the girls are telling the truth, the father is in need of help and might even molest the kids at school if he hasn't already.

You wonder how to best pursue the investigation and where to draw the line between arresting or not arresting.

Based on what you have read, answer the following questions:

1. What are the legal guidelines for gathering evidence in incest and child sexual molestation cases?

2. What are the characteristics of father-daughter incest and child sexual molesters in general?

3. Would you bring charges against Freddie Allen given the evidence at hand? How would you go about gathering evidence in this case?

Case 5

The Bust

You are a patrol officer responding to a call concerning a local high school. The dispatcher advised you that the school principal wanted to see a police officer.

Arriving .at the principal's office, you are given directions to the Guidance Counselor's Office. Upon entering the Guidance Counselor's office you see the principal, the guidance counselor, and a young girl approximately 15 years old. The principal introduces you to the counselor and the girl. The principal advises you that, during a locker check, he and the guidance counselor found a large packet of marijuana in the girl's locker. The principal hands the packet to you which appears to weigh close to a pound. The principal goes on to explain that the school board wants to "crack down" on the use of drugs in the schools. The principal further informs you that this is the first year as principal of the high school and he wants to set an example for the rest of the students.

Since you are unfamiliar with the procedures associated with the school system's methods of dealing with juvenile offenders at school, you are not sure how to respond. In addition, your department does not have a Juvenile Bureau to help with such matters.

When you ask the principal if he has called the girl's parents, he tells you that he wanted to wait and let you handle the problem. You then ask the principal whether or not he thinks the girl should be prosecuted. The principal quickly states that he will agree to prosecute or do whatever you think is right. It is apparent that he wants to leave the decisions up to you. After some deliberation, you suggest to the principal that he call the girl's parents. At this point the guidance counselor interrupts to say that this is the first time the girl has been in trouble. In fact, he goes on to say that she has had an excellent record at the school both in terms of attendance and grades. He continues by telling you how surprised he was to find this particular student in possession of marijuana.

The girl has been crying and is obviously very upset over the matter. You ask her if the marijuana is hers. Still sobbing, she explains that the marijuana belongs to her boyfriend and that she was only keeping it for him. She does not know where her boyfriend got the marijuana. With further questioning the girl reveals that she had smoked marijuana with her boyfriend on rare occasions. She also indicates that neither she or her boyfriend has used any other narcotic. While you are considering the options, the girl is escorted to the nurse's station in an effort to calm her down.

The guidance counselor informs you that the girl's boyfriend is Carl Balling. He adds that Carl is also a good student who has never been in trouble before as far as he knows.

The principal returns to the office and tells you that the girl's parents are on their way to the school. The principal advises you that the girl's parents are both active in the P.T.A. and appear to be very responsible parents. You ask the principal to have Carl Balling come to his office so that you can talk with him.

Waiting for the girl's parents and Carl to arrive at the counselor's office, you think about what the correct course of action would be to take. The girl has probably not been involved with drug offenses in the past. Both she and her boyfriend seem to have good records at school. However, the large amount of marijuana in the girl's possession constitutes a felony offense in your state.

The principal has agreed to follow any decision you make regarding the girl. What are you going to do?

Based on what you have read, answer the following questions:

1. According to your own State laws, what is the procedure for handling offenses on school grounds? Who prosecutes juvenile offenders? Who can file a petition with the courts?
2. What decision should the officer make in this case? What questions would you ask Carl?
3. If the girl were brought before the Juvenile Court, what do you think the Judge should do?

Case 6

Neighborhood Brat

You are a police officer assigned to the Juvenile Bureau and are presently responding to a request from a patrol officer to meet with you at residence in the outskirts of the city.

As you pull up behind the patrol cruiser at the residence, a patrolman comes up to your car and tells you that he believes you should handle the situation inside. The patrolman explains that he answered a call to the Baker's residence regarding an assault on the Baker's twelve year old son. He states that the Baker's next-door-neighbor, a Mr. Sutton, took a water hose and sprayed the Baker boy with it. Further explanation suggests that the Baker boy has been something of a trouble maker in the neighborhood. His previous escapades have included minor vandalism, fighting with other children, and generally being a nuisance to the neighborhood. In concluding his report the patrolman laughs and tells you that he believes the boy probably "got off easy."

You approach the Baker house to talk with the parents. The boy's parents are visibly upset and insist that their son is very well mannered and that Mr. Sutton intentionally tried to harm their son. They further explain that their son has a cold and might well become seriously ill as a result of the incident. The Baker's are very angry and want to press charges against Mr. Sutton. Trying to be diplomatic, you advise the Bakers that you will talk with Mr. Sutton and will return shortly for further discussion with them.

You find Mr. Sutton in his back yard waxing his car. You introduce yourself and ask him what happened to the Baker boy. Mr. Sutton seems friendly and is quite cooperative in explaining his version of what happened. He contends that the Baker boy is always bothering people in the neighborhood by breaking windows, destroying gardens, and being a nuisance. Mr. Sutton goes on to explain that the boy came over while he was washing the car and started throwing dirt and mud on the car and running away, then finally after warning the Baker's son several times he grabbed the boy and sprayed him with the water hose until he was soaking wet. After that the boy ran home crying. Mr. Sutton further informs you that despite many complaints from the neighborhood, the Baker's treat their son as if he were always innocent and everyong else is lying.

Apparently, the Bakers are unable or unwilling to control their son. They appear to be over-protective and reinforce the child's behavior by not disciplining him. You are beginning to wonder whether the real problem is with the son or with his parents.

Walking back to the Baker's house you must now decide what to tell them. It would be easier to advise the Baker's to take a warrant against Mr. Sutton and let the court handle the situation. On the other hand, the whole Baker family seems to need a different kind of help. You doubt they would be willing to commit themselves to family counseling, even if you tried to convince them it was needed. You mutter to yourself, "I am a police officer not a psychologist."

You knock on the Baker's front door still undecided what to tell them.

Based on what you have read, answer the following questions:

1. What should the officer say fo the Bakers?
2. Should Mr. Sutton be prosecuted for his actions? Why?
3. Could this matter be resolved in Juvenile Court? In Civil Court? Explain how either court could help the Bakers or be detrimental to them.

Case 7

The Hitchhikers

You are a State Trooper working interstate patrol near a metropolitan city. You are on your way to meet a fellow trooper to run radar for the afternoon traffic.

Just as you pass under a bridge, you see two subjects walking on your side of the interstate. Looking in the rear view mirror, you can tell that the subjects are both female and one appears to be very young. You decide to turn at the next exit and see if the girls are in need of assistance. Passing the girls on the opposite side of the interstate, you notice the oldest girl trying to hitch a ride. You pull across the median strip in order to stop the girls.

The oldest girl appears to be twelve or thirteen years old while the younger girl appears to be only five or six years old. When you ask the oldest girl to show some identification, she tells you she does not have any indentification. You open the passenger door and ask the girls to sit down in the front seat. Both girls appear to be scared and tired. They apparently have no baggage, money, or even warm clothing.

You ask the girls where they were going and they tell you they do not know. The oldest girl tells you her name is Lisa and her sister's name is Ann, but will not tell you what their last name is or where they live. It seems the girls are trying to run away from home.

The youngest girl, Ann, has bruises on her face and arms. Ann has remained silent, letting her older sister do all the talking. Lisa's face also looks somewhat bruised and one of her arms is crooked as though it had been broken and healed without being properly set. Both girls are dirty and seem to be malnourished.

You ask Lisa how the bruises got on her face. She only looks at you apprehensively and begins to cry, which starts her younger sister crying. You ask Lisa if she is afraid to go home and she tells you yes. In a choked voice she explains that her parents beat her and Ann frequently, especially Ann.

You call your partner on the radio and advise him that you have two juvenile hitchhikers in custody and will not be able to set up radar. You advise headquarters regarding the two runaways and indicate that you are transporting them to the county juvenile facility.

Lisa asks if you are taking them to the juvenile home and you tell them yes. Lisa grows more fearful and tells you that she has been at the juvenile home before and that they only returned her and her sister to their parents. Lisa asks if you will just take them home instead of to the juvenile facility. She adds that maybe their parents will not be too mad at them. You ask where she lives and she tells you her home is about four miles away. Advising headquarters that you are returning the girls home, you proceed to Lisa's address hoping that, at least, you will be able to talk with the parents. Maybe you can do some good. However, the sinking feeling in your stomach is not very reassuring.

The girls live in a shabby house out in the country. You decide to talk with the parents first and leave the girls in your patrol car. Both parents are home watching television. They ask what you want and you explain to them that you have their daughters outside in the patrol car. The mother asks you if they ran away again. Somewhat shocked that the parents act so unconcerned about the girls, you ask how long the girls have been gone. The mother tells you she does not know. The father is still watching television and does not speak to you. The mother tells you to let the girls come in and she will handle them. Lisa thanks you for bringing her home and goes into the house with Ann. Ann is sobbing and appears very scared. You begin to wonder just how the mother plans to "handle" the girls.

As you back out of the driveway you hear screaming and crying inside the house. You hear the father shouting at the girls as though he were whipping them. You also hear the mother pleading with the father. It becomes apparent to you what is going on inside the house. What are you going to do?

Based on what you have read, answer the following questions:

1. What should the Trooper do at this point?

2. Should the Trooper have handled the situation differently in the first place? If so, list what steps should have been taken.

3. What resources in the community can assist the police in these situations?

Section III

Selected Bibliography

Baron, R., and F. Feeney (1976). *Juvenile Diversion through Family Counseling*. Washington, D.C.: Government Printing Office.

Barry, R.J. (1984). "Incest: The Last Taboo," FBI Law Enforcement Bulletin, 53(2).

Barton, W.H. (1976). "Discretionary Decision-making in Juvenile Justice," *Crime and Delinquency*, 22:470-480.

Baxter, A. (1985). *Techniques for Dealing with Child Abuse*. Springfield, IL: Charles C. Thomas.

Burgess, A. (1985). *Rape and Sexual Assault*. New York: Garland Publishing Co.

Carey, J.T., and P.D. McAnany (1984). *Introduction to Juvenile Delinquency: Youth and the Law*. Englewood Cliffs, NJ: Prentice-Hall.

Cox, S.M., and J.J. Conrad (1987). *Juvenile Justice*, 2d ed. Dubuque, IA: Wm. C. Brown Publishers.

Crowe, T.D. (1985). *Directed Patrol Manual: Juvenile Problems*. Washington, D.C.: Office of Juvenile Justice and Delinquency Prevention.

Dyke, E.V. (1980). "Child Abuse," *New York Teacher*, (May 18).

Eldefonso, E. (1983). *Law Enforcement and the Youthful Offender*, 4th ed. New York: John Wiley and Sons.

Helfer, R.E., and C.H. Kempe (1976). *Child Abuse and Neglect*. Boston: Ballinger Publishing Co.

Meier, J.H. (1985). *Assault against Children: Why It Happens, How to Stop It*. San Diego, CA: College Hill Press.

Murrell, M., and D. Lester (1981). *Introduction to Juvenile Delinquency*. New York: MacMillan Publishing Co.

National Advisory Commission on Criminal Justice Standards and Goals (1976). *Juvenile Justice and Delinquency Prevention*. Washington, D.C.: Government Printing Office.

Pierce, R.L. (1984). "Child Pornography: A Hidden Dimension of Child Abuse," *Child Abuse and Neglect*, 8(4).

Rusinko, W.T., et al. (1978). "The Importance of Police Contact in the Formulation of Youth's Attitudes toward Police," *Journal of Criminal Justice*, 6:53-69.

Thornton, W.E.; L. Voight; and W. Doerner (1987). *Delinquency and Justice*, 2d ed. New York: Random House.

U.S. Department of Justice (1984). *Juvenile Law Enforcement: A Manual for Improving Productivity*. Washington, D.C.: Office of Juvenile Justice and Delinquency Prevention.

Section IV

The Police and the Emotionally Disturbed

Introduction

Police officers, although they may not always realize it, use psychology daily in their interactions with people in the community. Because police officers deal primarily with people who have problems, they must try to develop and utilize observation and communication skills in order to perform their job effectively and efficiently.

Communications make human interaction possible. The police officer should possess a variety of communication skills when dealing with people in their care. Police officers who are inclined to get involved in altercations and physical confrontations with citizens and suspects need to analyze themselves and may in some cases, need professional guidance. Exaggerated feelings of insecurity combined with self-doubt about his or her own identity as an authority figure can interfere with the process of becoming a professional police officer. Naturally, there are insecure citizens and suspects with poor self-control which may result in a physical assault against a police officer; this being the case, the officer should contain the individual with minimum amount of force. As police psychologist Martin Reiser (1973) states, "it is usually easier to talk a suspect into jail than to fight him."

Experienced police officers realize that "explaining things" is neither pampering citizens or a sign of weakness on their part. It is merely a professional approach in getting the job done in the easiest and least stressful manner.

Verbal communication is not the only form of communication. A police officer's words may be right, but the manner in which they are delivered may be incorrect or inadequate. Being too serious is an occupational hazard for many police officers. It comes, in part, from attempting not to get personally involved in a situation and playing an authoritarian role. Nevertheless, curtness and coldness during communication frequently leads to misunderstanding. A smile or kind word reminds the citizen that a police officer is really a human being and not solely a rigid authoritarian figure lacking in compassion or understanding.

Police Interaction with the Emotionally Disturbed

Dealing with an emotionally disturbed individual requires interpersonal skills; patience, and understanding on the part of the police officer. The majority of disturbed persons are afraid, withdrawn, passive, and unable to communicate rather than hostile, angry or aggressive.

There are some basic ground rules for police officers handling emotionally disturbed or mentally ill persons. First, a police officer should obtain as much background information about the individual and the situation as possible. Talking with witnesses, family, and friends will help provide a more realistic assessment of the situation and avoid unnecessary disruption or danger. Second, when in doubt, police officers should always call for assistance. Assistance may represent security for the emotionally disturbed individual and motivate him or her to respond more openly. It is always easier and more professional to call for assistance rather than resort to fighting with a mentally ill person.

Third, police officers should explain to the individual what they are going to do before they do it. Police officers should not lie to an emotionally or mentally disturbed individual, or talk as if the disturbed person cannot possibly understand what is going on. Police officers should, at least, attempt to communicate with the individual as if they were a relatively rational and normal person. Finally, the police officer should avoid threatening gestures, verbal abuse, or physical force except in extreme cases. Usually, emotionally disturbed individuals are compliant and agreeable if they are given adequate reassurance and the police officer communicates that he is a friend who will help rather than threaten the individual's already uncertain stability (Law Enforcement Study Center, 1970).

Mentally unstable individuals such as potential suicides, hostage-takers, or snipers are particularly dangerous. A police officer's main concern in such cases should be the safety of others and him or herself. If the police officer is convinced that prompt action is necessary to protect the interests of the emotionally or mentally disturbed individual and others, force may be required.

Zusman (1975) commented that police officers in dealing with mentally ill and dangerous individuals are in a "damned if you do and damned if you don't" situation. The threat of force or use of force by an emotionally unstable individual is a crime unless there are extenuating circumstances. If police officers attempt to make an arrest and hurt a mentally ill individual, the police are guilty of overreacting and of brutality. On the other hand, if the police fail to use force or arrest an emotionally unstable individual, the police are held liable if the individual injures himself or another person.

Police in the Helping Role

There are three recognizable components of the police in the helping role: 1) appeal for help, 2) immediacy, and 3) authority. Police officers are usually the first summoned when a crisis occurs (appeal for help); they have a highly organized mobile response capacity (immediacy); and they have the symbolic and legal power to do something (authority). Police officers constitute an often underutilized resource for the management of unpredictable mental health situations. The police are already delivering such services, but in some instances, the delivery is grudgingly performed and often inept. In effect, the police role is explicitly a control function and implicitly one of a helping dimension. Police officers, for a variety of reasons, often emphasize the control function and de-emphasize the helping role. This particular attitude is typically reflected in the common police expression, "we are police officers, not social workers." Although their role as a helping agent is denied by many police officers, it is the role which has become the predominant one in police work and one which requires the highest degree of skill and competence (Janis, 1958).

Since police officers should be especially sensitive to evidence of a crisis in victims of criminal activity, it is suggested that part of the police responsibility at a crime scene should be concerned with the mental health of the victim. Obtaining information necessary to determine if an offense has occurred and, if so, apprehension of the offender should, in an immediate sense, be a secondary concern for the police. The investigating police officer should take a few extra minutes to assess the immediate impact of the encounter upon the victim.

Police officers have more experience with rape victims and their families than do many mental health professionals. Since most investigating police officers are male, their gender alone may serve as a barrier to open communication unless care is taken to further the relationship with the victim. The investigating police officer, in this respect, would be best advised to approach a rape crisis as a counselor. Even concerning those investigations that appear to be false rape accusations, the investigating police officer must proceed with the assumption that each reported rape is genuine.

The range of unpredictable emotional crises that come within the purview of the police seems infinite. The police are positioned in time and place for an array of helping roles that coincide with their role as law enforcers. The immediacy of time and place regarding the police role cannot be achieved by any other group of persons in the helping system. This is not to say that the police should perform a clinical mental health or ministerial function, however.

Bittner (1967) indicated that in real police work provisions of law represent a resource that can be utilized to handle a vast array of problems. There are boundaries to legal guidelines that dictate when illegal offenses have taken place and when police action is necessary. However, these legal guidelines are broad interpretations and do not fit every situation exactly, particularly when police officers deal with the apprehension of mentally disturbed individuals. Police officers must rely on informal practices and experience in such cases rather than by strict interpretation of legal guidelines.

There are numerous situations where the police officer is inclined to ignore the behavior of persons who are apparently emotionally disturbed or mentally ill. The police frequently receive phone calls from persons who are under the delusions that others are trying to harm them. When a serious crime occurs which receives publicity, the police are besieged by persons ready to confess. Many of these are known to the police from past experience as relatively harmless individuals. It is a common practice for the police, in order to protect against false confessions, not to release certain information to the press about a serious crime. Although falsely confessing to a crime may constitute interference with the police and an obstruction of justice, criminal proceedings are rarely instituted against these people and, unfortunately, referrals to helping agencies are even more rare.

Police Authority for Handling the Emotionally Disturbed

The job of dealing with emotionally disturbed individuals is often left to the police. The problem of inadequate medical facilities and helping agencies are expressed by the numerous complaints of police officers. Despite the fact that most state laws appear to give police officers adequate legal protection when apprehending persons they reasonably suspect to be dangerously mentally ill and in need of emergency care, the statutes are, at best, complicated and confusing. Many police officers fear the possibility of civil suits for damages and refuse to act unless there is a clear violation of the law. Most police officers, when dealing with emotionally disturbed violators, prefer to make an arrest and let other agencies such as the courts decide whether to invoke the criminal justice system or provide medical care. This being the case, police officers usually wait until a legal violation occurs before taking action, rather than reporting or acting on obvious emotional or mentally disturbed individuals before a violation occurs.

There appears to be less accuracy with police recognition of persons who are emotionally disturbed than with other "normal" individuals (Green, 1976). However, there seems to be little point in heightening police perception of the emotionally disturbed individual unless concomitant measures give police officers some realistic hope of being able to deal with such cases by means other than arrest (Bae, 1981).

Summary

Police officers frequently find themselves placed in the role of psychologist and mental health counselor. Many police officers do not view intervening with mentally disturbed persons as a police duty. Nevertheless, police officers are expected to assist with emotionally disturbed individuals because of their potential for violence and their frequent disturbance of social order and peace. Police officers frequently come in contact with individuals who exhibit a wide range of mental and emotional problems. In each case, police officers are expected to make judgments, engage in some activity, and satisfactorily resolve the problem so that the public's safety as well as the safety of the disturbed individual is assured. Such decision and action-taking can be a most difficult and complex task, particularly when police officers are expected to resolve the problem successfully without adequate training or benefit of information regarding the individuals mental health history. Because it is difficult for most police officers to recognize mentally disturbed and emotionally unbalanced individuals all the time, it is important for them to receive as much training as feasible concerning the handling of emotional problems. Whether the police like it or not, they are the only immediate authority for helping mentally disturbed and emotionally unstable individuals.

References

Bae, R.P. (1981). "Ineffective Crisis Intervention Techniques: The Case of the Police," *Journal of Crime and Justice*, 4(1).

Bittner, E. (1967). "Police Discretion in Emergency Apprehension of Mentally Ill Persons," *Social Problems*, 15:278.

Green, E.J. (1976). *Psychology for Law Enforcement*. New York: John Wiley & Sons.

Janis, I. (1958). *Psychological Stress: Psychoanalytic and Behavioral Studies of Surgical Patients*. New York: John Wiley & Sons.

Law Enforcement Study Center (1970). *Mental Illness and Law Enforcement*. Washington, D.C.: Washington University Press.

Reiser, M. (1973). *Practical Psychology for Police Officers*. Springfield, IL: Charles C. Thomas.

Zusman, J. (1975). "Recognition and Management of Psychiatric Emergencies in Emergency Psychiatric Care," in H. Resnick and H. Ruben (eds.), *Emergency Psychiatric Care: The Management of Mental Health Crises*. Bowie, MD: The Charles Press.

Cases in the Police
and the Emotionally Disturbed

The next seven cases are designed to portray the numerous instances of emotional distress and related problems to which a police officer must respond. Emotional instability does not limit itself to mental illness, but may include a wide range of human emotions which may erupt into any number of unexpected events. The fact that human emotions sometimes result in unexpected behavior is a problem that the police officer should be aware of. Many times police officers have found themselves placed into the role of psychologist and counselor.

In the following cases, you will find yourself facing a variety of human emotions and mental disturbances. How you react in each of these cases will determine whether the emotional disturbance may be of a transient nature or may result in more permanent psychological damage or even physical harm to the individual, police officer involved, or the community.

Case number one, "The Chase," examines a common problem among a majority of police departments—how to handle high speed pursuits of intoxicated drivers. In most instances, the police officer must rely on his or her common sense and discretion. In this case, a police officer involved in a high speed chase with an intoxicated driver must decide if chasing the driver is the correct way of handling the problem.

Case number two, "A Victim of Rape," deals with an unsympathetic police officer investigating a possible rape incident. The officer finds difficulty in relating to the victim knowing that she has been sexually permissive in the past. The officer finds that his attitude seems to be contributing to the problem of the rape victim.

Case number three, "Police Psychologist," involves two police officers attempting to take a mentally disturbed individual into custody. Although the disturbed person has committed no crime, the officers must serve a court order to have the man committed to a mental institution. The technique of "arrest" the officers decide to use may mean the difference between a peaceful arrest or serious injury to the officers or the subject.

Case number four, "Suicide," portrays a police officer who is faced with a highly emotional individual threatening to commit suicide. Among a large crowd of bystanders, the officer must attempt to talk with the individual and persuade him not to kill himself. Although the officer is faced with many types of approaches to use and much advice from fellow officers and the growing crowd, he finds it is up to him to decide.

Case number five, "Hostage," focuses on an emotionally disturbed man on a rampage, shooting into a busy intersection. The man takes a small child as a hostage while a lone police officer finds himself in the position of making a decision.

Case number six, "I Did It," centers on a police detective who has realized that some mentally disturbed individuals confess to crimes they have never committed. In this case, the detective finds himself attempting to prove an individual's innocence rather than guilt.

Case number seven, "Prominent Deviance," deals with a police officer who apprehends a prominent citizen of committing a sexually deviant act with a small boy. The officer must decide on a course of action that will best treat an emotional problem as well as protect the community.

Case 1

The Chase

You are sitting in your cruiser, parked near an intersection on the outskirts of the city. It is two o'clock in the morning and you are thinking how much you would like to be asleep. The midnight shifts seem to get longer each night. Suddenly, a car speeds through the intersection, running a red light. You blink and watch the car for a second, thinking to yourself that the driver must be doing at least eighty miles per hour. You pull out of your parking place and begin pursuing the speeding automobile. You call headquarters and inform them that you are running one south on Papertree Road. As you start to gain on the car, you look at your speedometer which now reads 115 miles per hour. Getting close to the car, you reach and turn the spotlight on the speeding car. The driver begins to brake and pull off to the side of the road. As you pull in behind the car you try to note the license plate, but it is covered with mud, and is difficult to read. You call headquarters again and inform them that you have stopped the car and are going to check the driver.

You step out of your cruiser and begin to walk toward the car. Just as you approach the driver's window, the car suddenly jumps into gear and speeds off. You go back to your cruiser and resume pursuing the offender. You are becoming very angry. The driver is now driving erratically as though he or she were intoxicated. You call headquarters again and advise them of what happened adding that you may need some back-up intercepting the car. The dispatcher informs you that one back-up car is heading toward your area.

The car you are chasing is being driven more and more recklessly. The car has already exceeded ninety miles per hour and has almost crashed into a delivery truck. The car heads toward the interstate entrance ramp running another driver off the road. You have just pulled behind the offender and are beginning to wonder where your back-up car is? You also begin to wonder if you are doing the right thing by chasing the car. The car is doing over a hundred miles per hour and has almost wrecked two other vehicles which could have resulted in the death or injury of innocent people, not to mention placing your own safety in jeopardy. If you stop chasing the car, the driver may slow down and go home without incident. On the other hand, the driver may not only be intoxicated, but a wanted felon as well.

The car has just run another car off the interstate and into the median strip. Your back-up car has not arrived. What are you going to do?

Based on what you have read, answer the following questions:

1. List the options the police officer has at this point. Which option seems to be the best? Explain.

2. If the back-up car had arrived at this point, would it change the situation?

3. What policies would you make as a Chief of Police for similar encounters and situations?

Case 2
A Victim of Rape?

You are responding to a sexual assault call. The report is from an apartment complex in a poorer section of the city. The only information you were given is an apartment number which was relayed to the dispatcher by a neighbor of the victim.

As you approach the entrance to the apartment, a woman swings the door open and states that it is about time you showed up. You recognize the woman as Janice, a prostitute who works the neighborhood. Jokingly, you ask if she has been raped. Janice sneers at you and says no. Leading you inside the apartment she introduces you to a young lady sitting on a couch and crying. "She's the one that was raped," Janice says to you. You ask her if the young lady is a friend and she tells you that she is. You also ask Janice if the young lady is also a prostitute. Janice indignantly responds that the girl is not a prostitute.

The young lady is dressed in a short, see through, night gown. She does not appear to be injured physically. The apartment does not appear to reflect any recent violent actions. You begin to wonder if Janice is telling the truth to you about the girl not being a prostitute. You see no evidence of a husband or children living in the apartment with the girl. You have worked in this neighborhood for quite a while and have begun to realize how young girls living alone in apartment buildings like this one make their living — as prostitutes.

"What's your name?" you ask the girl. "Ann...," the girl answers as she looks up at you and wipes the tears from her face.

You ask Ann if she knows her assailant and she gives you a description, indicating that she knows his first name. "Pete, that's the only name I know him by," she explains.

"Then you do know him," you ask with some degree of skepticism.

"He's just an acquaintance," Ann snaps back.

You are now becoming more convinced that Ann is a prostitute and that Pete was probably a non-paying customer.

"Did Pete rape you here?," you ask while looking around the apartment.

"In the bedroom," Ann responds.

"Naturally," you think to yourself as you survey the bedroom.

"What do you do for a living?", you ask Ann.

Ann explains that she has just moved to the city a few weeks ago and is looking for a secretarial position.

"Well Ann, to be completely honest, this doesn't look good," you explain. "First, you say you're raped by some guy that you are acquainted with and only know that his name is Pete. Second, your apartment doesn't appear to have been broken into by force. Third, you don't have any bruises or cuts on your body that would indicate a man assaulted you."

"Well what the hell would you do if a guy has a damned knife at your throat?" Ann shouts at you angrily. You try to keep your composure as you say, "I don't mean to be an ass-hole about this, but if I went out and arrested this Pete guy, it would only hurt you. A trial jury would laugh you out of the courtroom. The jury would have you pegged as a prostitute by the time the defense attorney was through with you."

You continue by pointing out to Ann that it would probably be a waste of time if she went to the hospital for a checkup in that all the reports and procedures that would have to be done would more than likely be thrown out of court.

Ann begins to cry again and tells you to forget the whole matter.

Walking out the door, you turn and tell Janice to be sure that her new apprentice gets the payment in advance the next time. She responds with a glare.

Two days later at roll call your Sergeant makes an announcement. "Men, we've apparently got a rapist on the loose in the northeast section of the city. All we know is that he tells his victims his name is Pete. This guy raped a minister's wife last night and the boss wants us to catch him before the media come down on us."

As the Sergeant describes Pete and the M.O. he uses, you remember the rape call you investigated two days ago. The description and the M.O. matches the statement Ann had made to you. You are now faced with forgetting about the incident with Ann or returning to her and obtaining a statement. You realize you have probably made a mistake by treating Ann's rape as lightly as you did. If you go back now, she will probably be uncooperative, plus your supervisor will want to know why you didn't complete the investigation in the first place.

What are you going to do?

Based on what you have read, answer the following questions:

1. From the police officer's statements and thoughts, how would you describe him?
2. What can you, as the police officer, do at this point? List all the options and describe the probable consequences of each.
3. What does your own State law say about the evidence required for rape (i.e., force used, resistance by the victim, etc.)?

Case 3
Police Psychologist

"He's in here officer, I can't do a thing with him."

A frail elderly lady leads you and your partner down a hall and points to one of the bedrooms.

The document in your back pocket is a commitment order signed by a doctor and the judge instructing you to take a young man into custody for mental treatment.

"I just can't handle him anymore by myself. He's just gotten worse since his father died," the woman explains to you as she opens the bedroom door.

As the door swings open you see Bobby sitting in the middle of the floor. The room is a mess with broken furniture, clothing, and papers scattered over the floor.

"Is he violent?", you ask the woman.

"He does get upset sometimes and throws things, I'm scared of him," the old lady dejectedly replies.

Bobby is sitting on the floor his feet pulled up close to his body and his eyes fixed on the wall in front of him. Bobby is about six feet tall and weighs close to 200 pounds.

"Let's not get him mad at us," you whisper to your partner.

Your partner walks into the room next to Bobby and kneels down beside him. "Hi Bobby, how are you feeling today?"

Bobby doesn't respond and continues to stare at the wall in front of him.

"Would you like to go for a ride with us? We'd like to drive you to see a friend of ours."

Bobby begins to rock and his eyes widen still staring at the wall.

"Do you need some help getting up?", Brian asks attempting to get a grip around Bobby's arm.

"No!" Bobby screams as he lashes out with his arm and strikes Brian across the face.

The blow knocked Brian off balance from his kneeling position. Brian is now sitting on the floor rubbing his head.

Bobby runs to a corner of the room and sits down holding his legs up around him.

You enter the room quickly and kneel down next to Brian.

"You okay?"

"Yeah, I guess so," your partner replies.

"Please don't hurt him," the old lady says as she pleads with you and Brian to be careful.

You know from past experiences that if you try to take Bobby by force and he gets angry he will be afraid of everyone in a uniform. As a result it will be harder to handle him in the future for police or health personnel.

You survey the bedroom and notice there are two large windows. The bedroom is on the first floor of the house and it would not be difficult for Bobby to jump through a window and escape.

Brian is getting impatient and says, "C'mon, let's get the cuffs on him."

After several more moments of deliberation you agree with your partner. "Alright, but let's make sure he doesn't go out the window," you explain while getting your handcuffs ready.

Walking toward the corner where Bobby is seated you tell Brian to hold Bobby's legs and feet while you get the handcuffs on his wrists.

"Be sure to pull him out and turn him over on his belly so I can get to his arms," you explain to Brian.

Bobby's eyes begin to widen again as you and Brian start toward him.

Brian jumps at Bobby's feet and tries to get a grip around his legs. Bobby begins to scream and starts kicking with his legs. You try to grab Bobby's arms to turn him over. Bobby uses his leg to strike Brian in the stomach causing Brian to release his hold. Bobby jerks away from your grasp and retreats back into his corner.

"You okay?", you ask Brian, frustration written all over your face.

"Yeah. But this is getting ridiculous. Let's not baby him anymore or one of us is really going to get hurt. We're going to have to choke him down," Brian states as he pulls his baton from his belt.

"No, please don't hurt him. He doesn't know what he's doing. He's never hurt any-one before, the old lady begs running over to Bobby and holding him.

"Look, lady, we've got no choice," Brian tells the woman.

Brian seems to be right but you are not sure. You feel sorry for Bobby and his mother, but things were getting out of hand. Something has to be done.

Based on what you have read, answer the following questions:

1. What should the officers do?
2. What would be the probable consequences to Bobby's physical and mental health if the officers used force? Do you think the force used may be injurious to psychological treatments for Bobby?
3. Bobby appears to trust his mother. Can she help the officers in any way? Explain.

Case 4
Suicide

You are responding to a suicide threat. The call came from a subdivision on your beat. The subdivision is next to the city limits and is composed of middle class residents. As you approach the neighborhood you realize that you will be the first officer to arrive on the scene. The back-up units will have to fight the lunch hour traffic as they respond from further away in the city.

As you approach the area, you notice a group of people gathered in a field across the main street that services the neighborhood.

"Must be where it's happening," you think aloud to yourself.

You see an open gate and dirt road leading into the field and pull into it. Driving closer to the group of people you recognize what they are looking at—a large electrical cable support tower. There is a man halfway up on the tower, on a service ladder.

"That tower must be at least 200 feet high," you mutter to yourself.

You have never worked a suicide attempt before and certainly never a "jumper." The thought of someone jumping from a high structure in order to end their life is upsetting to you.

Walking up toward the crowd you see several individuals you know who live in the subdivision.

"Who is that on the tower?" you ask one of the men standing in the crowd.

"Bert Jacobsen. He's threatening to jump but won't do it," the man responds.

"Why does he want to jump?" you ask.

"Who knows, the guy's crazy."

You recognize Bert as a resident of the subdivision. You have never had any police dealings with Bert, but have stopped to chat with him on occasion. Bert always likes to work in his yard, trimming, planting shrubs, and flowers. That is how you met Bert. During the spring and summer you would see Bert working in his yard and you would pull up to the house and talk with him about gardening. You never realized that Bert had the kind of emotional problems that would lead to a suicide attempt.

The sound of sirens break your train of thought. Two more police vehicles and an ambulance have arrived. One of the police vehicles is carrying your shift lieutenant.

"What you got?" the Lieutenant asks. You quickly respond, "the guy's name is Bert Jacobsen. I just got here myself. I don't know what his problem is."

The Lieutenant begins to talk with the members in the crowd attempting to find out why Bert is threatening suicide.

Apparently, no one in the crowd of by-standers knows why he is on the tower threatening to end his life. The Lieutenant walks up to you and asks where Bert lives.

"524 Houston Place," you answer.

You continue to tell the Lieutenant that you believe Bert has a wife and a couple of children but that you have never met them. The Lieutenant motions for one of the other police officers to come over to where you are standing.

"Will you go over to 524 Houston Place and see if the guy's family is over there. His name is Bert Jacobsen."

"How well do you know this guy?" the Lieutenant asks you.

"He's just an acquaintance. I've talked with him before, just chit-chat," you explain.

The crowd of people is growing and some of the members are yelling for Bert to jump.

"That's all these people want to see. They want him to jump and then they'll blame us for not doing anything," the Lieutenant states in an aggravated manner.

The Lieutenant orders another police officer to try to disperse the crowd or at least to keep them quiet.

"I figured it wouldn't take long for them to get here," the Lieutenant gestures toward a local T.V. van and newspaper reporter entering the field.

"You say you've talked with him before. You're probably the best one to try to talk him out of jumping," the Lieutenant advises you.

Will comes back from Bert's house and advises the Lieutenant that there is no one home and no one in the neighborhood apparently knows where Bert's family is.

"They may have left him which could explain why he wants to kill himself," the officer suggests.

A television camera crew and newspaper reporter and photographer begin walking toward you and the Lieutenant.

"We had better figure out what we are going to do before they start making a big deal of this," the Lieutenant advises you.

The Lieutenant decides that you should go to your patrol car and use the P.A. speaker to talk to Bert.

"Ask him to come down and talk with us," the Lieutenant continues.

You run over to your patrol car as the T.V. and newspaper reporter gather around the Lieutenant. You begin to think how impersonal everyone is acting toward the situation. Several younger members of the crowd are shouting at Bert to jump and the ambulance team look like vultures waiting to scrape up the remains. You pick up the microphone and speak to Bert.

"Bert, Bert, this is Jim Wade with the Police Department. I'd like to talk to you. I'd like to help you. I'm going to come up to where you are and talk with you."

Bert makes no movement from his perch on the ladder. He is over half-way up the tower with his arms wrapped around the ladder and holding his head down against his right arm.

You begin to walk toward the tower and the Lieutenant stops you.

"I didn't mean for you to go up there and talk to him. It's too dangerous."

"I believe I can talk to him more effectively if I go to him," you explain.

"Alright, but be careful. If he is going to jump, don't let him take you with him," the Lieutenant warns.

"Use reverse psychology on him. Tell him to go ahead and jump and he won't do it," a fellow officer advises you as you approach the tower.

"Tell him anything he wants to hear, tell him his family is coming back to him and that they love him or something," another officer advises.

As you start up the ladder, you realize that it will be you alone who has to talk with Bert. You do not even know what Bert's problem is and you must try to solve it while perched over 100 feet above the ground. You have never liked heights much, but you know you have to try.

Based on what you have read, answer the following questions:

1. Is the officer doing the right thing in going up to see Bert?
2. Assuming that the officer is successful in getting close to Bert, what should the officer say and/or do?
3. Is the crowd creating a confusing situation for Bert? How would you deal with the crowd and the press?

Case 5

Hostage

It's a warm spring afternoon; you and your partner, Harry, are patrolling the west side, which is one of the busiest sections of town. It has been a quiet day and you are looking forward to getting off-duty and attending a cook-out that evening.

As you pull into the intersection of 17th and Pine, you see people stopping their cars and jumping out. Some of them are running and shouting hysterically. You see a man with a rifle running in the street. He fires several rounds randomly toward the fleeing crowd.

Harry is on the radio barking for assistance. Stopping your vehicle you turn on the emergency lights and grab the shotgun from it's rack.

The man with the rifle grabs a young woman with a small child in her arms. She and the child are both young. The man forces the child from her arms and knocks her onto the pavement. Harry mutters, "Oh, my God!" The sniper, carrying the child in one arm and holding the rifle in the other, fires one or two more shots into the crowded intersection and runs into an alley.

You and Harry instinctively pursue the assailant. Two people are lying in the street motionless and many others are screaming and running for protective cover. Harry stops to check the injured people and the woman the sniper had knocked down. You run into the alley and see the sniper climbing up fire escape stairs at the side of a building. Spotting you the sniper points his rifle at you. You clumsily back up and stumble into a couple of trash cans sitting next to the other building—as he fires, narrowly missing you. Red dust powders your uniform from the bricks struck by the bullet. You aim your shotgun at the sniper who is now continuing up the fire escape. You hold your fire because you realize the sniper still has the child in his arms. You know that your shotgun would mean death for the child and sniper. You sit under cover of the trash cans until the sniper reaches the roof of the building.

The scream of sirens are now filling the air. You decide to continue the pursuit for fear of losing sight of the sniper. There is no time to wait for a back-up or Harry. You climb up the fire escape and once on top of the roof, you see the sniper, still holding the child close to his body. The sniper is looking over the edge of the building onto the street below. He fires two more rounds taking careful aim this time. Several thoughts run through your mind, "who has he just shot on the street?" "Why is he doing this?" "Does he have other weapons in his possession?" You wonder how many bullets the sniper has left. His weapon is a .22 automatic and could have as many as 10 or 12 bullets remaining.

There is an air conditioning unit between you and the sniper. You run toward it for cover. The sniper sees you and fires one round, hitting the unit. You lay the shotgun down, draw your revolver, and peer over the top of the air conditioning unit. The sniper is looking at you, a glazed look in his eyes. He points the rifle at you and holds the child close to his chest. The child is a very young boy, two or three years old at most. The little boy is no longer crying, but seems to be in a state of shock.

You point your revolver toward the man and order him to drop the rifle. The sniper yells at you to stay away or he will kill you and the boy.

You still cannot risk a shot for fear of hitting the child. You ponder the sniper's position. He could shoot more people in the street, the child, himself, or even you. You are shaking and can hear your own heart beating. You feel you must act because the sniper is becoming more nervous and agitated.

You hear footsteps on the fire escape stairs. They are probably police officers coming to back you up. The sniper could shoot them as they come onto the roof unless you do something.

Based on what you have read, answer the following questions:

1. Did the officers perform their moves in the correct manner? What changes would you make in their procedure?

2. List the options the officer has at this point and discuss the probable consequences. What option appears to be the best?

3. If the officer had a high powered scoped rifle with him in the same situation, would this change the option you made?

Case 6

"I Did It"

When you joined the police department four years ago, you realized that you would come in contact with many different types of people. You have become concerned that most of the individuals you came in contact with regarding police problems are either poorer people or persons with emotional problems. Your concern was increased when you were promoted to the criminal investigation's bureau. You rarely arrest or convict anyone who is wealthy or who is involved in "white collar" crimes. Those individuals are generally investigated by state or federal agencies and not by the local police force.

As a police officer, you have seen poorer people and emotionally disturbed individuals receive treatment and punishment that people with wealth and power never seem to receive. As a result, you have tried to treat everyone as equally and fairly as you can.

You have been working the Crimes Against People unit of the Detective Division for two months. During that period you have investigated several rapes and numerous robberies and assaults. You have recently been assigned to investigate a series of rapes that have occurred at the city's university.

The city university is a resident four year college with less than 10,000 students. There is a small security force that patrols the campus but has neither the manpower nor the facilities to investigate major criminal acts such as rape. You have been assigned to work with the campus security force in the current investigation involving four rapes which occurred on campus during the past three weeks. All of the rapes have been at night and all but one have been outside the dormitories. The attacker apparently selects girls who are walking alone from a night class back to their dormitory and assaults them under the cover of many shrubs that surround the dormitories. The one inside assault was committed in the laundry room of one of the dormitories late at night.

The description of the attacker is sketchy but all the girls agree that the man is white, 20-25 years old, five feet nine to six feet tall, and smells like a mechanic. The girl who was attacked in the laundry room only caught a glimpse of the man before he placed a pillow case over her head. You have been concentrating your investigation around the many service stations in the area in order to locate a suspect.

The girls on campus are living in fear and are beginning to carry hammers, knives, and even firearms with them. The campus police have been giving lectures about rape prevention in the girl's dormitories but have not been very effective in reducing the fear. The university administration and the news media are demanding that the suspect be apprehended. There is even pressure from the police administration to make an arrest as soon as possible.

One morning as you sip on a cup of coffee and review some of the statements of witnesses you have been interviewing, you receive a telephone call from campus security.

"Allen, this is Jeff from the campus police. I believe we've got the rapist, you want to come down and talk to him?'' You respond affirmatively and gulp down the last of your coffee. Leaving the office, you hope that this is not just a false alarm.

Driving to the campus you think how great it would be for you and everyone concerned if the suspect was the rapist. You have been hassled by several police administrative officers to get the case cleared. The newspapers have been calling you every day wanting to know progress and you feel relieved to be able to have something definite to report when they call today.

Walking into the campus police office, you meet Jeff, one of the security officers, waiting for you with a grin on his face.

''Craziest thing I've ever seen. This guy just came in early this morning and confessed to all the rapes. Said he wanted to get it off his chest,'' Jeff says enthusiastically.

''Let's make sure we don't violate any of his rights or mess this thing up,'' you warn.

''Hell, he just came in and said he did it. One of those spontaneous confessions. Didn't want a lawyer or anything. Already got his statement,'' Jeff proudly announces.

Walking into the small conference room you see the suspect sitting in a chair, looking out the one window in the room.

''You a detective?'' the young man asks as he turns to you.

''My name's Allen Osborne, I'm with the city police, what's your name?''

''David Farrows,'' the young man answers as he pulls a pack of cigarettes from his pocket.

You notice the suspect's fingernails as he lights a cigarette. His fingernails have black grease under them as if he had been working on an automobile engine.

''You a mechanic?'' you ask Farrows remembering that the rape victims all smelled the odor of gasoline on their assailant.

''Yeah, I tinker around with cars a little. I got a part-time job at the race track helping out.''

''Were you advised of your rights by the campus police?'' you ask worried that the investigation may be thrown out on a technicality.

''Yeah, I signed one of them waiver forms. I don't need no lawyer. I just want to get this over with. I already gave a statement to the campus cops.''

Jeff hands you the waiver of rights form and a handwritten statement.

''Did you write out this statement yourself?'' you ask David.

''Yeah, might have some misspelled words in it, but I never was no good in English.''

You read over the statement and find it to be somewhat sketchy. There is little detail about how the suspect actually committed the rapes. The statement reflects everything the newspapers have carried about the rape accounts. You ask Dave about the fine details of the rapes and he becomes angry.

''Look, I did it and I confessed to it, so let's get it over with. Take me to jail!''

''Has the suspect got a record of sex offenses,'' you ask Jeff.

''Sure does, nothing like this, but he's been busted for indecent exposure and voyeurism on campus,'' Jeff explains while looking down at a clipboard.

You pull out the case file from your briefcase including the evidence list. There is little physical evidence to associate anyone with anything. There is no stained clothing, no semen samples from the hospital, and no blood samples. The rape victims either took a bath after the rapes or the doctors could find no external semen samples. You look over the newspaper accounts and compare them with David's statement.

"Damned newspapers have to print everything and makes it harder to do a good investigation," you mutter to yourself, noting the similarities between the newspaper stories and Farrows' statement.

One thing the newspapers did not describe was the knife the assailant used.

"Did the suspect have a knife on him?" you ask.

"Yep, right here," Jeff acknowledges as he empties a property envelope and pulls out a folding hunting knife.

The type of knife used in the rapes was a folding hunting knife that is very common. You think to yourself how coincidental and circumstantial this evidence is. Pushing aside any doubts you might have, you thank Jeff and carry the suspect down to headquarters for booking.

Several days later the campus police send you a report in which several witnesses observed the suspect on campus during the times of the rapes. You also know that the rape victim, who was in the laundry room, positively identified David as her assailant in a line-up.

After reading the report you are still unsure of the suspect's guilt. All the evidence is circumstantial and corroborated by one girl's identification of David, and the description of the knife. It is enough evidence for a conviction, especially since the suspect admits to committing the rapes. But somehow you are still doubting David's guilt. The fact that he is unable to give a detailed account of the rapes and appears to enjoy the attention he is receiving has lead you to believe that he is not the rapist.

Your superiors have not supported your beliefs about the suspects innocence. They appear to be more concerned that an arrest has been made and the media are "off" their backs. The administration has ordered you to close the case and to begin work on other pressing investigations.

The fact that there have been no rapes or sexual assaults on campus since the suspect was placed in custody does not relieve you. Especially since a young man was arrested on campus the previous evening for stealing gas from parked vehicles. Has the real assailant been apprehended or is it just a matter of time before another attack occurs? What are you going to do?

Based on what you have read, answer the following questions:

1. List the evidence against the suspect. List the investigator's reasons for not believing the suspect is indeed the offender. What defenses would the suspect have in court?

2. Does the investigator have any options to pursue the investigation longer?

3. How does the news media affect police investigations for better or worse?

Case 7

Prominent Deviance

You are a police patrolman assigned to a walking beat near a city park. It is early spring and the favorable weather has increased the number of persons visiting the park. On weekends the park is almost overrun with small children and teenagers. Since you have to work the three p.m. to eleven p.m. shift, you must handle all the minor problems associated with young people in the park. Lost children, injuries, teenagers necking, and occasionally alcohol and drug problems arise that you have to try to resolve. Your town is small and fortunately does not have the major problems associated with big cities.

One evening, just as the sun is setting, a young girl in her early teens comes running up to you while you are making your rounds. She is obviously upset.

"Officer, I need to talk to you."

"What can I do for you?" you ask, smiling at the girl.

"A man tried to attack my little brother in the restroom at the park," the girl exclaims, her voice shaking.

The girl leads you into the park where her little brother and an older boy are sitting on a bench. The girl introduces you to her brother and her boyfriend.

"This is Adam, my brother, and Jackie, my boyfriend."

"What happened son?" you ask.

Adam doesn't appear as upset as his sister.

"Nothing, really. I went in the restroom over there and a man was inside. He wanted to touch me and offered me money," Adam tells you while pointing toward the Park's public restroom.

"What did you do Adam."

"I ran. I was kind of scared of him."

You determine from Adam's remarks that the incident happened about twenty minutes ago. Adam tells you that he never saw the man before and didn't know him. The older boy tells you that he and his girlfriend were sitting on a park bench talking when Adam ran up to them.

"Me and Susie were sitting over there when her brother came running up to us and told us what happened. I ran over to the restroom to see if the man was still there and he was gone. Then Susie saw you and decided she'd better report it."

"How old are you Adam?" you ask taking out your notebook.

"Eleven next month."

"Can you describe the man in the restroom?"

"He was old, about forty and big and fat. He had on a dark suit, black hair and was bald on top," Adam explains.

"Would you recognize him again if you saw him?" you ask Adam.

"Sure would." Adam exclaims.

You obtain the full names, addresses, and other information for your report from the children and tell Adam to advise you if he ever sees the man again. You spend the rest of the shift walking around the park area looking for a possible suspect.

At the end of the shift you give the motor patrol officers on the relief shift a description of what happened in the park.

"Hey, I had a similar report like that last month," one of the relief officers added. This woman complained that a man tried to pick up her little boy in the park restroom. In fact, it was on the 3-11 shift before I rotated to graveyard."

"Did you file a report?" you ask the officer.

"No, I didn't think it was important at the time. You know how upset mothers get if somebody looks crosseyed at their kids. Besides, the kid didn't appear too upset about it. However, he did give a description that matches the one you have of the man."

You arrive at work a little earlier the next day so you can check with the Records and Complaints Bureau about similar reports in the park. You find two complaints of attempted sexual molestation of young boys in the park from last summer. The description of the man that Adam gave closely resembled that of the suspects in the complaints.

You decide to watch the restroom in the park closely to see if anyone matching the description appears. As darkness grows near you reason that it might be a good idea to go inside the restroom and wait for awhile. The restroom is empty and you look for a stall in which you can wait undetected.

After thirty minutes of waiting and watching people come and go to the restroom, you begin to feel somewhat like a deviant yourself.

"If somebody sees me in here, they might assume I'm a sex deviant, you think to yourself.

Just as you decide it's time to leave and make your rounds, two young boys enter the restroom. The boys are about ten to twelve years old and appear to have been playing baseball. Within a few seconds, another individual enters the restroom and from your stall you can only see the man's back. You carefully open the stall door in order to observe more clearly. The man matches the description from the reports. He is a big man dressed in a suit. You are unable to see the man's face from your vantage point. The man approaches the two boys. "Hello boys, what are your names?" the man asks.

"I'm Timmy and this is Giles," one of the boys answers.

"How would you two boys like to make ten dollars apiece?" the man asks as he takes out his wallet.

"What do we have to do?" one of the boys replies somewhat suspiciously.

"Just something that will make us both feel good," he explains in a soft tone as he begins to hold and fondle one of the startled boys.

Leaving your stall, you state, "Mister, I want a word with you. I am a police officer."

Turning toward you, the man's eyes are wide with fear. You recognize his face immediately. He is Charles Tussell, a prominent citizen in the community. Tussell is a member of the school board as well as several community organizations, and an alderman on the city council. He is also president of a bank in your city.

"Why, Mr. Tussell, what are you doing here?" you ask in a surprised manner.

"I, uh...I uh...just came to...uh...wash my hands, officer." Tussell answers perspiring heavily.

After obtaining the names and addresses of the two boys, you advise them to wait outside for you. You know that you have seen and heard enough to convince you that Tussell is the sex deviant you have been looking for but the two boys will have to make a statement.

"Mr. Tussell, I want to inform you of your rights..."

"Please officer, I...uh...I can't afford any bad publicity. I have a wife and two daughters.

Please let me go. I'm receiving professional help from Dr. Anders in Bakerville. You can check with him. Please.

You ponder the situation. You have heard of Dr. Anders, a psychiatrist in the neighboring town of Bakerville. Tussell is very embarrassed and scared. He may be telling the truth or he may be lying just to get you to let him go. No one has been physically hurt by Tussell's propositions, but then again, there is no way to measure the emotional damage that may have been caused by his behavior. If you make an arrest it could cause a lot of complications in your town. If you let Tussell go, he could continue his sexual deviance somewhere else or he could continue to receive treatment for his problem. Your gut reaction is to "throw the book" at him. Yet, you want to use your mind as well as your emotions to do what is most appropriate.

Based on what you have read, answer the following questions:

1. What should the officer do?
2. If Tussell is arrested and brought up on charges of sexually molesting children, what do you think his penalty would be?
3. Can Tussell's problem be treated or should he be placed in a penal institution?

Section IV

Selected Bibliography

Bae, R.P. (1981). "Ineffective Crisis Intervention Techniques: The Case of the Police," *Journal of Crime and Justice,* 4(1).

Bittner, E. (1967). "Police Discretion in Emergency Apprehension of Mentally Ill Persons," *Social Problems,* 14:287-292.

Ellison, K., and R. Buckhout (1981). *Psychology and Criminal Justice.* New York: Harper and Row.

Feldman, P.M. (1977). *Criminal Behavior: A Psychological Analysis.* New York: John Wiley and Sons.

Frederick, D.L., and F.H. Mason (1979). "Prediction of Violent Behavior," *Journal of Crime and Justice,* 1(1).

Kerber, W., et al. (1977). "Citizen Attitudes Regarding the Competency of Female Police Officers." *Journal of Police Science and Administration,* 5:337-347.

Monahan, J. (1976). *Community Mental Health and the Criminal Justice System.* New York: Pergamon Press, Inc.

Russell, H.E., and A. Beigel (1982). *Understanding Human Behavior for Effective Police Work,* 2d ed. New York: Basic Books.

Olin, W.R., and D.G. Born (1983). "Behavioral Approach to Hostage Situations," *FBI Law Enforcement Bulletin,* 52(1).

Polk, K. (1985). "Rape Reform and Criminal Justice Processing," *Crime and·Delinquency,* 31(2).

Taylor, W., and M. Braswell (1978). *Issues in Police and Criminal Psychology.* Washington, D.C.: University Press of America.

Wilson, J.Q. (1968). *Varieties of Police Behavior.* Cambridge, MA: Harvard University Press.

Section V

Police Stress

Introduction

Police officers are the subject of continual scrutiny by the people they serve. They are routinely faced with complicated and frequently dangerous problems in which they are supposed to react quickly and, at the same time, correctly. As police psychologist Martin Reiser (1970) points out:

> The police officer is in the middle of forces pushing for social changes on the one hand and forces which want to severely punish anyone who deviates from society's norms on the other.

The police officer finds his or herself often locked into a "no-win" position—"there will always be someone to voice disapproval of police behaviors (Reiser, 1970).

Police departments are typically organized in an authoritarian, quasi-military fashion. This organizational structure of the police profession has been adopted by virtually every police department in the United States. The military model was designed so that people within the system could efficiently receive and respond to orders issued by superiors. Soldiers, especially in the lower ranks, are not expected to make complicated decisions—only respond to orders. Police officers, however, are constantly expected to make decisions and solve complicated problems (Keller, 1972).

The police officer occupies a difficult role. He or she must be effective interpersonally, but usually has little or no training for such skills. The police organization often fails to reinforce improvement in police officers' use of crisis counseling and human relations skills. The officer must always try to maintain control of situations which he or she may misperceive—yet, at the same time, must avoid conflict. The officer also finds it necessary to adapt to an occupation in which one moment may bring a threat of death while other extended periods of time may be boring and routine. The police professional must attempt to be an effective decision-maker and independent problem-solver within a system which encourages dependency by its

101

very structure (Keller, 1972). The result of such occupational paradoxes has been partially responsible for developing what is currently referred to as "police stress."

Police Stress as an Occupational Hazard

Several studies of health and safety among occupational groups have identified the police profession as having a high incidence of stress due to police social components. Keller (1978), Bennett (1978), and Vastola (1978) found that police officers adapt to their occupational situations. The psychological makeup of the police officer develops from a sociological framework of the police profession. Many new police officers "lose" the friends they had as civilians and develop friendships with other police officers during this adaptation period. Individuals who had no prior history of stress-related diseases or accidents prior to becoming police officers, in some instances developed these diseases and accident-prone characteristics after employment as police officers (Keller, 1978; Bennett, 1978; Vastola, 1978). The period of time during which police officers seem to go through the most stress is when the new officer begins to acquire police personality traits. This adaptation period frequently leads new officers into stress-related characteristics such as divorce, increased smoking habits, increased use of alcohol and drugs, heart disease, and accidents (Kroes, 1985). A second adaptation period seems to develop after police officers retire or resign from the profession. After adapting to the stress of police work, officers who leave the profession must readjust to the general social environment which frequently leads to a high incidence of alcoholism and, in some instances, suicide (Maslach and Jackson, 1979).

The concept of "police stress" seems to have formally evolved in 1974 when Kroes, Margolis and Hurrell researched the police profession to determine the effects of job stress on the health of police officers. Kroes, Margolis and Hurrell (1974) found that, as an occupational group, the police profession was the second most stressful occupation in the United States (air-traffic controllers were first). Kroes, Margolis and Hurrell (1974) identified different types of stressors the police frequently encountered including court schedules, shift work, administrative frustrations, community relations, poor equipment, and role ambiguity. In addition, the fear of civil litigation is often cited as a major cause of stress. The decade of the 1980's depicted a proliferation of lawsuits against the police ranging from improper use of force and false arrest to failure to provide appropriate protection and services (Stafford, 1986).

All police officers are subject to police stress, but many officers are capable of handling stressors in a variety of ways and in varying amounts depending upon their own personal capabilities and the particular police environment in which they work. Attempts have been made to identify the potential for stress in individual police officers and the police environment (Dantzken, 1986). Police officer characteristics which have been identified as "stress indicators" include divorce rates, cigarette smoking, alcohol and drug use, headache frequency, high blood pressure, and stomach ailments (Miller, 1981). Police environment characteristics which have been identified as "stress indicators" include size of the police department, administrative support regulations, salary ranges, employment duties, and number of hours worked (Miller, 1981).

Stress and the Police Family

The family of the law enforcement officer often find themselves in a unique and frustrating position. Other non-law enforcement families may view them with some degree of suspicion and distrust because of the police occupation. This can create a potential for the family to become alienated and isolated from the rest of the community, which, of course, can have a devastating impact on relationships within the family as well. If the family is isolated, family members may break down into separate and sometimes antagonistic relationships. In some instances the parents may join together and exclude the children. Sometimes the mother forms a relationship with one or more of the children and excludes the father. The excluded father may form a closed relationship with a favorite daughter or with someone outside the family (Braswell and Meeks, 1982).

It seems apparent that family communication is particularly important for the law enforcement officer, since they often find themselves in a social vacuum with their primary and sometimes only friends being fellow officers and their families. The family is, perhaps, the most continuous intimate communication environment available to an individual (Elliott, 1986). The criminal justice professional brings his or her work experiences home, whether they are talked about or not, and carries his or her home experiences into the work environment. As a result, open and healthy family communication is a vital contribution to and reflection of the police officer's level of effective communication and human relation skills while at work.

The excessive job pressures a police officer may experience trying to maintain control of a variety of situations and to make complicated decisions, can drain his or her energies, leaving the officer depleted and unable to cope with minor or major family problems. The police officer's family who need and expect some time and attention themselves, are often confronted with a person who simply lacks the emotional resources to deal with his or her family problems. "Whether the problem is large and important or small and trivial is irrelevant to the emotionally depleted officer; he is unable to deal with it (Territo and Vetter, 1981)."

A police career is more than just an occupation for an individual; it is a way of life for the officer and his or her family. Police marriages are susceptible to stresses inherent in the police profession. Changing work schedules, pressures on the job, long hours, and the threat of danger are but a few factors that can drive a wedge between a police officer and his or her spouse. Stratton (1978) notes that police officers have one of the highest divorce rates in the United States.

Stress and the Police Image

One major stress area involves how one defines the role of the police officer in today's society. The police profession includes substantial contradictions and inconsistencies. The duties of a police officer depend upon such factors as the oath of office, statutes of law, court decisions, departmental policies, politics, community pressure, informal quota systems, common sense, and the personalities of superiors (Ward, 1971). Police officers who patrol the streets find that legalistic solutions to human problems are often inappropriate or unjust, and common sense solutions are frequently second-guessed.

The role conflict and ambiguity inherent in the police profession are multiplied by distorted media images of the police officer. The media often create a fictionalized image of police work that promotes unreal expectations in both citizens and new police recruits. Many young police officers like to identify with the "macho" image of the media's representation of police work. Reiser (1974) refers to one "macho" form of mistaken role identity as the "John Wayne Syndrome." The public and the police alike, are constantly being bombarded with the tough, aggressive cop; an image which is in contrast with the helpful, friendly, professional police officer that modern training academies and criminal justice academic programs are trying to graduate today.

The nature of police work requires officers to face situations in which they are likely to experience frustration and anxiety during interactions with people. Police officers are expected to deal with serious matters among people who possess a life style different from their own. They may experience "culture shock" when they move from one sub-culture to another and may find it difficult to interpret accurately, to predict, or to influence the behavior of those around them (Strecher, 1971). Such discomfort and social confusion often lead the police officer to develop negative attitudes toward those individuals who are different.

Many officers experience trauma after being involved in highly emotional situations. Some officers find it difficult to cope with certain instances of social injustices, injuries, and deaths. Often police officers become deeply and personally involved in certain cases involving victims, injustices, public apathy, and shooting situations (Cohen, 1980). The officer, however, is expected by the public and by his or her peers to approach such situations in an objective and professional manner. The result being the repression of his or her emotions in order to maintain a professional image (Turco, 1986).

The police officer is trained to display a certain image and to react with authority to given situations. This image is not only provided by the media's representation and public expectations, but by the training academy as well. Police officers are trained to be somewhat suspicious and to perceive events or changes in the physical environment that indicate a probability of disorder (Skolnick and Gray, 1975). Training movies depict police officers injured or killed in any number of situations that other individuals would consider normal. Many "shoot—don't shoot" films portray police officers encountering young children, elderly individuals, beautiful women and other unexpected persons bearing weapons. Such training is intended to "alert" the police officer to his or her vulnerability as a target of assault and to prompt preventive measures. Such training may create substantial stress for a police officer; possibly to the extent that the officer may be unable to relate with other non-police officers as meaningfully as he or she would like.

Coping with Stress

There have been many suggestions for reducing stress or learning to cope with stress in the police profession. The International Association of Chiefs of Police (1978) made the following recommendations for handling police stress:

1. More efficient pre-employment screening to weed out those who cannot cope with a high-stress job.
2. Increased practical training for police personnel on stress, including the simulation of high-stress situations.
3. Training programs for spouses so that they may better understand potential problems.
4. Group discussions where officers and perhaps their spouses can ventilate and share their feelings about the job.
5. A more supportive attitude by police executives toward the stress-related problems of patrol officers.
6. A mandatory alcoholic rehabilitation program.
7. Immediate consultation with officers involved in traumatic events such as justifiable homicides.
8. Complete false arrest and liability insurance to relieve the officer of having to second-guess his decisions.
9. The provision of departmental psychological services to employees and their families.

More specific programs designed to increase effectiveness in coping with police stress have included:

1. The enhancement of self-awareness and self-esteem. The individual police officer can often decrease the impact of stress by increasing his/her understanding of the problems they face in police work.
2. Physical exercise and diet. Activities such as aerobic exercises, jogging, swimming, tennis, and similar activities allow a means of ventilation for built up stress. Diet is another important contribution to the physical well-being of police officers who find themselves under shift changes and long hours which often has the officer eating nutritionally deficient food.
3. Biofeedback and relaxation training. Instructing police officers how to relax and control their physiological responses has been successful in many stress management programs.
4. Psychological services and counseling programs. Police officers know what the stresses of police work are but either cannot or are reluctant to talk about them with anyone other than fellow police officers. By training selected police officers in counseling and psychological techniques under the supervision of a clinical mental health professional, police agencies have reported successes in reducing stress related symptoms in police officers such as alcoholism, drug abuse, and marital problems (Territo and Vetter, 1981).

Summary

The police profession has been identified as having a high incidence of stress and stress related diseases. The causes of stress within the police profession are numerous, but are usually related to the social and political environment police officers find themselves working and living in. Stress in police work has been demonstrated by a relatively high rate of divorce, alcoholism, drug abuse, heart disease, and accidents to name a few. Police officers are trained to be suspicious of potentially dangerous individuals. Unfortunately, almost everyone a police officer comes in contact with is potentially dangerous. Maintaining a suspicious attitude of others creates a substantial amount of stress in the police officer. Consequently, it could be suggested that police training provides an atmosphere conducive to stress. Several police agencies have developed programs designed to provide ventilation and resolution of police stress for officers and their families. Many police agencies have incorporated counselors, chaplains, ride-along programs for spouses, and auxillary police services for officers and their families. Many of these programs appear to help relieve the stresses of police work, but much more needs to be done before the police profession clearly resolves the problem of police stress.

References

Bennett, B. (1978). "The Police Mystique," *Police Chief*, 45.

Braswell, M., and R. Meeks (1982). "The Police Officer as a Marriage and Family Therapist: A Discussion of Some Issues," *Family Therapy*, 9(2).

Cohen, A. (1980). "I've Killed that Man Ten Thousand Times," *Police Magazine*, July.

Dantzken, M.C. (1986). "A View into Police Stress," *Journal of Police and Criminal Psychology*, 2(1).

Elliott, M.L., et al. (1986). "Marital Intimacy and Satisfaction as a Support System for Coping with Police Officer Stress," *Journal of Police Science and Administration*, 14(1).

International Association of Chiefs of Police (1978). *Training Key Number 257*. Gaithersburg, MD: IACP.

Keller, P. (1972). "Situational Set and Need for Approval as Variables in Police Recruit's Perceptions of Ghetto Residents" Diss. University of Miami.

Keller, P. (1978). "A Psychological View of the Police Officer Paradox," *Police Chief*, 45.

Kroes, W.; B. Margolis; and J. Hurrell (1974). "Job Stress in Policemen," *Journal of Police Science and Administration*, February.

Kroes, W. (1985). *Society's Victims - the Police: An Analysis of Job Stress in Policing*, 2d ed. Springfield, IL: Charles C. Thomas.

Maslach, C., and S.W. Jackson (1979). "Burned-out Cops and Their Families," *Psychology Today*, May.

Miller, L. (1981). "Police Officer Involvement in Motor Vehicle Accidents within the State of Tennessee" Diss. The University of Tennessee-Knoxville.

Reiser, M. (1970). "A Psychologist's View of the Badge," *Police Chief*, 38.

Reiser, M. (1974). "Some Organizational Stresses on Policemen," *Journal of Police Science and Administration*, 2.

Skolnick, J., and T. Gray (1975). *Police in America*. Boston: Educational Associates.

Stafford, A.R. (1986). "Lawsuits against the Police: Reasons for the Proliferation of Litigation in the Past Decade," *Journal of Police and Criminal Psychology*, 2(1).

Stratton, J. (1978). "Police Stress: An Overview," *Police Chief*, 45.

Strecher, V. (1971). *The Environment of Law Enforcement*. Englewood Cliffs, NJ: Prentice-Hall.

Territo, L., and H. Vetter (1978). *Stress and Police Personnel*. Boston: Allyn and Bacon.

Turco, R.N. (1986). "Police Shootings: Psychoanalytic Viewpoints," *Journal of Offender Therapy and Comparative Criminology*, 30(1).

Vastola, A. (1978). "The Police Personality: An Alternative Explanatory Model," *Police Chief*, 45.

Ward, R. (1971). "The Police Role: A Case for Diversity," *Journal of Criminal Law, Criminology and Police Science*, 61.

Cases in Police Stress

Police officers have a tremendous responsibility regarding the maintenance of the social order. Police officers must act in an authoritative capacity, represent the law at all times, be compassionate in some situations and be prepared to take a life in another instance, help remove a lifeless body from a highway and, within the same hour, bear the tragic news to an unsuspecting widow. He or she must witness countless injustices and yet, be expected to lead a normal life. It is not surprising that those persons in the police profession often experience high divorce, suicide, accident, and alcoholism rates. Many police officers will face and make more crucial decisions in an eight hour shift than many nonpolice persons will make during the course of an entire year. One of the keys in becoming a successful police officer is learning to cope with the varieties of stress that the position inherently involves.

As you react to the following seven cases, make an attempt to identify with and to place in perspective the personality characteristics portrayed.

Case number one, "Decisions," concerns a police officer who is faced with two situations at the same time. The officer must make an on-the-spot decision as to which deserves his attention first. The officer finds that sometimes the first decision may not always be the best. There is little time for deliberation in an emergency, and there is no room for error.

Case number two, "A Trained Machine," involves an internal affairs investigation into a police shooting incident. An officer has shot an innocent person by mistake. Some feel the officer should be punished for negligence. It is the officer's fault—or is it?

Case number three, "Eviction Notice," deals with a police officer forced to serve an eviction order on an elderly couple. The couple has nowhere to go and no one to turn to for help. The officer must do his duty and evict the couple regardless of his emotional feelings about the situation. The officer finds that what is legal is not necessarily just.

Case number four, "Should I Shoot?," explores the stress of deciding when to use deadly force in a police situation. A female officer is faced with a situation that requires her to make a split-second decision whether or not to squeeze the trigger.

Case number five, "Family or Job," deals with one of the more common police stressors—how to be a career police officer and have a stable family life at the same time. A police officer sees his family pulling apart from him and friends making inappropriate demands on his limited free time. Although the officer is happy with his job, can he find a way to prevent his family from breaking up because of it?

Case number six, "The Concert," involves the use of police discretion. Discretion is a powerful tool in police work. The stress of knowing when and how to use discretion becomes an important part of the police role. A police officer finds that one arrest situation is not like others.

Case number seven, "Civil Liability," explores the popularity of civil suits against police actions. Police effectiveness is sometimes marred by the always present threat of a civil suit. A police officer must decide if the fear of litigation will impede his performance as an officer of the law.

Case 1

Decisions

It is your first day back on the seven a.m. to three p.m. shift. You are in the roll call room of the State Police Barracks waiting for your Sergeant to address the shift before you go on patrol. Sipping on a cup of coffee and trying to wake up, you wonder what the weather will be like.

"Hope it doesn't rain. There will be a lot of traffic accidents to work if it rains," you think to yourself.

The Sergeant, looking a little sleepy himself, enters the roll call room.

"Alright men, I don't have any new items for you, but I do want to remind you about the mental patient who escaped from custody yesterday. The city and county have not had any luck locating him and they have asked us to keep an eye on the interstates. He may be trying to get home. Remember, he can be dangerous. For those of you who have been off for a couple of days, I have some copies of this guy's description and background. Pick one up before you go out. Any questions?"

The room is quiet for a few seconds. When you realize that no one else is going to say anything you raise your hand.

"Sergeant, have you heard what the weather's going to be like today?"

"Oh yes, it's supposed to rain so be sure you all have enough accident forms," he warns.

After picking up a copy of the escaped mental patient report and checking out your patrol car, you proceed toward your patrol zone. Your patrol zone consists of approximately fifty miles of interstate and nearly one hundred square miles of suburban area near a metropolitan city.

Traffic accidents kept you busy during the first few hours of the shift. Your Sergeant was right about the rain. It began raining just after you left the State Police Barracks and needless to say, has contributed to a number of commuter accidents in your zone. It is now eleven a.m. and you decide to eat an early lunch and work on some reports at a nearby truck stop. As you start to obtain clearance on the radio, the dispatcher provides new information on the escaped mental patient.

"All units prepare to copy. Be advised that city P.D. has informed us that a homocide has occurred in Fairbanks Subdivision last evening. Suspect is described as being the escaped mental patient from the state hospital. Suspect last seen in the Fairbanks Subdivision running from the scene in a northerly direction at about 7 a.m. this date. Consider suspect armed with a knife and dangerous."

The report surprises you. You didn't realize that the escaped mental patient was that dangerous. You fumble through your attache case and pull out the report on the mental patient. After a closer reading, the report indicates that the individual is criminally insane and extremely dangerous. You now wish that you had read the report in more detail since Fairbanks Subdivision is only a few miles from your patrol zone. You decide to telephone headquarters at the truck stop in an effort to acquire more information on the fugitive.

The records clerk at headquarters advises you that the mental patient stabbed an elderly woman to death last night. The patient had broken into a residence at Fair-banks Subdivision where the elderly woman lived alone with her two small dogs. The records clerk also informs you that the mental patient also stabbed the dogs to death.

Hanging up the telephone you decide to skip lunch in favor of some peanut butter crackers and a soft drink. You feel that you should spend the time patrolling the areas near Fairbanks Subdivision looking for the mental patient.

It is still raining hard and you hope that there will not be any more traffic accidents to work before you get off-duty. The radio dispatcher interrupts your thoughts.

"Attention all units in zone 26 and vicinity. An armed robbery has just occurred at the Pike Street Liquor Store. Two suspects seen heading north in a 1973 red Duster. City Police were in pursuit of suspect vehicle until lost near interstate 26 and the Brookcastle Highway.

Zone 26 is your zone and you're only a few miles from the Brookcastle exit. You begin to head south on I-26 watching the north bound traffic for the red Duster.

You observe a man hitchhiking on the north bound side of the interstate. The man is dressed in only a shirt and pants and you think about why the man isn't under a bridge for cover from the rain. You realize that the man could fit the description of the escaped mental patient. As you look for a level area in the median strip to turn you notice that a black Volkswagon—with what appears to be two girls—stopping to pick up the hitchhiker. Just as you begin to pull into the median strip a red Duster speeds by on the north bound side of the interstate. It is raining hard and you are unable to make out the occupants of the car or its license plate. Pulling onto the north bound lane you realize that you must make a decision. The hitchhiker who was just picked up by the girls may or may not be the patient. The red Duster could be the robbers or just someone driving too fast in the rain. You have enough probable cause to stop either the Duster or the Volkswagon.

Making a radio call for assistance would result in at least a five or ten minute delay for a back-up unit. By that time the vehicle you decide not to stop would probably be lost. You cannot waste any more time. You have to act now.

Based on what you have read, answer the following questions:

1. What should the Trooper do?
2. If, in fact, there were no police units close to the Trooper's location, would your decision change?
3. What probable cause exists for pursuing the red Duster? For pursuing the Volkswagon?

Case 2

A Trained Machine

Female police officers are looked upon with curiosity, humor, and sometimes, contempt. As a female investigator in the Internal Affairs Bureau, you occasionally feel that other officers view you with more than the usual amount of contempt. Traditionally, internal affairs officers have been feared by other police officers, and traditionally internal affairs officers have been men.

You have been educated and trained to perform as a law enforcement officer in your city. You have never been assigned to work any "real" police functions during the three years you have been on the force. You were first assigned to the Identifications Bureau where you worked as a crime scene technician for two and a half years. Desiring to become involved in criminal investigation work, you took and passed the detective exam. Evidently, the administration felt that you were more suited to work internal affairs investigations than criminal investigations.

You are getting bored with having to perform background investigations on police applicants and have been requesting more important assignments from your Lieutenant. Your Lieutenant, a sexist, has promised to give you the next important case that comes along.

A telephone call at 3 a.m. from your Lieutenant has just made that promise a reality.

"June, you awake? Listen, you've been wanting a good assignment and I've got one for you. A patrolman shot and killed an unarmed man a couple of hours ago and we need a case report on it. Get down to headquarters and get on it. The patrolman's name is Frank Schmidt. We're going to see how good a job you do."

You have finally gotten that one important case. Regardless of how distasteful the situation is, you are excited about being assigned as the investigating officer.

Arriving at your office, you find that officer Schmidt and his Sergeant, Joe Banks, are waiting for you. Schmidt is a young officer, probably in his mid-twenties. He is pale and appears to be very scared. Sergeant Banks is chewing a cigar and looking at you with no small amount of animosity.

You introduce yourself and ask Officer Schmidt and Sergeant Banks into the internal affairs conference room.

"I understand there's been a shooting," you say, attempting to hide your nervousness.

"Look, the kid blew away this bastard out behind an all night market that was robbed. The bastard made a sudden move and Schmidt shot him. The kid did all right," the Sergeant retorted.

"Thank you Sergeant, but I need a statement from officer Schmidt himself," you advise, noticing that Sergeant Banks is impatiently rolling his cigar from one corner of his mouth to the other.

"Now, officer Schmidt...Frank, tell me as completely as you can what happened."

"Well, I was patrolling the Baker Section when I got this silent alarm call at the all night market on Duke Street. It was about 1 a.m. and I was only a couple of blocks away so I got there in a few minutes. As I approached the market, I cut my lights and engine and coasted to the rear of the market. That's when I saw the guy come running out of the market with a bag. The guy ran around to the back of the market and I hollered for him to stop. He turned real fast and looked like he was grabbing something inside his jacket and that's when I shot three times and I guess I hit him all three times.''

"O.K. Frank. Did the man you shot rob the store?''

"No, the store clerk said the guy was a frequent shoplifter and he wanted us to catch him this time so he turned in the alarm. That clerk's not supposed to use the alarm unless it's an armed robbery attempt. He shouldn't have turned in the alarm.''

Officer Schmidt is obviously upset. You notice that he is beginning to perspire and rubbing his hands together nervously.

"Frank, did the man you shot have a firearm or any other type of weapon on him?''

"No, not even a pocket knife,'' Schmidt replied.

After three hours of questioning officer Schmidt and obtaining additional details about the shooting incident, you excuse Schmidt and his Sergeant.

"Oh Frank, you can go home now. I'll have to obtain statements from some other people then I'll get back in touch with you. Sergeant, remember that officer Schmidt will be assigned to day shift in the Records Bureau until this is cleared up.''

Assignment to desk duty in the Records Bureau is standard procedure for officers in your department who have been involved in a shooting incident. The assignment is supposed to be a "cooling off'' period for the officer, but in some cases seems to create more stress as the officer waits to see if his or her career will be ended.

After reviewing the statements and circumstances surrounding the incident, you decide with some reluctance, that the shooting was unjustified. Newspaper, radio, and television accounts of the incident have also ruled the shooting unjustified and are calling for the prosecution of officer Schmidt.

Several days later Sergeant Banks enters your office while you are writing your final report to the Review Board.

"Well, what's going to be in your report to the Review board,'' Sergeant Banks demands, chewing on what appears to be the same cigar he had three days ago.

"I'm recommending that disciplinary action be taken against officer Schmidt for unjustified shooting,'' you answer, not looking up from your typewriter.

"What do you mean?...That kid did exactly what he's been trained to do. He got an armed robbery in progress call, got to the scene and saw a man running from the store. He told him to halt, but the man wheeled around and grabbed at something in his jacket. What the hell would you do?'' Sergeant Banks yells, getting angrier by the moment.

"He should have made sure the man was pulling a gun,'' you answer, trying to maintain your calm.

"By that time it could've been too late. Schmidt could be lying in a grave right now like a lot of other young cops who waited to make sure,'' the Sergeant states as he storms out of your office.

You begin to think about Sergeant Banks' statement. You remember that you have never been on patrol or had to face any of the situations line officers must face in their day-to-day activities. You also remember the training that you received on the use of deadly force at the police academy three years ago. You remember all the training movies and how you joked with other members in the classroom about how hard it was to differentiate a shooting situation from a non-shooting situation.

You begin to think about officer Schmidt and what your report may do to his life and career. The Review Board relies heavily upon the internal affairs investigation report for making their decisions. Looking down at the report still in the typewriter, you wonder if you are doing the right thing.

Based on what you have read, answer the following questions:

1. Why would the Lieutenant give this case to June rather than an experienced investigator?
2. Do you think police firearms training tends to make officers paranoid?
3. What should June do? What would you place in the report if you were the investigator?

Case 3
Eviction Notice

You have just finished working the morning school traffic at a county elementary school. Looking at the pile of court process papers laying in the seat of your cruiser, you realize that today is going to be a very busy one. Fumbling through the papers to separate the subpoenas and warrants, you find one eviction order.

"Never had to serve one of these before," you think to yourself as you read the order.

The eviction order states that you are to remove two individuals, Mr. and Mrs. Enoch Hall, and their belongings from a rented house. The order further states that Mr. and Mrs. Hall have not paid their rent in over two months and the landlord is attempting to find "relief" from the courts.

"Probably a couple of welfare bums who are too sorry to pay their rent," you think to yourself.

You decide to stop at the landlord's home and talk to him about the eviction. The landlord lives only a few miles from where the Hall's house is located.

"Good morning, Mr. Hughes, I'm deputy White with the Sheriff's Department. I understand you have a problem with your renters."

"Did you get an eviction notice to serve?" Hughes asks.

You show Mr. Hughes the order and again ask what the problem is.

"The problem is they won't pay their rent. They've been living there for I don't know how long. I inherited the place from my uncle who died last year. I'm going to rent the place to some more responsible people," Hughes explains to you.

"When's the last time they paid their rent?" you ask.

"Oh, they pay a little here and a little there. I can't keep track of it. I raised their rent last year hoping they would move but they didn't," Hughes states.

"How much is their rent?" you ask, somewhat curious about the situation.

"I charge 'em $300 a month. They were paying $175 when my uncle owned the place. They should've moved when I upped the rent. They're on a fixed income," Hughes continues.

From the conversation with Mr. Hughes you begin to realize that the Hall's must be an elderly couple. It seems obvious that Mr. Hughes apparently just wants the Halls off the property.

"Mr. Hughes, I don't know too much about civil law but can you evict a renter if they indicated good faith in paying the rent? You indicated that they have paid some on their rent."

"Look officer, that order has been signed by the judge. I went up to the courthouse and talked with him myself. Known him a long time. We go fishing together. If you've got a question about it why don't you call him?" Hughes responds somewhat irritated.

Remembering what your academy instructor advised about not getting involved in civil actions caused you to stop questioning the rationale of the order. Your job is to serve court processes and not question whether they are just or not. You advise Mr. Hughes that you are going to serve the eviction order and leave.

Arriving at the Halls' home, you notice that the house is a small frame structure.

"It sure isn't worth $300 a month," you think to yourself as you pull into the driveway.

Mr. Hall comes to the door after you step on the porch of the house. He is a small, frail man who appears to be in his seventies.

"Mr. Hall, I'm deputy White with the Sheriff's Department. I'm afraid I have some bad news for you."

"Morning officer, would you like to come in?" Mr. Hall asks as he opens the screen door.

The inside of the house is what you expected. There are a few furnishings and the living room is dark. You sit down on an old, worn-out couch. Mrs. Hall comes into the living room and asks if you would like a cup of coffee. Declining the coffee and being as courteous as you can, you explain the eviction order to them.

Mr. and Mrs. Hall do not appear surprised about the order.

"Figured he'd get around to throwing us out," Mr. Hall remarks.

"Have you folks paid anything on your rent to Mr. Hughes?" you ask, still concerned about Mr. Hughes' motives.

"Yeah, we've been paying 175 a month for five years now. Mr. Hughes took this place about six months ago and came by and told us we'd have to start paying 300 a month or get out. We're on a fixed income, Social Security. We've been trying to pay Mr. Hughes on time but sometimes we have to pay two or three payments a month rather than the whole 300 at one time. The wife's been sick and medicare doesn't pay all the doctor and drug bills, so we have to pay some." Mr. Hall explains.

"Then you have paid some on your rent and are not trying to get out of paying?" you ask.

"I'll pay Mr. Hughes what he wants but I can't pay the whole $300 at one time," Mr. Hall continues.

It is apparent to you that Mr. Hughes is only concerned with making the Hall's leave. Hughes either lied to the Judge about the Halls not paying their rent or else the judge is just a good friend of Hughes and is "helping him out."

"You know, Mr. Hall, I believe you'd have a good case against Hughes in a Civil Court," you suggest.

"Too much time, trouble, and money. Besides, if Mr. Hughes wants us to get out there ain't no way to stop him," Mr. Hall states.

"Where are you going to go?" you ask, wondering if the Halls have any children.

"Don't know. Don't have any children to live with. I guess we'll just have to find somewhere else to live. Don't have any money. Maybe the county poorhouse will take us," Mr. Hall says with a small grin.

The situation sickens you. You know there must be some underlying motive why Hughes wants to evict the Halls. You could call the State Department of Human Services and talk with them about the situation; but you are not supposed to get involved in Civil matters. You are a law enforcement officer, not a social worker. Still, it doesn't seem right.

Based on what you have read, answer the following questions:

1. Should law enforcement officers become involved in civil matters?
2. What legal grounds, if any, do the Halls have? What can they do about the situation?
3. What should the deputy do in this case? Are there any resources or institutions available that could aid the Halls?

Case 4
Should I Shoot?

Although you have been a police officer in the patrol division for over two years, you still have a difficult time convincing your fellow officers that you are capable of performing your duties. You are a female officer. You are rather small in stature and would have never have been a police officer had the equal rights legislations not been enacted. Your supervisor was reluctant to assign you to patrol duty but you were finally able to convince him that you were just as capable as a male patrol officer. Nevertheless, the administration assigned you to a two man patrol so your partner could "protect" you.

Having a male partner does create problems. You are attractive and several of the policemen's wives have complained to the chief about their husbands' riding in a patrol car with you. This has caused somewhat of a high turnover rate in partners for you. Most recently the chief assigned a young unmarried patrolman as your partner who apparently wanted more than just a partner. He seemed to be more "interested" in you than in his job. Finally, the chief assigned an older officer as your partner. Your partner, Jim, is old enough to be your father and his wife does not seem too concerned that you are an attractive female. Jim, however, treats you like a daughter and is very protective of you. When Jim thinks there will be trouble in a situation, he orders you to stay in the patrol car.

On the other hand, having a male partner like Jim does have certain advantages. Because you are female and not big and strong, some individuals you come in contact with do not take you seriously. There was the time you were attempting to put handcuffs on a male drunk driver and the driver almost overpowered you. You were relieved that Jim was there to control the driver, although you would never admit it to him. There have also been other altercations with males that Jim has had to "pull you out of."

Despite these occasional mishaps, you enjoy your job and would like to remain in the Patrol Division. You have been offered other assignments, such as Juvenile Bureau and Traffic Division, but you enjoy the variety of patrol work.

You and Jim are working the 4 p.m. to midnight shift patrolling a lower income neighborhood. You both have just finished eating dinner and have checked back on the radio to headquarters as "in-service." The dispatcher informs you that two black males have mugged an elderly black woman in your area. You are requested to back-up another patrol car that was assigned to the call.

Jim turns the cruiser around and heads toward the location of the mugging. Pulling behind the other patrol car, you see two officers on the sidewalk talking with the victim. The victim is holding a handkerchief to her head and is apparently injured from the mugging incident. One of the officers walks over to your cruiser.

"Hi. Lady here got knocked down and had her purse taken from her. Don't have much of a description of the assailants, just two young black males. The lady says they ran through the alley after they knocked her down."

"We'll drive over to the next block and see if we can see anyone fitting their description," Jim advises.

"Okay, we're going to stay here and wait for the ambulance. I think the lady should be checked over at the hospital. I'll try to get a better description from her there," the other officer explains.

Jim pulls into the alley and drives slowly looking for evidence of where the two males may have gone.

"I tell you what, you drive down to the next street and come back up and around the block. I'll get out here and walk. Might be able to come up on'em. If you see anything give me a call, I'll have the walkie-talkie." Jim tells you as he puts the walkie-talkie in his back pocket.

You begin to drive along the other street looking between alleys. About a block from where Jim got out of the car you notice a purse lying in an alley near some trash cans. You get out of the cruiser and walk over to the purse. The purse matches the one belonging to the victim of the mugging.

"You're right Slim, it is a honky fox cop," someone says, very close to you.

You are startled and back up against the alley wall. You see two black males standing not more than five feet from you. You hadn't seen them because they were standing behind a large trash container next to where the purse was laying. You glance toward your cruiser parked on the street thinking about the radio.

"C'mon Slim let's have some fun with this lovely lady," one of the boys comments as they both begin to move toward you.

You cannot run. You think about using your revolver. Your night stick is laying in the seat of your cruiser and your revolver is the only weapon you have at your side. A warning shot is out of the question. If you made a move toward your holster, it would have to be fast and you would have to shoot because the two males are too close to you. You are concerned. Should you try to talk to them or go for your gun? You only have a few seconds more...

Based on what you have read, answer the following questions:

1. What should the officer do? Describe the options she has and choose the option that appears to be the best.
2. If the youths produced a weapon, would this change the situation? If the officer were a male rather than female, would this change the situation?
3. If there was no time to talk with the youths (i.e., the youths suddenly tried to reach out and grab the officer) and the officer fired her revolver killing one or both of the youths, what would her judgement be? What would it be if she were a male?

Case 5
Family or Job?

It's nine p.m. and you are on your way home from police headquarters. After working twelve hours on a burglary detail, you are bone tired. As a detective working in the Property Crimes unit of the Criminal Investigation Division for the past seven weeks, you have been involved in a Sting investigation attempting to break a burglary ring that has been operating in your city. You enjoy your work, especially since you were transferred from Traffic Division to C.I.D. nine months ago. There seems to be more excitement and more reward for you in investigative work.

Pulling into your driveway, you notice that the family car is gone.

"They must have gone out to eat," you think to yourself as you rummage through your pockets for the house key.

Entering the house, you notice dishes in the kitchen sink. Suddenly, you remember that your nine year old son is participating in a school play. There was a P.T.A. meeting and school play scheduled for tonight. You were supposed to go with your family but somehow it slipped your mind. You even forgot to call and inform your wife that you would be late getting home tonight.

"Damn," you think, remembering how important your attending the play was to your son.

It is too late for you to go to the school now. The meeting and play is supposed to be over at 9:30. You open a soft drink and sit down in a living room chair and begin to think about how you are going to apologize to your son.

Working investigations seems to take much more of your time than when you were in Traffic Division. Your schedule in the Traffic Division was more structured. You worked eight hours and came home, the same thing everyday. But, you were not happy in the Traffic Division. You are very happy in investigations because you are actually doing something that you feel is important. You are making major arrests and getting "real" criminals rather than traffic offenders, nevertheless, you realize that your new position has been hard on your wife and son.

A couple of weeks ago you had to stay out overnight on a surveillance. It just happened that the night was your 10th wedding anniversary. You remember how understanding your wife was. Sure, she was hurt and disappointed but she seemed to realize how important this case was to you. Especially since you have been working so hard, over sixty hours a week for the past seven or eight weeks. You chuckle to yourself thinking of your work as work. It is more fun than work and you are getting something accomplished that is worthwhile.

You hear the family car entering the driveway and you go to the door to greet your wife and kids.

"Sorry, this case is really big. We've got thirty or so people we can get closed indictments on already. But, we're going to get to the big ones at the top of this ring...," you stop short noticing that your wife does not seem to be very interested in hearing about the case.

"Hi Daddy, how come you didn't come to my play?" your son asks.

"Sorry Billy, but I had to work late. How was your play?" you ask kneeling down to him.

"You always have to work late," Billy says sadly, walking away.

"Honey, just as soon as this case is over, I'll make it up to you and Billy. I promise," you explain to your wife.

"As I recall, that's what you said during your last **big** investigation and then this one came up. For the past nine months it's been one **big** investigation after the other. Billy and I are both getting a little sick of it. Apparently you would rather be at work than here with us," your wife states, almost in tears.

You walk away not wanting to get into an argument. Your wife is upset now and you decide to let her "cool off." Maybe you can talk to her tomorrow.

The ringing of the telephone awakes you at 6:30 the next morning.

"Hey, it's time to get up. Remember you've got to get down here and relieve Martin at the surveillance site."

The voice at the other end of the line is your partner, Dave. You remember that you asked him to call you this morning to make sure you were awake. You are supposed to relieve Detective Martin who has been on surveillance all night. You decide not to wake your wife and go into the kitchen to make some instant coffee.

"I'm going to try and take off early today," you say to yourself, realizing you should spend some time with your son and maybe even take your wife out to dinner.

Later that day you ask your partner if he will cover for you so you can take the afternoon off. Dave agrees to the arrangement and you go home at 2 o'clock that afternoon.

Your wife and son are not home. Billy must be at school and your wife is probably out shopping. You change into some comfortable clothes and gaze out the window. "Lawn needs cutting. I'll cut it this weekend if I have a chance," you mumble to yourself.

The telephone starts to ring and you think about not answering but then decide to answer since it could be something important about the case you are investigating. The call is not about your case, but is from one of your friends.

"Hey, I caught you home. Remember you were supposed to help me get that gun permit this week."

Your friend, Andy, works in a jewelry store in town and wants you to help him obtain a concealed weapons permit. Andy must carry large sums of money and expensive jewelry from time to time and is worried about getting robbed. You told him you would help him obtain the permit. Andy gives you a good discount on the items he carries in his store because you are a friend. With some reluctance, you tell him that you will be over shortly to pick him up and take him downtown to obtain the permit.

Arriving back several hours later, you notice that the family car is in the driveway. You wish now that you had stayed home and arranged to help Andy some other day. Your wife approaches you as you enter the house.

"Where have you been?" I've been miserable worrying about you. Dave called several times wanting to know where you were and said you were supposed to be home. I didn't know if you had been shot or what," your wife states growing angrier by the minute.

You remember turning off the radio in your car when Andy was with you. You realize that Dave may have tried to contact you on the radio.

"I was with Andy, getting the gun permit I promised him," you sheepishly try to explain.

Your wife begins to explain that Dave wants you to call him. Apparently something is wrong at the surveillance site and you are needed. As you reach for the telephone to call Dave, your wife makes another comment.

"Before you call and rush out again, let me tell you something, I can't take anymore of this. I am worried about Billy and I am sick of the way your work dominates our lives. It has come to the point that you're going to have to decide between your **big** important investigations or us. I mean it, I'll take Billy and leave you," your wife warns, tears streaming down her face.

You find yourself feeling more frustrated than angry. Dave is waiting for your call. Your family is waiting for your time. You have got to make some hard decisions.

Based on what you have read, answer the following questions:

1. Describe the officer portrayed in terms of being a police officer, family man, and his general disposition.
2. Briefly, discuss the officer's point of view. Discuss the wife's point of view.
3. If you were the officer, what would you do? What resources are available to him? To his wife?

Case 6

The Concert

You have just placed your name on the "Available To Work" roster thumb-tacked to the departmental bulletin board. Reading over the roster you notice that there are two public events scheduled for the month that will require police security. There is a drag-race and a music concert scheduled on the same nights. You have placed your name on the roster to work the music concert. You have worked drag races before and did not like the noise. You do not particularly like to work concerts, but they are usually not difficult to work and, besides, the concert hall management pays well for police protection. Since your department allows off-duty officers to work special events for extra pay, you try to take advantage of the benefit whenever you can.

On the night of the concert you arrive at the auditorium to check with the supervisor and to get your assignment. You are usually given the parking lot detail to protect the vehicles from burglary or theft. Tonight there are only eight men working rather than the usual fourteen, probably because the drag races were on the same night. Your supervisor assigns you to work inside.

"Stout, you're inside on the left side of the stage down front. You'd better take some cotton for your ears," your supervisor chuckles.

Your supervisor is right about the cotton. The concert is a rock special and the music gets very loud up front near the stage.

As you stand down front you wonder if the drag races are any louder than what you are now experiencing.

Situating yourself near the stage, you try to find an area that will not make you conspicuous to the audience and will position you away from the large speakers. You turn off your walkie-talkie, knowing that when the music begins, trying to listen and transmit on the radio will be futile even with the earphone jack attached.

You notice that there is an unusually large crowd of young people at the concert. The music group playing is a popular one that attracts teenagers and young adults. You begin to think about the stories other officers have told about working rock concerts on the inside. Stories that tell how some people in the audience bring alcoholic beverages and narcotics into the auditorium and how the police cannot make an arrest for fear of being attacked in the crowd.

"If they want to smoke pot and get drunk they can. I'm not going to try and stop them in this crowd," you think to yourself.

About halfway through the concert a man you recognize as a newspaper reporter, approaches you. The reporter's name is Mike Jackson and you are familiar with his reputation for trying to write articles that make the police department look bad.

"How you doing officer? Enjoying the concert?" Jackson addresses you.

"It's okay," you reply.

"It's a wonder you're not high with all the marijuana smoke in the air. Look at that guy there; he's even snorting on something," Jackson states as he points out an individual sitting a few feet from the stage.

Jackson is, of course, right. The individual is apparently sniffing cocaine as are two other individuals sitting with him.

"I guess anyone can do anything illegal as long as they're at a concert. You agree?" Jackson asks.

"Well, I don't plan to go in there and arrest him in that crowd," you answer without thinking.

"You don't mind if I quote you, do you?" Jackson asks as he takes out a pad and begins writing.

You notice that Jackson has already gotten your name from your nameplate and is in the process of writing down what you have said. You are beginning to think about what the police chief will say after reading Jackson's article about the police not doing anything about the use of narcotics at concerts because they are intimidated by the crowds.

You realize that attempting to arrest the individuals in the crowd may create a problem for you and the other officers, particularly if the person is not disturbing anyone else. You also realize that not doing something about the narcotic users will make the police look bad in the newspaper. You cannot wait until the concert is over to make the arrest because the individuals could be "lost" in the crowd. On the other hand should you make an arrest at all?

Based on what you have read, answer the following questions:

1. Should Officer Stout attempt to make an arrest? What procedures should he follow at this point? What could happen if Officer Stout attempted the arrest in the concert hall?
2. What should Officer Stout say to the reporter?
3. What policies could be formulated about making arrests in similar situations? Could the problem of alcohol and narcotics be eliminated from such gatherings? What can the police do to prevent or limit these illegal activities at such gatherings?

Case 7
Civil Liability

You have just placed an intoxicated driver under arrest. Having handcuffed the subject's hands behind his back and placing him in the cage car, you notify head-quarters that you have a prisoner in custody and are en-route to the city jail. The man you have just arrested is an attorney in your city. The man's name is Jefferson and specializes in civil law. You are aware of Jefferson's reputation as being an "ambulance chaser" who obtains clients by talking them into suing. You do not like his type of attorney, and you are rather pleased with yourself for arresting him on a DWI charge.

Jefferson is not very drunk, but has had enough to drink to render him legally intoxicated. He is very upset at you and has been making threatening remarks to you.

"I'm not going to sit still for this. I'm not drunk. I only had a couple of drinks at a party. I'll have you in court for this," Jefferson continues.

You do not respond to Jefferson's threats but just glare at him in the rear view mirror and smile to yourself.

"Mr. Jefferson, you'll have to submit to an intoximeter test when I get to the jail," you advise.

"I'm not going to take an intoximeter test," Jefferson responds.

"Well, you don't have to, but you may lose your driver's license under the Implied Consent Law," you add.

"Look, don't tell me about the law. I'm an attorney, I know what the law says. I want to take a blood analysis test and not an intoximeter test," Jefferson tells you.

According to your state law, an individual arrested on a DWI charge has the right to refuse a breath analysis test and request a blood analysis test. The blood analysis is more accurate than the intoximeter test. A qualified doctor or nurse must admin-ister the blood test, however. The hospital is several miles from your location and it will take quite a while to arrive at the hospital. Also, the hospital emergency room is frequently busy and you usually must wait several minutes before a nurse can administer a blood test on a DWI offender.

"He's killing time so he can sober up," you think to yourself.

"O.K. Mr. Jefferson. A blood test it is," you state as you turn your cruiser around and head toward the hospital.

Jefferson is still threatening you with civil action for false arrest as you explain your situation on the radio to headquarters. You have been lucky so far in your police career. You have never been sued. Some police officers have told you that a cop is not doing his job if he has not been sued. Civil action against police is popular and sometimes profitable. You know several officers who have had to pay out of their own pocket in civil actions against them.

Just as you are turning onto the street leading to the hospital, a car backs out of a driveway into your path. You slam on the brakes to avoid hitting the backing vehicle. Jefferson, unable to catch himself with his hands cuffed behind him, strikes his head against the cage frame in the back seat of your cruiser. You look into the back seat and see Jefferson trying to get back into the seat.

"You alright, Mr. Jefferson?" you ask in a concerned manner.

Jefferson does not acknowledge your question. He looks at you and begins to smile. Blood is trickling from Jefferson's nose and there is a large bruise on his cheek.

"This'll cost you son. You shouldn't have hit me. That's police brutality," Jefferson states with confidence.

You do not say anything and continue toward the hospital. You notice that Jefferson has stopped threatening to sue you.

"He doesn't have to threaten now, he's going to do it," you think to yourself.

As you pull into the hospital parking area, Jefferson asks you a question.

"Son, we can forget this whole thing. All you have to do is drive me back to my car and let me go home and I won't say anything about it. If you'll drop the DWI charge, I won't sue. Believe me if I sue you I'll win. Especially with my bloody nose and bruised face. You'll be paying me for the rest of your life and all I'll get is a small fine. What do you say?"

Based on what you have read, answer the following questions:

1. Could Mr. Jefferson sue the officer? Do you think Mr. Jefferson would win a judgement? Even if Mr. Jefferson lost the civil case, would it hurt the police image in the public eye?
2. If you were the officer, what would you do?
3. If Mr. Jefferson sued the officer, what defense evidence could the officer produce?

Section V
Selected Bibliography

Barrineau, H.E. (1987). *Civil Liability in Criminal Justice.* Cincinnati: Anderson Publishing Co.

Carter, R.M. (1974). "The Media Image of Law Enforcement," *Crime Prevention Review,* (January).

Cohen, A. (1980). "I've Killed that Man Ten Thousand Times." *Police Magazine,* (July).

Goldstein, H. (1977). *Policing a Free Society.* Cambridge, MA: Ballinger Publishing Co.

International Association of Chiefs of Police (1984). *Police Work and Family Life.* Gaithersburg, MD: IACP.

Kirkham, G.L. (1975). "Doc Cop," *Human Behavior,* 42(May).

Kroes, W.H. (1985). *Society's Victims - the Police: An Analysis of Job Stress in Policing,* 2d ed. Springfield, IL: Charles C. Thomas.

McEvoy, D.W. (1976). *The Police and Their Many Publics.* Metuchen, NJ: The Scarecrow Press.

Neiderhoffer, A. (1976). *The Ambivalent Force: Perspectives on the Police.* Hinsdale, IL: The Dryden Press.

Reiser, M. (1976). "Stress, Distress and Adaptation in Police Work," *The Police Chief,* 43 (January).

Stratton, J.G. (1984). *Police Passages.* Manhattan Beach, CA: Glennon Publishing Co.

Territo, C., and H. Vetter (1981). *Stress and Police Personnel.* Boston: Allyn and Bacon.

Terry, W.C. (1985). *Policing Society: An Occupational View.* New York: John Wiley and Sons.

Section VI

Police Ethics

Introduction

Police ethics involve a broad spectrum of behavior that includes not only corruption, but also malpractice, mistreatment of offenders, racial discrimination, illegal searches and seizures, suspect's constitutional rights violations, perjury, evidence planting, and other misconduct committed under the authority of law enforcement.

Various forms of police ethics exist and are influenced by numerous factors. For instance, one might distinguish between the overzealous narcotics officer who plants evidence on suspects and the corrupt narcotics officer who takes bribes to forego enforcement of the law. Regardless of the motivations, when police officers violate their professional responsibility to uphold the law, they create image problems both within the police department and within the community. The violation of police ethics affects the public image of all police officers, eroding public confidence in the police profession and increasing the difficulties encountered on the job.

The police profession is unlike other vocations in a number of ways, all of which contribute to the problem of police malpractice and the number of citizen complaints regarding police actions. Some of the factors which influence police misconduct and the frequency of complaints against police officers include:

1. Because police have the unique responsibility for law enforcement, they are sometimes asked by others to ignore violations of the law for one reason or another.
2. Most police are visible in their uniforms and in their vehicles, making their actions — both good and bad — more noticeable by the public.
3. Enforcement of the law often creates resentment which sometimes becomes vindictive and personal.
4. Police officers are exposed to temptations not often found in other forms of work.
5. Officers in the field usually work without direct supervision, a fact that creates additional opportunity for misconduct and unethical practices.
6. The public tends to be more critical of police because the police are expected to exhibit a higher level of conduct and behavior than others.

When they do not exhibit this higher degree of good conduct, complaints may be expected.

7. The nature of police work occasionally attracts persons who have antisocial or brutal tendencies which creates a need for psychological screening.

8. Emotional charge of situations are frequently encountered during police contacts such as arrest, interviews at crime scenes, and so on. Such emotion can obscure reason and judgement of both police officers and citizens (Wilson and McLaren, 1977).

Degrees of Police Ethics

While the public may disagree or be unfamiliar with what constitutes police malpractice and ethics, the police cannot afford the same luxury. There are degrees of wrongdoings which must be defined and prohibited by police agencies. There are three basic forms of police malpractice: 1) legalistic, 2) professional, and 3) moralistic (Goldstein, 1975).

Legalistic malpractice may also be referred to as police corruption. Varying degrees and types of police corruption exist in nearly all police agencies. Police corruption includes: 1) the misuse of police authority for personal gain; 2) activity of the police that compromises their ability to enforce the law or provide police services impartially; 3) the protection of illegal activities from police enforcement; and 4) the police involvement in promoting the business of one while discouraging that of another. Police corruption is defined, therefore, as "acts" involving the misuse of authority by a police officer in a manner designed to produce personal gain for himself or for others (Bopp and Whisenand, 1980). Even this definition produces a problem of "where to draw the line." A police officer who frequently eats at a restaurant where he/she receives free meals or is given a discount because he/she is a police officer, would constitute police corruption under this definition.

Professional malpractice can range from physical and verbal abuse of an individual to "conduct unbecoming an officer." Physical abuse may exhibit the characteristics of police brutality and use of excessive force in arresting a suspect. Verbal abuse may display characteristics of improper communication with suspects and witnesses or the violation of civil rights in interrogations with accused individuals. Professional malpractice may take two basic forms: one of law, and one of professional conduct. Illegal conduct would include excessive physical force and violation of civil rights. Professional misconduct would include improper police behaviors (i.e., police officers drinking alcoholic beverages in the public view).

Moralistic malpractice includes the discretionary powers of police officers. Personal feelings, prejudices, and friendships may influence a police officer's decision regarding whether to take police action or to ignore situations that warrant such actions. A police officer may feel that a person or group of persons are more deserving of police attention than others. Police officers may consciously and unconsciously label and stereotype certain types of individuals as being good or bad. Such attitudes may cause a police officer to look more closely for violations by one type of individual while only giving a cursory glance at others. A police officer may decide to arrest one type of individual because they are "deserving of it," while deciding not to arrest another individual because they are "alright."

Social and Psychological Influences on Police Ethics

It has often been said that nothing is wrong with the police profession that is not wrong with the entire society. Law enforcement does not exist in a vacuum. The police profession represents a cross-section of the community. In communities where the majority of the population are not prejudiced, one might expect to find very little prejudice in the police. Police officers in highly prejudiced communities are rewarded for their prejudiced attitudes by the general population; and therefore, may often find it beneficial to exhibit such attitudes.

Police officers do not enjoy the prestige, salary, dignity, or esteem which they believe their profession is worthy of. Police officers face complex situations daily which are perplexing, frustrating, at times, dangerous. A police officer's education and training often does not adequately prepare him or her to face responsibilities with enough confidence. There are few police agencies which provide enlightened leadership and clear policies. Most police officers are left to make their own decisions, often without proper guidance. Police officers are seldom praised for their good deeds, but are quickly reminded of their bad ones. Police officers often find it difficult to enforce laws or professionally assert themselves with upper class citizens. This leaves only the lower and middle classes, especially minorities, with which to enforce the full authority of the law. These groups seldom have the influential lines of communication to those in power which may give them relief from police actions.

The complex nature of law enforcement and the myriad of problems the police face requires a tremendous number of discretionary decisions. As noted previously, few police agencies have clear policy guidelines or enlightened supervision. Without such, the police officer is under substantial stress to act or not to act in given situations. If the officer takes action, will he/she be ostracized? If the officer does not take action, will he/she be criticized for not performing properly?

Many police administrators have stated, "the public gets the kind of law enforcement they want," or "the people don't want good law enforcement." These statements reflect the social influences on police actions. The influential elements of a community, the more socially and economically powerful citizens are often in a position to direct and dictate police actions. These are the groups that typically comprise the leaders and respected citizens of a community. It is not uncommon for these groups to comment on quality law enforcement as long as the enforcement does not interfere in their lives.

Political Influence on Police Ethics

Most recruits enter the police profession with an idealistic attitude. Most of them believe police work involves keeping of the peace, protecting citizens from criminal activity, and preserving the social order. While such an idealistic attitude has some merit, many officers change their attitude regarding police work after a relatively short time on the job. Many officers find that an unwritten policy of discrimination exists concerning police work. Officers become frustrated when tickets are "fixed" or prominent citizens are treated too generously by the courts. Officers also become frustrated when they find injustice within the criminal justice system. Officers often become demoralized when they invest their time and risk their lives to make an arrest and find that the offender is given a minimum sentence. Such frustration can easily lead a police officer to assume a more realistic attitude regarding police work. The officer finds that police work is a part of our democratic society that tends to tolerate a variety of injustices. As a result, some police officers may resort to unethical police procedures, corruption, and even close their eyes to violations of the law (Barker, 1986). Such police actions may result in an increase in using "drop guns," excessive force, violating constitutional rights of offenders, planting evidence, acceptance of bribes, and discriminatory enforcement of the law (Sherman, 1986).

Improving Police Ethics

There is a need for change in the police profession. Not all police officers are unethical and not all police officers who are unethical necessarily prefer it that way (Miller and Braswell, 1985). Social and political influences on the police profession may create a polarization regarding police ethics. When such influences dictate police actions, such actions may become ethical because they conform to the reality of the system. Those within the system that oppose the influences become outsiders and are, thus, viewed as unethical (Maas, 1973). Therefore, it may become unprofessional or unethical to, relatively speaking, initiate police action or arrest a member of the upper class, a politician, a judge, or even a fellow police officer.

Police ethics can be improved by a number of ways, including the following:

1. Improved selection and screening techniques for persons entering police service and, especially, those selected for leadership positions.
2. Increasingly stringent personnel requirements, such as advanced education and formal training including the encouragement of higher education for in-service police ethics.
3. Basic research and development in police organizations, policy-setting techniques, and community attitudes toward the police.
4. Policy guideline formulation and training in policy application and practice within the department.
5. More control over discretionary decisions making by police officers.
6. Facilitating change of citizen perspective of the police by developing supportive services within the community as well as the department.
7. Increased review of police actions by independent agencies and media representatives knowledgeable of the police profession (Parsons, 1973).

Summary

Police ethics include a broad range of police behavior and "misbehavior" including corruption, discrimination, violation of constitutional and civil rights, and other police misconducts. Various forms of police malpractice include mitigating as well as aggravating circumstances. For instance, many police officers may condemn fellow officers for being corrupt, while dismissing practices of perjury, gratuity acceptance, and evidence planting as a necessary part of the police job or as a fringe benefit of policing. In the final analysis, there seems to be degrees of police ethics and malpractice ranging from major offenses to minor infractions or even acceptable behavior. There are both social and political influences on police ethics that may increase or decrease police malpractice. When the community is corrupt, the police department often follows the same inclination. If political pressures influence the population and other organizations within the community, one may be assured that the same political pressures will influence police actions or non-actions. Unethical police practices can be decreased in increased monitoring of police actions by the public as well as more stringent selection and promotion procedures for police personnel.

References

Barker, T., and D. Carter (1986). *Police Deviance*. Cincinnati: Anderson Publishing Co.

Bopp, W., and P. Whisenand (1980). *Police Personnel Administration*, 2nd ed. Boston: Allyn and Bacon.

Goldstein, H. (1975). *Police Corruption: A Perspective on Its Nature and Control*. Washington, D.C.: The Police Foundation.

Maas, P. (1973). *Serpico*. New York: The Viking Press.

Miller, L., and M. Braswell (1985). "Teaching Police Ethics: An Experiential Model," *American Journal of Criminal Justice*, 10 (Fall).

Parsons, J.C. (1973). "A Candid Analysis of Police Corruption," *Police Chief*, March.

Sherman, L.W. (1986). "Becoming Bent: Moral Careers of Corrupt Policemen," in R.G. Culbertson, and M.R. Tezak (eds.), *Order under Law*, 2d ed. Prospect Heights, IL: Waveland Press, Inc.

Wilson, O.W., and R.C. McLaren (1977). *Police Administration*, 4th ed. New York: McGraw-Hill Book Co.

Cases in Police Ethics

Members of the police profession have, perhaps, more power than any other component of the criminal justice system. Police officers possess the discretion to make an arrest or to ignore criminal activity. This "power" attracts many police applicants. It also attracts attention from professional criminals, politicians, business people, and the "man next door" who wants a ticket "fixed."

It is not only corruption that destroys the police image. Unethical procedures utilized to bring a law breaker to justice also have a devastating effect upon the public's view of law enforcement.

In the following seven cases, you will have the opportunity to make decisions regarding corruption and ethics. You must be able to define police corruption in your own terms and decide what is ethical or unethical in each situation presented.

Case number one, "Fringe Benefits," involves a rookie police officer who is realizing that law enforcement work may bring many unexpected benefits. "Police discounts" may be one method the public uses to thank police officers for performing their duty. These discounts may also be the means to provide police officers with the incentives not to perform their duty.

Case number two, "Corrupt Community—Corrupt Police," explores the relationship between the elected law enforcement administrator and the constituency. A newly elected Sheriff is faced with an important decision. Should he enforce the law in his county or bow to the political pressures of certain community members? If he enforces the law, he may not be re-elected. If he performs selectively, the way the citizens want, he will perpetuate a tradition of corruption.

Case number three, "Super Cop," deals with the methods of solving crimes some police officers utilize. One of the best police officers on the force is using unethical techniques to solve crimes. By using these techniques, the officer is solving crimes and getting sound convictions. When another officer questions his methods, the other department members advise him that "that's the way it is."

Case number four, "Drop Gun," involves a police officer who has questioned his partner about the use of a "drop gun" in a shooting incident. The partner advises him that if he did not use the drop gun, it could mean a civil suit and even his job. The officer is now faced with a choice between going to his superiors about his partner's use of the drop gun or remaining silent.

Case number five, "Employment or Ethics," deals with a police officer who has stopped the Mayor's son for drunken driving. Weighing all the responsibilities, the officer decides it is his duty to make an arrest. Later, the Chief of Police advises the officer to drop the charges or face the possibility of termination.

Case number six, "Constitutional Rights," discusses how the police "get around" the legal requirements of rights of the accused. A newly appointed police detective finds that not every suspect receives their right to remain silent or to have an attorney present during questioning. A veteran police detective shows the young officer how to "get around" the constitutional rights requirement with suspects.

Case number seven, "Missing Evidence," concerns a Confiscations and Property Bureau officer who finds that not all stolen or confiscated property is properly disposed of. The officer realizes that there are some extremely good "buys" at the Bureau stores.

Case 1

Fringe Benefits

Crawling into the passenger side of a patrol car you position yourself beside your new partner, Bert Thompson. You have been working in the city jail as a detention officer since you graduated from the police academy three weeks ago. It is standard policy for your department to have new officers work inside prior to patrol duty.

"Name's Bert. Bet you're glad to get out of jail duty and onto some patrol," Bert remarks with a big grin.

"Sure am. My name's Warren," you reply.

"O.K. Warren, let's go fight crime," says Bert as he pulls out of the parking lot.

Bert breaks the silence. "Warren, its almost eight thirty and looks like our side of town is pretty slow this morning, how about a cup of coffee?"

"Fine, there's a coffee shop over there," you point out.

"No, No, not that place. Higher than a cat's back on prices. I know this doughnut place just up the road." Bert says.

Bert pulls into a franchised coffee and doughnut shop and tells you to wait in the cruiser and monitor the calls from headquarters.

"How do you like your coffee, Warren?" Bert asks as he steps out of the car.

"Black," you respond.

You see Bert through the large windows of the doughnut shop joking with one of the waitresses as he orders the coffee. You notice the waitress handing a large bag to Bert and begin to wonder how much coffee he bought.

"What did you do, buy out the whole place?" you ask as Bert climbs back into the cruiser.

"Well, I thought a few doughnuts wouldn't hurt along with our coffee," Bert says as he takes coffee cups from the bag.

"How much I owe you for mine?" you ask Bert.

"Not a thing, this was on the house, if you know what I mean," Bert responds with a grin.

"They told us at the academy we weren't supposed to take gratuities or anything like that," you state, trying to remain objective.

"Look Warren, on the salaries we make and the type of work we do its not a gratuity to take an occasional free-ride. Most merchants in the community enjoy giving the cops a free meal or a discount now and then, it makes them feel like they can contribute. When we eat lunch today we'll get it for free or at least at a discount. Restaurant owners like to see cops in their establishments, it makes for good business."

"Yeah, but what if they want something in return?" you ask.

"Warren, in twelve years of police work I've had maybe two or three ask me for a favor. Anyway, they weren't big things, fixing tickets, and stuff like that," Bert responds patiently.

Berts' argument seemed pretty convincing. After all, Bert had said that everyone in the department does it to some extent, including the chief.

That night, as you prepare to go to your night class at the university, you check your work schedule for the next month and notice that you will be rotating to the three to eleven shift in three weeks.

Rotating onto the afternoon evening shift poses a problem for you. You are working on an Associate degree at the University and are going to two night classes a week. Rotating to the three to eleven shift means that you will miss two weeks of classes. It is too late in the semester to drop the classes without penalty so you decide to talk with the instructor concerning your problem.

Your first instructor, Dr. Whitaker was very understanding and provided you with a research paper assignment to make up for the lost time. You have one more instructor to contact.

"Dr. Rowland, I'm sorry but I've been switched over to an evening shift and I'll have.to miss the next couple of classes. Is there anything I can do to make up the work that I'll miss?"

"Warren, your grades have been very good, but you know how I feel about student absenteeism, unless you can work something out with your supervisor so that you can come to class, I would suggest that you withdraw from the course or face a serious grade reduction," Dr. Rowland suggests.

You do not want to withdraw because you currently have an A in the course and the semester will be over in six more weeks. You decide that you will talk with your Lieutenant and see if you can get your off-days changed.

"No way, Warren. You know the policy. Unless there's illness or an emergency, we can't change the schedule. It would screw up the whole shift," the Lieutenant explains.

A couple of days later you receive a phone call from Dr. Rowland.

"Warren, this is Jim Rowland. Did I wake you up?"

"No, Dr. Rowland, today is my day off. By the way, I guess I'll try to stick with the class and take my chances. I wasn't able to get my work schedule altered but I figure I can make a C if I make all A's and miss a couple of classes," you explain.

"Warren, I'm not calling about that but, well, I need a favor. My son got his third speeding ticket in a year yesterday and I was wondering if there was anything you could do to help."

"Well, I don't know Dr. Rowland. Who gave your son the ticket?" you ask reluctantly.

"An officer Thompson. Listen if you can help, I would certainly appreciate it. I believe I could work out your class problem and give you a final grade for the work you have already accomplished. I believe you have an A in the course up to now," Dr. Rowland adds.

Officer Thompson is Bert. It would be very easy to persuade Bert to "fix" the ticket and alleviate your problem with the class. By fixing the ticket you would be guaranteed an A for the course. On the other hand, you consider yourself a "straight" cop and not one to take "pay-offs." You wonder if it would be corruption to fix the ticket. It does not really seem like such a big deal. Still, there was no mistaking what the instructor at the Academy said.

Based on what you have read, answer the following questions:

1. What should Warren do?
2. If Warren refused to "fix" the ticket, what course grade would he likely receive? Could Warren seek help from other sources?
3. Discuss where an officer should "draw the line" on accepting gratuities? Is an officer corrupt when he or she accepts a free cup of coffee? Give your definition of Police Corruption.

Case 2

Corrupt Community—Corrupt Police

As a newly elected Sheriff of a small rural county, you were extensively supported by the news media and influential people of the county during the campaign. Your qualifications are excellent considering the types of Sheriffs the county has had before you. You have a Bachelor's degree in Criminal Justice and seven year's experience as the Chief Investigator for the Sheriff's Department. During your seven years as Chief Investigator, you came into contact with many people and are very much aware of the workings of your county.

During your campaign for Sheriff, you promised to uphold the law and to enforce it to the best of your ability if elected. You promised to run the Sheriff's Department in an ethical and professional manner and to keep the office free from corruption. Now that you have been elected, you intend to stand by those campaign promises and develop your department into a professional law enforcement organization.

Shortly after becoming Sheriff many of your campaign supporters came to you requesting jobs as deputies or for deputy sheriff identification cards. You expected this and were not too concerned. After all, you should employ qualified individuals as deputies and give reserve deputy sheriff cards to those you trust.

Several upstanding members of church organizations visited you and called for action on vice and immoral businesses operating in your county. You began to respond to the fullest legal extent of the law against massage parlors and adult book stores in the county. These businesses are considered "shady operations," and are the source of many law enforcement problems in the county. One adult book store could not take the "heat" you were putting on them and had to fold. You arrested the owner of one of the massage parlors for attempted bribery when he offered you five thousand dollars to "look the other way," regarding some of his illegal activities.

The news media and the community are supportive of your position against the massage parlors and adult book stores. You feel that you are beginning to live up to your campaign promises.

One day, one of your deputies informs you of certain illegal gambling operations in the county. Apparently some of the fraternal clubs in the county were operating slot machines and holding high stakes poker games. Your deputy had enough information to obtain a search warrant on one of the clubs—a veteran's organization. After reviewing his evidence you decide to make a raid on the club.

Your raid was very successful. Twenty-two slot machines and several thousand dollars of poker money was confiscated. Eighteen persons were arrested for illegal gambling operations.

The next morning you received a visitor in your office. The visitor was Max Snelling, one of your stronger campaign supporters and a retired criminal court justice.

"Morning Sheriff. I'd like to talk with you for a moment if you're not too busy," Max asks with a smile.

"Hey, I've always got time for you Judge, after all the support you gave me during my campaign," you respond shaking Max's hand.

"Sheriff, it's about that raid last night on the Vets Club. Now you know I don't like to get politically involved in such things, but I got a lot of phone calls last night. You know it's hard being a retired Judge when people continue to contact you about their problems. It seems a lot of folks want to know whether or not you are going to continue raiding fraternal clubs?"

"Not if I don't have to, Judge. If these clubs don't learn to obey the state law against gambling, then they're just as illegal as massage parlors and dope pushers," you respond.

"I know Sheriff, but this is a little different. You've got a lot of people worried that you're going to raid some of the other fraternal clubs in the county. Some of those people are pretty influential and helped to get you elected. John Phelps, publisher of the newspaper, belongs to one club and countless county officials are members of almost all the fraternal clubs here."

"There's nothing different about the law, Judge. You should know that. If those places are involved in illegal activities, then I will have to do something about it. I promised to uphold the law and that's what I'm going to try to do," you exclaim.

"Look Sheriff, it's alright to bust these little shady places like massage parlors and such, because they're out in the public eye and make communities look bad, but the fraternal clubs are different. They're not open to the general public, but to members only. Besides, all of them donate generously to charities and most of that money comes from the slot machines," Max explains.

"Judge, I appreciate your situation, but I promised the people of this county when I ran for Sheriff that I would enforce the law and that's what I'm doing," you argue.

"The people don't want that kind of law enforcement. They want a County Sheriff who will support them, and nothing the big shots at the State Capitol say is going to change that. You've got to enforce the law the majority of the people want you to enforce or you're out of office next term. It's as simple as that," Max argues.

You realize that what Max has said is probably true. If you enforce the law the way the majority of the people want you to enforce it, you could be Sheriff for a long time. If you ignore what the people say and enforce the law equally, you may not be re-elected.

"What it boils down to then, Judge, is I can either keep my job as Sheriff, or my values, but not both. Is that right?" you ask.

"I'm sorry son, that pretty much is the picture," Max states with a sad look on his face.

"What do you want me to tell the concerned citizens that are contacting me?" Max questions.

Based on what you have read, answer the following questions:

1. What should the Sheriff tell Max? What should the Sheriff do?
2. Would there be any difference in the situation if the Sheriff were a Chief of Police (not an elected law enforcement official)?
3. Does the Sheriff have any options that would allow him to continue to be a non-corruptable law enforcement official? List and explain.

Case 3
Super Cop

Bill Hammond's name appeared on the "Best Detective of the Month," roster. It was the sixth time in a row that Hammonds had received the honor. Hammonds had only been promoted from patrol to investigations nine months ago.

"How does he do it?" you ask yourself aloud.

"Hammonds is doing a damn good job isn't he?" Pete Rowe comments as he steps up to the bulletin board.

"That's not the word for it. Look at the difference in all of our case load and conviction rates and then look at Hammond's. His conviction rate is almost eighty percent while the average is around twenty percent," you point out.

"Well, I've heard that he's got a whole army of snitches working for him," Pete says as he walks away from the bulletin board.

"Snitches" is a slang work for informants. Without good informants, an investigator can do very little with an investigation. But, it takes time for an investigator to develop good informants. Hammonds did not seem to have any trouble developing informants during his first weeks as an investigator. It took you almost two months to develop a couple of snitches and Hammonds seemed to have an "army" of snitches working for him during the first several weeks of his detective assignment.

"How does he do it?" you ask yourself, again.

That afternoon your Captain calls you into his office.

"Mike, how's that investigation coming on the Country Club burglary?" the Captain asks.

"It's a pretty tight case, Captain. I've got a couple of leads and I'm waiting for a response from the crime lab," you explain.

"I've been getting some pressure up the ranks to get this thing resolved. You've been working on the case for about two weeks. I'm going to put you and Hammonds both on the case and see if we can't get this thing solved," the Captain says.

Walking out of the Captain's office, you feel as though you have been slapped in the face. It seems obvious that the Captain felt that you were not as competent as Hammonds in solving this case. It was an insult, but one you would have to live with.

The next day, Hammonds walks up to you sporting a grin.

"Mike, I hear you are having trouble with a burglary at the Country Club?" Bill asks somewhat snidely.

"Very funny, Hammonds. C'mon let's contact some of your snitches and see if they know anything," you retort as you grab your overcoat.

Hammonds will not allow you to talk with any of his informants. Hammonds always suggests that you stay in the car while he gets out to talk. You did not become very concerned because several detectives are "protective" of their sources and do not like others around while talking with them. After a while, you begin to wonder what kind of informants Hammonds has working for him. Almost all of Hammonds snitches seemed to be either drug users or pushers.

"Now all we have to do is set back and wait for a phone call," Hammonds says as he begins to drive back to the station.

"Did one of your snitches know anything?" you ask.

"No, not yet. But one will turn up something real soon," Hammonds responds confidently.

That afternoon, Hammonds comes into the detective office with a warrant in his hand.

"This is it, Mike. I've got a warrant for Jake Lennon, the one that broke into the Country Club," Hammonds says as he waves the warrant in your face.

"O.K., Hammonds, now tell me how you did it," you say, looking over the warrant.

"It was easy, Mike. My snitches came through with the information. Besides I think there is a real good chance that Mr. Jake Lennon will want to talk and confess to the break-in as well as return the stolen property," Hammonds comments.

You look at Hammonds in disbelief. Hammonds noticing the expression on your face, continues to explain.

"Look, if this Jake guy doesn't talk and confess I'd sure hate to be in his shoes when my snitches get hold of him."

Hammonds' last statement put a thought in your mind. Apparently Hammonds is using his informants to do the investigation work for him. Hammonds informants may even be using force on suspects like Jake Lennon to confess and return stolen property. It seemed Pete was right about Hammonds having an army of snitches. You begin to wonder what Hammonds is giving his informants in return for their services.

"What are you paying your snitches for doing your work for you?" you ask with increasing skepticism.

"Nothing much. I may let them slide on a few things they may be involved with," Hammonds responds as he turns and walks away.

It is becoming more apparent to you that Hammonds may be solving cases by using his informants to do the investigation work as well as engage in other inappropriate activities. Hammond's use of drug addicts and pushers as informants leads you to other possible conclusions. He could be ignoring violations of narcotics laws by his informants in return for information and services. You decide to confront Hammonds with your suspicions.

"Well why not? I'm solving more cases than anyone else here. Why not let snitches slide on some things in return for good convictions. I haven't put one thug in jail that didn't deserve to go. It's throwing back the little fish for the big ones," Hammonds argues.

Hammonds continues to explain to you how he has been using his informants to "catch" the crooks and making them confess to their crimes.

As you think about what Hammonds said, you wonder if that is the way an investigation should be handled. His argument seems to have some merit and does produce results. It does not seem right to you that a police officer should ignore illegal activities of one group and arrest others. You decide to ask your Captain.

"Look, Mike, in our business it's give and take. We have to look at our priorities. We have to look at the worst offenses and let the others slide. We can use that to our advantage the way Hammonds is doing. We've all done it as investigators — maybe not to the extent that Hammonds has, but if all of us would take that advantage like Hammonds does, we would solve more cases," your Captain explains.

The Captain's statement still does not satisfy you. You still believe Hammond's methods are unethical, even if "that's the way it is" in detective work.

You wonder what you will have to do to become "Detective of the Month."

Based on what you have read, answer the following questions:

1. Discuss the arguments of both sides for using such investigative techniques. What would you do in this situation?

2. How could a criminal investigator develop informants without using money or "promises?"

3. In your opinion, when does a police officer have justification in "throwing back the little fish" in favor of apprehending serious offenders? Explain your answer.

Case 4

Drop Gun

You and your partner are responding to a robbery in progress call at an all night service station. As you pull into the service station you see two black males run out of the side door. Your partner jumps out of the cruiser and tells you to go around to the left side of the building as he begins to run toward the right. The two subjects have split up and you are now pursuing the one who ran toward the left. Spotting the subject trying to hide in some brush, you pull your revolver and shine your flashlight on the subject.

"O.K. come on out. Don't make me have to start shooting," you warn.

The youth steps out of the bushes with his hands raised. You handcuff the subject and search him. You find a toy pistol in the subject's back pocket.

"This what you used to try and rob the place?" you ask holding the toy pistol in the youth's face.

"All we had, man. Can't afford no real gun," the youth responds.

You lead the subject over to the cruiser and place him in the back seat. You walk into the service station and see a middle-aged man wiping perspiration from his forehead with a handkerchief. You ask the man if he is uninjured.

"Yeah, I'm O.K. officer. I see you got one of them," he replies.

Suddenly, you hear three gunshots ring out and become concerned about your partner. Running out of the service station toward the area where the shots came from, you hear a fourth gunshot. After running a couple of hundred feet, you see your partner standing over the body of the second youth.

"What happened, Jim?" you ask your partner.

"Damned kid pulled a gun on me, had to shoot him," your partner replies, his eyes wide with fear.

You kneel down beside the body and confirm the youth is dead. You pick up the small handgun laying next to the body. The handgun is a cheap blue steel .25 caliber automatic with white plastic grips. The weapon had apparently been fired once as you notice one shell-casing on the ground.

"Couldn't help it. I cornered the kid here and he swung around at me with that gun. I shot three times and he shot once into the ground. I guess I'm pretty lucky," your partner explains.

"You sure are. You know this gun looks like that one you took off of that guy in the park last month," you comment.

"Well you know about those types of guns. They're floating around everywhere," your partner responds.

You remember what the other youth said about not having enough money to buy a real gun and the fact that he had a toy pistol on him.

"Jim, I caught the other kid and he had a toy gun on him. He said that they didn't have a real gun," you state, looking to see what your partner's reaction will be.

"Hey, look, you're my partner. We've got to stick together on this. I'll level with you. This kid didn't have a gun; it was dark and he jumped out of the bushes here trying to run away. It startled me and I shot him. After I noticed he didn't have a gun I put that .25 in the kid's hand and shot into the ground. I've been carrying that .25 just in case something like this happened," your partner explains.

"Jim, you don't have to use a drop gun. It was just an accident. I'd have shot too. You'll get in worse trouble if the boss finds out you used a drop gun," you try to explain.

"No way, I'm not going to be criminally or civilly liable for shooting this thug. I could be sued, criminally charged with manslaughter, loose my job, or all three. I'm not taking any chances. I'm a cop who's just shot a kid. What do you think the media is going to do with that?" your partner explains.

What your partner did is wrong. He is right about possibly being civilly and criminally liable for his misjudgement. The same thing could have happened to you. You know that it is wrong for your partner to use a drop gun. If you go to your superiors and report the drop gun, Jim will certainly be dismissed from the department and may be criminally charged. If you say nothing and the truth comes out at a later date you could be considered an accomplice. What are you going to do?

Based on what you have read, answer the following questions:

1. Answer the question, "What are you going to do?"

2. If the officer did not use the "drop gun," what would be the consequences from a) a shooting review board; b) the news media; and c) the black community?

3. If nothing was said about the "drop gun," what would happen? Include in your discussion the internal affairs investigation steps and the probable results.

Case 5

Employment or Ethics

With the third blast of the siren, the black Lincoln finally pulls over against the curb. The driver is apparently intoxicated—a common occurrence on Saturday nights such as this one. You step out of your cruiser after calling in your location and the license plate of the Lincoln. Approaching the massive black car, you can see the driver is alone.

"Step out of the car, please," you politely ask the driver.

The door swings open and a young man in his late teens staggers out. The smell of beer permeates the air and an empty beer can falls from inside the Lincoln onto the pavement.

"Been drinking, son?" you ask the young driver.

"Look, don't bug me, mister. I may have had a couple, but I can handle it," the young man sullenly retorts.

Looking over the young man's driver's license, you recognize the name as being the son of your city's mayor.

"John P. Stone, Jr., nineteen years of age, 1633 Wessex Drive. Your father the mayor?" you ask.

"That's right and if you know what's good for you, you'd better let me go. My dad won't appreciate one of his cops harassing me," the young man warns, becoming more belligerent.

"I'm not one of his cops. I work for the same boss as he does. Besides, you can barely walk let alone drive in your condition," you tell young Stone.

You think about driving the young man home and explaining the circumstances to Mayor Stone, but the young man's arrogance is upsetting you.

"Why should I give him a break when I would otherwise make an arrest. So what if he's the mayor's son?" you say to yourself. You could see the look of disbelief from the other officers when you took John P. Stone, Jr. down to headquarters and booked him for DWI.

Monday morning the Chief of Police calls you to come see him at headquarters.

"Bill, sorry to have to drag you from home early like this but I have a problem. You arrested Mayor Stone's son Saturday night for DWI and the Mayor isn't too happy about it. He wants me to try to talk you into dropping the charges," the Chief advises you.

"Why should I, Chief? The kid was too drunk to walk. He could've killed somebody driving in that condition. I wouldn't have given anyone a break in that condition," you argue.

"Look, Bill, I'm not asking you to drop the charges, I'm telling you to. We need the Mayor's support. Let me put it to you this way; you can either drop the charges or face the possibility of being fired over "something." I know you're a good cop but this is a difficult situation. Believe me if you don't drop the charges, you had best be looking for another job. The Mayor has a long memory," the Chief warns.

After being dismissed with the instructions to think it over, you stare at your lukewarm cup of coffee feeling both angry and helpless. You wonder if police work is really for you.

Based on what you have read, answer the following questions:

1. What do you think the population of this city is? Would this case be different in a metropolitan sized department? How?

2. Apparently, it is up to the officer to decide what to do about dropping the charges. If the officer refused to drop the charges, what would most likely occur in court? What would happen to the officer?

3. What options does the officer have?

Case 6

Constitutional Rights

You have been transferred to the Detective Division in a medium sized police department. You were a traffic patrolman for three years prior to your transfer. The only experience you have had in investigations is what you have gained in training and in accident investigations. You are excited about your transfer and are anxious to get started in criminal investigations.

Your partner is Will Madden, a veteran police detective who has been assigned to "break you in" on criminal investigation procedures. Will is somewhat gruff, in his mid-fifties, and has been an investigator for twenty-two years. You feel that you are lucky to have someone like Will to give you some pointers on detective work. Will, wearing a hat that went out of style years ago, comes up to you and introduces himself.

"How ya doing, kid. Looks like it's me and you for the next few weeks," he states.

Will explains to you that he is working on an armed robbery case and has a good suspect.

"C'mon kid. Let's go out and pick this guy up and see what he's got to say about it," Will tells you as he lights up the stub of a cigar he has been chewing on.

Driving to the suspect's residence, Will tells you some "war stories" of investigations he was involved in back during the "old days."

"It must have been more exciting work back then than it is now," you comment.

"I dunno if it was more exciting or not. I know police work was easier back then. Didn't have to worry about all the paper work and legal "mumbo jumbo" we do now," Will remarks, chewing on his cigar.

"Here we are, let's go see if the boy knows anything," Will states as he pulls up to the apartment building where the suspect lives.

Will knocks on the door and there is no answer. He then checks to see if the door is locked and finds that it is not.

"Let's go in and see if the boy's in bed or something," Will tells you as he enters the apartment.

"Isn't this breaking and entering illegally? I mean, we don't have a warrant or anything," you question as you follow Will inside.

"Don't worry about it, kid. Hey, I think the boy's taking a shower. I hear the water running in the bathroom," Will states as he saunters toward the sound of running water.

The suspect is taking a shower and there is no one else in the apartment. As you wait for the suspect to come out of the shower, Will searches around the apartment looking for evidence of the robbery.

"Well, look what I found. Looks like the gun the store owner described as being the one the robber used," Will says as he holds up a blue steel .45 automatic he found in a dresser drawer.

The bathroom door opens and a startled man looks at you and Will. Will is toying with the .45 automatic he found in the dresser drawer.

"How ya doing, son? Looks like your luck has run out," Will comments to the dripping man.

"What you guys doing in here? You got a warrant?" the suspect asks angrily.

"Don't need no warrant, son. I got what we call probable cause. See, you probably caused that armed robbery two nights ago and I'm holding the evidence. Now what you got to do is give back the money you stole," Will continues.

"Hey, man. You can't do this. I got rights you know," the suspect argues.

"You ain't got no rights, boy. You can either go down hard for this or make it easy on yourself," Will advises.

The man sits down and looks very scared.

"Look son, we got eyeball witnesses that saw you do it; we got your fingerprints; we got this gun, and now we got you. We got you good on this and it ain't no sweat off our backs if you want to cooperate or not. If you cooperate, it might relieve us of some paper work and we'd be grateful for that. In fact, I could talk to the judge and tell him how cooperative you were and he'd probably make it easier on you. Or, I could tell him that you were uncooperative and he'd probably send you away for a long time."

The man looks worried and confused.

"Hey man, this ain't right..." he begins.

"It's not right or wrong, friend. That's the way it is. Now you want to cooperate or not?" Will asks.

"Sure, man. I mean, I got no choice do I?" the man says with disgust. "Money's in the closet over there in a paper bag. Didn't even get a chance to spend any of it," the suspect comments dejectedly looking out of a window.

Will tells you to call a cage car to transport the offender to headquarters while he searches through the closet. Finding the money he begins to count it.

"It's all there, man. Like I said, I never had a chance to spend none of it," the man advises Will.

After the patrol car leaves the apartment building with the offender, you decide to question Will about his methods.

"Will, everything we did was in violation of that man's constitutional rights. We broke and entered his residence, made an illegal search and questioned him without advising him of his rights. Is this how you conduct all your investigations?"

Will looked at you as an adult might look at a child.

"Look kid, you've got a lot to learn about interrogation. We were lucky to find that gun he used in the robbery. We've got him dead to rights with that piece of evidence. Hell, I lied to him about us having eyeball witnesses and fingerprints. If he hadn't have copped out he may have gotten off with it. He'll sign a waiver of rights form when we get to headquarters and get a statement from him. Besides, if he had wanted to be uncooperative and not talk, he knows we could make it rough on him. All you have to remember is when we get into court you'll say the same thing I do —that he let us in and that the gun was out in the open, we gave him his rights and he decided to talk without a lawyer. C'mon. I'll treat you to a cup of coffee. We deserve a break."

As you leave the apartment building you consider your options—go along with Will, or report him to his supervisor. You strain to think it over.

Based on what you have read, answer the following questions:

1. What constitutional rights were violated? How were they violated?
2. What would have been the proper investigative steps to take?
3. If the suspect had refused to answer questions and demanded that he be appointed a lawyer, what "pressures" could Will place on the suspect?

Case 7
Missing Evidence

You have been assigned to fill a vacant post in the Property Bureau of a large City Police Department. The Property Bureau is responsible for keeping all pieces of evidence, confiscated property, and recovered stolen property. You are one of four police officers assigned with administering and maintaining the Bureau's inventory.

Lt. Hanson introduces himself and shakes your hand.

"Welcome aboard, I'm Tom Hanson, Lieutenant in charge of this operation."

"Glad to be here. I have to admit, though, I know nothing about this kind of operation," you comment to the Lieutenant.

"Don't worry, Sue. We'll show you the ropes. It gets pretty boring and there's a lot of paper work," the Lieutenant explains.

You meet the other members of the Property Bureau and begin to learn what your specific duties are.

"You'll be responsible for recording the recovered stolen property inventory, Sue. We get a lot of recovered property that is apparently stolen, but we are unable to locate the owners. Some of the property can't be returned to the owners because they can't positively identify it. In other cases the property has had the serial number removed like this stereo set here," the Lieutenant explains as he shows you around the property room.

After several weeks, you feel that you understand your function and duties in the Bureau. Although your job is not as exciting as being on the streets in patrol, you do enjoy working with everyone and the Lieutenant is easy to get along with. However, you have seen some incidents that have caused you to be somewhat concerned. You have noticed that the inventories of Evidence and Property have been juggled around and are not kept very accurately. This is especially true on pieces of evidence, such as guns, that have been checked back in after trial. You remember one such incident last week when a patrol officer returned a handgun which had been used as evidence in court. The patrol officer asked if he could keep the handgun since it was "through with" in court. The Lieutenant handed the officer the handgun and told him to "just keep it." The officer did not even have to sign for it. The Lieutenant had marked "Destroyed" on the inventory form. This did not seem to be very ethical to you, but you had noticed many officers keeping weapons they had confiscated from individuals and you had decided not to say anything.

You also noticed that several of the officers you work with in the Property Bureau go through the property room like it was a candy store, picking things out that they would like to have. You even observed the Lieutenant arranging for two officers to carry out a color console television set and place it in his personal car. The Lieutenant laughed and made the comment that since no one claimed it, he might as well watch it.

One day the Lieutenant calls you into his office.

"Sue, I'm sure you see a lot of things here that you would like to have. Stuff like T.V.'s, stereos, guns, and the like. The rule is to wait and make sure that whatever you want is finished in court or will not be claimed. Then check with me so we can take care of the paper work on it. One more rule. We don't say anything to anyone about taking stuff home. There's no need in having every officer in the department coming down here like this was some kind of wholesale store," the Lieutenant advises.

Apparently, everyone in the Property Bureau is taking advantage of the opportunity to get "free goods." At first it does not seem ethical to you. However, you begin to think about the fact that property not claimed is usually auctioned off once a year and guns are, in most cases, destroyed. It seems a shame to waste all the property in that manner. You have seen many items in the property room that you would like to have, but could not afford if they were purchased at a store. In some ways, it would be a good opportunity for you to take advantage of the situation. After all, you are really not stealing the items. But then again...

Based on what you have read, answer the following questions:

1. What should Sue do?
2. If Sue decided against taking advantage of the "opportunities," what effect would her decision have on her status in the Bureau?
3. Is this operation unethical? Is it illegal?

Section VI

Selected Bibliography

Ahern, J.F. (1972). *Police in Trouble*. New York: Hawthorne Books.

American Academy for Professional Law Enforcement (1977). *Ethical Standards in Law Enforcement*. New York: AAPLE.

Armstrong, M.F. (1973). *The Knapp Commission Report on Police Corruption*. New York: Braziller.

Barker, T., and D. Carter (1986). *Police Deviance*. Cincinnati: Anderson Publishing Co.

Burnham, D. (1976). *The Role of the Media in Controlling Corruption*. New York: John Jay Press.

Culbertson, R.G., and M.R. Tezak (1986). *Order under Law*, 2d ed. Prospect Heights, IL: Waveland Press.

Felkenes, G. (1984). "Attitudes of Police Officers toward Their Professional Ethics," *Journal of Criminal Justice*, 12(3).

Goldstein, H. (1975). *Police Corruption: A Perspective on Its Nature and Control*. Washington, D.C.: The Police Foundation.

Manning, P.K. (1977). *Police Work*. Cambridge, MA: M.I.T. Press.

McCarthy, W. (1976). *A Police Administrator Looks at Police Corruption*. New York: John Jay Press.

Miller, L., and M. Braswell (1985). "Teaching Police Ethics: An Experiential Model," *American Journal of Criminal Justice*, 10(Fall).

Muscari, P.G. (1984). "Police Corruption and Organizational Structures: An Ethicist's View," *Journal of Criminal Justice*, 12(3).

Radano, G. (1974). *Stories Cops Only Tell to Each Other*. New York: Stein and Day.

Sherman, L.W. (1974). *Police Corruption: A Sociological Perspective*. New York: Anchor Books.

Wilson, J.Q. (1968). *Varieties of Police Behavior*. Cambridge, MA: Harvard University Press.

Section VII

Police Administration and Supervision

Introduction

Police officers have many basic responsibilities and work in a variety of ways. They drive patrol cars, direct traffic, counsel juveniles, intervene in family disputes, enforce laws, write reports, interrogate suspects, interview victims and complainants, testify in court, investigate accidents, prepare budgets, render first aid, provide security checks at residences and businesses, collect and preserve evidence, give public talks, and engage in numerous other functions that come within the purview of their mission. Their duties are numerous and often conflicting.

Because a police organization cannot have a separate unit to perform all the tasks for which the police are charged, it becomes necessary to combine and administer them in some systematic way. The police organization has, for decades, operated in a paramilitary fashion. Sir Robert Peel recommended in 1829 that the police be organized along military lines. The military is organized in a fashion that makes the most of effectiveness and efficiency theories. As a result, many police agencies have utilized military organizational theories to develop a model for police organizations. Police rank, chain of command, lines of authority, span of control, unity of command, and even uniforms are based to a large extent on the military model of organization.

Although there are many similarities between the police organization and the military, there are also many differences. The separation of the ranks in the police organization is not as diverse as in the military. Patrolmen do not have to salute lieutenants or captains in most police departments. Also, it is not uncommon to find police captains socializing with police patrolmen. Most higher ranking police officers acquired their rank by moving up from patrolmen. Police chiefs in the United States usually were once patrol officers. There is no R.O.T.C. or O.C.S. for police recruits entering the profession. In addition, there are very few lateral transfers between police agencies (Beckman, 1980).

Police organizations are typically led by an elected leader. City police departments are usually under the control of the mayor or city council, while county police departments are under the control of the Sheriff, and state police agencies are under the control of the governor. Of course, this does not mean that mayors and governors make detailed decisions regarding police matters. Generally, such decisions are made by officers in the department who are experienced in police matters. The highest official in the police department is usually a police chief or commissioner. The chief is responsible for running the police department and advises the mayor or city council under whom he serves.

Below the chief of police, police agencies are frequently organized into two broad divisions: line and staff. Staff services perform technical, advisory, and support services, while line services comprise the law enforcement area of the department (i.e., patrol, traffic and investigations). Within line and staff services, specialty divisions may be formed (e.g., homicide, juvenile, patrol, jail, crime lab, etc.)

Police Chain of Command

A chain of command exists in most police departments. The chain of command, also known as the scalar principle, is an organizational mechanism which establishes formal lines of communication within the police agency. The line of communication stretches from the chief through supervisory officers such as captains, lieutenants, and sergeants, to patrol officers and detectives. The chain of command normally means that information travels up the chain from the patrol officer to sergeant, to lieutenant, to captain, and finally to the chief. Direction and discipline flow down the chain. The chain of command is an invaluable organizational tool because it establishes formal communication links. If a police department is to be properly organized, these communication links should be used by everyone within the organization to communicate formally in any way. If the chain of command is not utilized for all formal communicating, serious organizational difficulties may arise. For example, a chief of police who disregards the chain of command by issuing orders directly to patrol officers is breaking the chain and dissipating the authority of all those within the chain who have varying degrees of authority over the patrol officer's duties. Patrol officers may quickly learn that the chain of command is inconsequential in internal communications and that they can also disregard it in their efforts to communicate upward in the police organization.

Ranking officers who neither command nor supervise line officers are usually staff personnel. Although these officers may hold rank, they usually do not have command or supervisory authority over anyone. For example, a lieutenant assigned to staff services as a crime lab technician is in a staff position, not a command-level line position such as a lieutenant in patrol division.

The Police Chief

A police chief is by far the most important planning, organizing, staffing, directing, controlling, and system-building position within a police department. Because the position of chief of police is so precarious, many chiefs try to do everything themselves, attempting to become personally involved in all aspects of the police role. Career success is not achieved, however, through interference in activities for which others have been delegated authority.

Initially, all police chiefs should be able to perform successfully the following seven organizing tasks:

1. Group similar functions within the organization to facilitate task accomplishment.
2. Construct spans of control that are sensible and designed to strengthen supervision.
3. Apply the principle of unity of command in order to develop good working relationships between supervisors and subordinates.
4. Delegate necessary authority.
5. Hold those to whom authority has been delegated fully responsible for their actions.
6. Establish a meaningful and relevant chain of command designed to enhance organizational communication.
7. Organize so that decision making and problem solving may take place at all organizational levels (Sheehan and Cordner, 1988).

Police Discipline

Leadership is a most important skill for a police administrator. Qualities of leadership that induce subordinates to render their best service vary widely. Wilson and McLaren (1977) point out that "superior leaders are nearly always intelligent men, emotionally stable and physically strong, who have contagious enthusiasm and forceful personalities that seem to reach out and grip people who come under their influence." Unfortunately, such an example of police leadership is often not reflected in many police chiefs. If these qualities were found in police chiefs, many current problems of morale and discipline within police ranks would not exist.

Most police administrators and supervisors were once police patrol officers. As patrol officers many of these persons experienced the same temptations, corruption, violations of regulations, and unethical police practices that many patrol officers now engage in under their command. The only difference between the police administrator and the patrolman in this respect is the administrator must discipline those officers violating regulations, if they are caught. There seems to be a wide gap between supervisors and subordinates in many police organizations. Patrolmen do "their thing" while supervisors "do theirs." In some departments this process can become a "cat and mouse" game. Supervisors try to catch subordinates goofing off or in violation of department regulations while the subordinates are trying to stay one step ahead from being caught. Clearly, this is not proper leadership but is too often a common occurrence within police agencies (International Association of Chiefs of Police, 1985).

In some cases, a promotion to a supervisory level for an officer increases police morale. Lower ranking officers know the supervisor is "one of them" and tend to feel they have more freedom. In many instances this higher morale disappears when officers find their new supervisor adjusting to a supervisory role rather than remaining the same.

Police Unions

Police strikes are forbidden in most states and within all police agencies. However, such regulations have not deterred police unions from participating in such disruptions. Police unions are one of the primary concerns of every police administrator.

Police unions may appear legally and formally within a police organization or they may be organized informally. Typically, informal unions are organized under police associations such as the Fraternal Order of Police (Bopp and Whisenand, 1980). In most police agencies, these unions are organized for the purpose of collective bargaining with police administrators and with local government leaders. Police unions are not necessarily bad, but do often come under heavy criticism because of strikes or the threat of strikes (Anderson, 1976). When strikes do occur, the statements of President Woodrow Wilson made during the Boston police strike of 1919 usually appear in newspapers: "A strike of policemen of a great city, leaving that city at the mercy of an army of thugs, is a crime against civilization (Ayres, 1977)."

It is important to realize that a police strike is the last possible hope for police officers seeking redress of grievances from local government officials. Police employee dissatisfaction develops from poor communication and management's lack of concern and appreciation for employees and the work they do. Such dissatisfaction does not materialize overnight, but develops slowly over a period of years. One of the first allegations police officers make when a strike is threatened is "bad faith bargaining." Collective bargaining is a viable procedure for airing grievances and communicating between management and police employees. Collective bargaining works when both parties are genuinely interested in both the welfare of the community and the needs of the workers. When this communication deteriorates to the point where one or both parties becomes disinterested in the needs of the other, bad faith bargaining is the result.

Not all bad faith bargaining leads to a full-blown police strike. Police officers have devised many methods for "hurting" their employers without striking. The "Blue Flu" is a common occurrence short of striking. The "Blue Flu" usually occurs when the police department is at its busiest time with traffic or when carnivals, fairs, and concerts are in town. Police officers individually call in sick to protest management's bargaining practices. Police officers may also reduce the issue of citations for parking and traffic violations which deprives the local government from revenues generated by such activity. Police officers may refuse to answer all but emergency calls while on-duty. This type of activity allows the community to complain to government leaders that police service is not being provided.

Police unions may have a permanent place in modern police organizations. However, police strikes and work slow-downs can be avoided if the police and management will follow guidelines such as the following ones:

1. Police and government officials should work toward developing an atmosphere of trust and cooperation important for good faith bargaining.

2. Police administrators must get politically involved in decisions made

by government officials that may have an impact on the efficient operation of the police agency.

3. Internal communication between supervisors and subordinates must be developed in an effective manner.

4. Better communications and selection between the police administrator and government officials must be established.

5. Government officials and police officers must be made aware of the problems facing each with a genuine interest in meeting the needs of the police, government, and the community (Ayres, 1977).

Summary

Most police departments are organized on a para-military model. The military model of organizations can allow for an efficient and effective delivery of services. However, the police organization is unlike the military in that the lower ranking police officers are expected to make complicated decisions rather than just respond to orders. In view of this, it is most important that police agencies make optimum use of supervision and leadership skills. Following basic organizational principles of chain of command and lines of communication and supervision is very important if the police organization is to be efficient. These principles can also create a high degree of morale in the police agency.

The police chief or chief administrator has the scale which is responsible for insuring that the police organization is working in an efficient and effective manner. The police chief may accomplish this task if he/she has utilized the basic principles of organizational management, delegated proper authority, and kept lines of communication open. Police unions and collective bargaining by police officers and police management has become a growing concern of many police administrators. A major concern of police administrators is the threat of police work slow-downs or strikes. These actions can be prevented if both management and police officers work together and respect each other's needs and priorities at the bargaining table.

References

Anderson, R.O., et al. (1976). "Support Your Local Police - On Strike?" *Journal of Police . Science and Administration*, March.

Ayres, R.M. (1977). "Police Strikes: Are We Treating the Symptoms Rather Than the Problem?" *Police Chief*, March.

Beckman, E. (1980). "Police Career Planning among University Students: The Role of Agencies Perceived Reputation," *Police Studies*, Spring.

Bopp, W., and P. Whisenand (1980). *Police Personnel Administration*, 2nd ed. Boston: Allyn and Bacon.

International Association of Chiefs of Police (1985). *Police Supervision: A Manual for Police Supervisors*. Gaithersburg, MD: IACP.

MacNamora, D.E.J. (1979). "Discipline in American Policing," in D.O. Schultz (ed.), *Modern Police Administration*. Houston: Gulf Publishing Co.

Sheehan, R., and G. Cordner (1988). *Introduction to Police Administration*, 2nd ed. Cincinnati: Anderson Publishing Co.

Wilson, O.W., and R.L. McLaren (1977). *Police Administration*, 4th ed. New York: McGraw-Hill Book Co.

Cases in Police Administration and Supervision

Our police systems often follow a more military style of organization and administration. The police officer in a command position needs to possess leadership capabilities as well as qualities that will promote morale within the department. As a result, contemporary police administrators not only have the responsibility to satisfy the needs of the community, but also the needs of department members.

In the following seven cases, you will find yourself in police supervisory positions. In each case you must make a decision based on what you know from the narrative and the available resources given to you.

Case number one, "Mrs. James Thorton, III," deals with a member of the city council demanding that punitive action be taken against a police officer. The council member is threatening to turn down the police Chief's request for additional salaries and equipment for the police department unless punitive action is taken against the officer. The Chief finds that the officer performed his duty in the correct manner. The Chief must decide what to do and how to do it.

Case number two, "Good Officer—Poor Commander," concerns a police Lieutenant who has been promoted to shift commander. While having an outstanding record of achievement as a Lieutenant, the commander is finding it difficult to provide effective leadership.

Case number three, "Blue Flu," explores a frustrating experience for any police administrator. A police chief faces a possible strike if he does not act to procure an additional salary increase for his men. Officers are beginning a work slowdown by calling in sick. The chief must decide what course of action to take.

Case number four, "Chain of Command," is concerned with an assistant chief of police who becomes frustrated with the Chief of Police. The assistant chief finds himself burdened with a great deal of responsibility but very little authority when the chief overrides several decisions.

Case number five, "Discipline," deals with a newly appointed chief who finds himself having to be an administrator rather than just one of the officers. The chief experiences conflict between the officers that were his friends and whom he must now discipline.

Case number six, "Over the Hill?" involves a Chief of Police nearing retirement and his conflict with deciding whether to remain on the force and correct current problems or take the easy way out and retire.

Case number seven, "An Out-of-Shape Department," is concerned with the problem of poor physical fitness in police agencies. A Chief of Police must decide how he is to persuade his officers to begin and maintain proper physical fitness habits.

Case 1

Mrs. James Thorton, III

You are the Chief of Police in a city with a population of approximately 25,000 people. You are respected and admired by your officers. You became Chief three years ago when the city council appointed you from Assistant Chief to fill the retired Chief's post. You have always had a good relationship with the members of the city council, although a city election was held recently and two new council members were elected. You met briefly with both of the new council members at the last meeting and felt they would be supportive of your department. City Council support is extremely important at this time because you are in the process of developing the next year's budget for the police department.

Budget work is one area of police management for which you have not developed any affinity. It seems more and more difficult to justify and obtain funding, particularly since federal grants have become more difficult to procure. Your goal is to include a substantial salary increase for your officers as well as some additional equipment for the department in next year's budget. Apparently, the city council is pleased with the accomplishments and progress of your department and should be responsive to your requests.

While working on the budget proposal, your secretary advises that you have a phone call from one of the council members.

"Yes. This is Chief Phillips, may I help you?"

"You certainly may, Chief. This is Mrs. James Thorton, the third. I have a complaint about one of your officers."

Mrs. James Thorton, III is one of the new members of the city council. Mrs. Thorton married into a wealthy family in your city and is the former president of the city school board. Mrs. Thorton considers herself a socialite and projects a bit of arrogance because of her wealth and power. She has a substantial amount of influence on the city council. She indicated to you at the last council meeting that she would be supportive of your new budget proposal.

"A complaint, Mrs. Thorton? Who was the officer and what did he do?" you ask in a surprised manner.

"Patrolman Everett Bailey. Officer Bailey stopped me this morning next to Cedar Bluff school and issued me a ticket for speeding in a school zone. I explained to officer Bailey that I was late for an appointment and am a member of the city council. He insisted on giving me a ticket anyway. I knew if I called you, you would clear this up. Doesn't your new budget proposal come up at the next meeting?" Mrs. Thorton went on.

"Yes, Mrs. Thorton. Let me check into it and I'll call you back. I'm sorry this happened. Goodbye," you respond.

Mrs. Thorton was very upset and practically threatened to veto your new budget proposal if you weren't acquiescent to her request. You decide to consult Officer Bailey for the details.

"Everett, I received a phone call from Mrs. James Thorton. She said you issued her a speeding ticket..." You are interrupted by Officer Bailey before you can finish.

"I certainly did, Chief. That woman has been speeding through that school zone for some time. I've warned her several times but she insists on speeding. I was working radar at the school zone this morning and clocked her at 55 mph. I stopped her and she threatened that she would have my badge and that she could speed if she desired since she was a city council member on an important errand. She became more and more obnoxious and I issued her a citation. One of these days she's going to hit a child over there. I've got two children in that school myself," Officer Bailey explains.

"O.K. Everett. You were correct in issuing her a speeding citation. Now, let me explain the problem," you explain to Officer Bailey about the circumstances surrounding the incident.

"Everett, I'm going to have to make a tough decision. If we fix the ticket, Mrs. Thorton will never learn to stop speeding in this city. On the other hand, if we don't we may not get the salary increase or the equipment we need next year," you explain hoping that Officer Bailey will understand the predicament.

Officer Bailey appears puzzled.

"I don't know, Chief. If we fix the ticket, Mrs. Thorton will have no respect for us. This may happen time and again if we don't follow through this time. I'd rather us take our chances with the remainder of the city council as far as the budget is concerned," Officer Bailey reasons.

Officer Bailey is probably correct in assuming that Mrs. Thorton would have less respect for the police department. It is also true that if you fix the ticket this time there may be another ticket and another threat. Mrs. Thorton has a great deal of influence on the other members of the city council and if she votes against your budget request, a substantial number of the other board members may follow her lead.

Based on what you have read, answer the following questions:

1. What should the Chief do in this situation? What are his options?
2. Was the Chief correct in checking with Officer Bailey about "fixing" the ticket?
3. Could the ticket be "fixed" without Officer Bailey knowing about it? How does overriding an officer's decision in such a case as this affect the morale of the department?

Case 2

Good Officer — Poor Commander

You are the Chief of Police of a medium sized police department. After reading an evaluation report from your Deputy Chief in the Patrol Division, you are concerned over the evaluation of the second shift patrol unit. It appears that morale is low among the officers of that shift and the unit's efficiency is down.

Three months ago the Commander of the second shift unit, Captain Owens, retired. The vacant position was filled with a young Lieutenant, Bob Kingston. Kingston's background is full of accomplishments. He joined the police force seven years ago when he was 21 years old. He has a Bachelor's degree in Criminal Justice and has just finished his Master's degree in Sociology. Kingston spent 18 months on patrol before he was promoted to Sergeant. A year later, Sergeant Kingston was placed in the Records Division. Three years ago, Kingston was promoted to Lieutenant and placed in charge of the Communication's Bureau.

Lieutenant Kingston is well-educated, highly motivated, responsible, and mature. He performs every task assigned him with careful accuracy and logic. Lieutenant Kingston has increased the effectiveness and efficiency of every division bureau he has worked in.

Seven months ago, when your department was seeking someone to fill Captain Owen's position as Shift Commander, you were pleased to see Lieutenant Kingston's name on the promotion list. Lieutenant Kingston received the highest score on the Shift Commander's written examination. He also scored high on the promotion board's oral interview.

In view of Lieutenant Kingston's past performance, high scores, and his potential, you readily accepted the promotion board's recommendation to promote Kingston to Captain and Shift Commander.

Now, looking at the poor evaluative report of Captain Kingston's shift, you are puzzled. You decide to confer with the Deputy Chief about the problem.

"Dave, I've been looking at your evaluation on the second shift patrol. What seems to be the problem?"

"I was concerned too, Chief. The Personnel Bureau has had several requests for transfer from the second to another shift. Apparently, no one's pleased with the way Kingston is running the show," Deputy Chief David Pike answers.

"Just how is he running the show?" you ask, somewhat perplexed.

"By the book. Kingston is following departmental policy and regulation by the letter. Best shift Commander we've ever had as far. as the paperwork goes. All the reports are accurate, neat, and detailed. I'd say his evaluation report will improve next time, after all he's only been on the job for three months. Give him some time, he'll be alright," Pike advises.

Deputy Chief Pike's comments does not satisfy your concerns. Pike only knows what he reads about the shift's operations. Pike has already commented on the report's accuracy and details. However, Pike did not explain the low morale of the officers on the second shift. Reports can be deceiving and the only way to find out what is happening on the second shift is to observe. You decide to call in one of the Sergeants on the second shift patrol.

"Hello, Sergeant Bellows....I just thought I'd call you in to see how things are going on your shift."

"I guess you should ask Captain Kingston about that, Sir," Sergeant Bellows responded.

"Well, I would, except I want to know how he is doing in his new position. Know any problems. Don't worry about telling me, nobody's going to know about our meeting except you and me, O.K.?"

"Well sir, if you really want to know...Captain Kingston's a good officer, really knows his stuff. But he goes by the book too much, I mean, there's no flexibility. And, he thinks reports are more important than our doing the jobs," Sergeant Bellows explains.

"Sergeant, why don't you give me a couple of examples."

"Well, just last week when we had that armed robbery on Cecil Street. The suspects were travelling in a white sedan heading west on Clairemont in Alpha sector. We had a unit not two blocks from there in Beta sector and Captain Kingston ordered him not to pursue because he was the only unit in Beta sector and its against policy for a unit to leave his sector unprotected. He's also more interested in how we write our reports than how we do our jobs. Seems like he's more concerned with details than the real reason we're out on the streets. Some of the officers like to switch off-days on occasion. Yesterday, one of my patrolmen, Kim Berry, wanted to switch off-days with Tim Sheets because his daughter was in a school play; Captain Kingston refused because it's against departmental policy. Captain Owens was never that strict." Sergeant Bellows contends.

What the Sergeant said about the former Captain was true. Efficiency was important, but so was flexibility.

Based on what you have read, answer the following questions:

1. What should the Chief do at this point?
2. What problems might arise if Captain Kingston continued to perform "efficiently" and "by the book"?
3. What kinds of evaluation can be utilized to identify good leaders in a police organization?

Blue Flu

You are the Chief of a Police Department numbering 248 officers. You have been with the police department for seventeen years, with the last four years as Chief. You moved up through the ranks of the department to your present position as Chief. You were promoted from Deputy Chief to Chief by the newly elected mayor you supported during the recent campaign. There was no bitterness concerning your appointment. The former Chief had resigned to accept another position and you were highly qualified for the job. You hold a Bachelor's degree in Criminal Justice from the local university and are presently working toward a Master's degree. Realizing that the Chief's position in your department is a political appointment, you are pursuing a graduate degree so that you will be qualified to teach Criminal Justice if, and when, you are ever "removed" from office.

At present, your department is going through some budgetary problems. The Board of Mayor and Aldermen have attempted to cut back on expenditures for next year. They have decided to limit salary increases to 6½% for all city employees which includes police officers.

Members of your department attempted to obtain a substantial pay increase last year by threatening a strike. The Board of Mayor and Aldermen temporarily resolved the problem by promising a 14% pay increase for all members of the police and fire departments, effective the following year. Apparently, the Board of Mayor and Aldermen are "backing out" of this agreement by limiting all city employees salary increases to 6½%.

As Chief, you addressed the Board of Mayor and Aldermen about the problem of a salary increase for your officers. You reminded them of their previous commitment to your officers. They apologized to you and explained that there was not enough money in the budget and that they did not want to raise taxes.

For several months you have attempted to pass through the Board of Mayor and Aldermen a proposal for collective bargaining.

The Board was ready to accept a collective bargaining system, but were staunchly against third party arbitration. Recognizing that the police department may attempt to unionize, the Board of Mayor and Aldermen advised you of the State law prohibiting police unions and strikes. The Board further advised you to "pass the word" that any officer joining a police union or participating in a police strike would be terminated immediately.

Collective bargaining is a good system as long as both the administration and labor act in good faith. Realizing that the Board of Mayor and Aldermen are not receptive to the problems in your department, without third party arbitration, collective bargaining may be ineffective in meeting your department's needs.

After hearing that the Board of Mayor and Aldermen are refusing the 14% pay increase, members of your department organized themselves within the local chapter of the Police Association. Several leaders of the Police Association attempted to bargain with the Board at the last meeting. The Board refused to recognize or hear grievances from the Police Association. The Police Association leaders defined the Board's actions as "not in good faith" and threatened to strike. The Board of Mayor and Aldermen harshly reminded the Police Association leaders that any officer who attempted to strike or unionize would be terminated.

Three days later you receive an early morning telephone call at your home.

"Chief, sorry to call you so early but we've got a problem."

The caller is Deputy Chief Waller, commander of the graveyard shift.

"Chief, almost everyone on the day shift is calling in sick. It's 6:30 now and not one officer has shown up for work," Waller comments.

The day shift begins at 6:00 a.m. and ends at 2:00 p.m. There are 67 officers who are supposed to work day shift. Waller explains that only a few high ranking officers have shown up for work.

"I'll be right in," you tell Waller, an uneasy feeling growing in your stomach.

While driving into headquarters, you hear on your police radio that members of the fire department are also calling in sick. You are not prepared for this type of action. You were aware that the Police Association held a meeting two days earlier to discuss the problems with the Board of Mayor and Aldermen but are apparently unaware of the total results of this meeting.

Deputy Chief Waller meets you as you walk into your office.

"Chief, only five patrol officers have shown up for work. We've got a total of 12 officers working the day shift which includes all higher ranking officers," Waller explains.

"We'll have to call in all off-duty and vacationing officers," you advise Waller.

"Already tried that. Everyone has been saying that they are going to call in sick until the Board of Mayor and Aldermen grant them the 14% pay increase," Waller advises.

"How long can they do that?" you ask, wondering if what the officers are doing is legal.

"I've figured it up, Chief. According to our policy, an officer can—provided he has enough sick days built up—call in sick for seven consecutive days without a doctor's excuse. Tabulating the number of sick days the officers have built up, we'll average a 75 to 80% loss of strength for the next few days and there's nothing we can do. This city's going to be a mess without police protection for seven days," Waller comments.

You have a crisis on your hands. The dispatcher's office has called to advise you that there are no officers to answer calls for service. You know you must call the Mayor and advise him of the situation. You also know that you are responsible for the police department's operations. Something has to be done.

Based on what you have read, answer the following questions:

1. Apparently, the Chief is concerned about the welfare of his men. Is it the Chief's responsibility to "fight" for benefits before a city council (i.e., collective bargaining agreements)?

2. What forms of collective bargaining exist? Why are there laws prohibiting union-ization and strikes? Do these laws work?

3. What options does the Chief have open to him? Could he fire the men? What would the city council tell the Chief?

Case 4
Chain of Command

Stepping into your office to begin the day's work, you notice a pile of reports and memorandums stacked on your desk. Seeing the mountain of paperwork produced a sickening feeling in your stomach. In addition to your administrative duties of running Staff Services with its many daily problems, you are expected to review and disseminate stacks of reports and memoranda. Being an Assistant Chief of Police takes more of your energy now than it did twenty-two years ago when you joined the police force as a patrolman. You were younger then and twelve hour shifts and six day work weeks did not seem to bother you. Now, however, life is different. You are an Assistant Chief of Police in charge of 185 people in Staff Services.

It took you nineteen years to work your way up from Patrolman to Assistant Chief. Your accomplishments are satisfying, promotions were earned through performance rather than political maneuvers. The only other Assistant Chief, Richard Hall, became Assistant Chief last year when Brad Mason became Chief of Police. Mason and Hall had been long time friends and were partners in patrol twenty-six years ago. Hall is nothing more than a "yes man" to the Chief. Hall has never been a good leader, administrator or planner, but instead had the right contacts to get promoted. Chief Mason, on the other hand, is well educated and ambitious. Mason will probably run for Mayor in a future election.

Chief Mason is a good planner and organizer, but lacks leadership qualities. Mason tries to be the "good guy" of the department to satisfy his own ego. Mason generally leaves the duty work of discipline and the personnel problems up to his subordinates. More frequently than not, their tasks have fallen into your hands.

Chief Mason has never been a close friend of yours. He probably recognizes that you have the leadership and administrative qualities he and Hall lack. It is probably the reason that he has maintained you in your position.

Sipping a cup of coffee and checking over your calendar for the day you notice there is a staff meeting at 10:00 a.m. You cringe at the thought of another staff meeting. Staff meetings are held once a month with all the police executives including the Chief. Usually, staff meetings last for two hours and accomplish little. Apparently, staff meetings are the Chief's way of holding the reins on the departmental activities. You look at the stack of paperwork and realize that you will have to work overtime to clear up the important tasks since two hours will be lost in the staff meeting. Disgusted, you gather up your notes for the meeting.

Walking into the conference room, you greet the police administrators gathered around the table joking and drinking coffee. At five after ten Chief Mason and Rick Hall walk in the conference room together. Mason always likes to walk into the staff meetings late. It's his way of demonstrating his power. Hall shadows his every move. An audible chuckle escapes you as you ponder Chief Mason turning a sharp corner and breaking Hall's nose.

The first ten minutes or so are generally spent with the Chief telling the gathered members old jokes and memories of past endeavors.

Now men, I guess we should get down to some serious business. Chief Hall would you like to fill us in on how your people are doing in Line Services?" the Chief mutters while lighting his pipe.

"We've had no problems in Patrol or the Detective's Division this month. Had one officer resign in Juvenile Bureau to take a job with Human Services in the city as a counselor. Nothing else has happened," Hall responds.

"Human Services? Ha, wants to be a social worker does he?" the Chief laughs and everyone follows suit.

"O.K., how's Staff doing?" Chief Mason glances in your direction.

You pull out your notes and begin to highlight the activities of the Records, Jail, Planning, and other bureaus and divisions under your command. Glancing around the room, you can see that your statements on the statistics you have prepared are not receiving much attention.

"At any rate, I've prepared a monthly report detailing the activities of the Staff Services and I will give each of you a copy for your review and comments," you state, trying to finish up.

"That's fine. Oh, by the way, just a couple of things I need to fill you in on. I told the Chief Jailer to get rid of those two T.V.s for the prisoners. We're running a jail, not a Holiday Inn," the Chief laughs as everyone else echoes his sentiments.

"Excuse me Chief, but I authorized the prisoners to have two T.V.s from the property room. I told the trustees that if they would paint and clean the cell blocks, they would be allowed to watch T.V. They've done a good job and there's nothing for them to do in their leisure time. I feel that in order to alleviate some of the stress and boredom they might be more manageable watching..."

"No T.V.," Chief Mason interrupts.

"They're here to be punished. They can watch T.V. over at the county jail but not while they're here. Let'em read those law books we had to put there for them," Chief Mason adds, chuckling to himself.

You reluctantly acknowledge his order. You wish he had explained this to you before you made the authorization for the T.V.s. Now you are going to look bad in the eyes of the prisoners and your subordinates in the Jail Division.

"Another thing I should mention to you. Captain Joe Reynolds in Records has requested a transfer into Planning and Research. There's only a Lieutenant over the Planning and Research Bureau and we've got two Captains in Records so I approved the transfer. Joe's a good guy, known him for years," Chief Mason advises you.

"Chief, I refused that request for transfer. We don't need a Captain in Planning. Besides, Lieutenant Watts is a trained specialist in statistics and grants management. If we put Captain Reynolds over him it will decrease the efficiency of that unit. Captain Reynolds doesn't have any background in grants management," you argue.

"Well, he's got the rank and he's been in that records room so long now he's beginning to look like a file cabinet," the Chief laughs as the others in the room follow his actions.

It has been three weeks since the staff meeting. You are still frustrated with the Chief's overriding your decisions, but this is how your job has been since Mason became Chief. Mason enjoys running the department when it is convenient. He leaves all the responsibility to his subordinates and blames them when things go wrong.

The intercom line on your desk phone buzzes. It is Chief Mason.

"Thought I'd better tell you that Lieutenant Watts in Planning threatened to quit if Captain Reynolds didn't go back to Records. I told Reynolds to tell him to quit if he didn't like the way things were being run around here. You'd better go down there and see what business there is to take care of. You know, Reynolds doesn't know too much about research and I told him you would come down and help get things straightened out."

After the Chief is through, you stare at the intercom. You think to yourself, "Nineteen years of police service is a long time. Maybe too long." With a sigh you lean back in your chair. There must be some way to straighten this mess out.

Based on what you have read, answer the following questions:

1. Draw an organizational chart of this police department.
2. Define chain of command, Scalar Principle, unity of command, and span of command.
3. What are the administrative problems with this department and how could the assistant chief cope and/or handle these problems?

Case 5

Discipline

You have been Chief of the Fulton City Police Department for nearly three weeks. You were appointed Chief by an emergency meeting of the city council after the former Chief and several of his administrative officers resigned. The resignation of the former Chief and his aides came after several months of a State Attorney General's investigation of illegal activities within the police department. Recognizing that you are an honest individual and well liked and respected by the community as well as your officers, the city council has asked you to become the Chief.

You have been with the Fulton City Police Department for over 12 years, with nine years as Patrol Sergeant. The offer was shocking since the jump from Sergeant to Chief is a rare occurrance in your profession. You eagerly accepted the offer, not merely for the status, but because you felt you knew the problems and could handle the administration better than any of the other thirty-two officers in the department.

It has taken three weeks for you to adjust to your new position. Much of your time was spent re-organizing and re-scheduling shifts due to the recent "loss of manpower." A meeting was held with all your officers the day you took the office as Chief. You conveyed that no promotions would be made until the department "got back on its feet." You urged all the officers to work together until you could identify those officers with leadership qualities and make appropriate promotions. By informing the officers to put forth extra effort in the performance of their duties for evaluative purposes, they seemed especially pleased that they would all have a chance to show what they could do. You have always gotten along with people and tried to be a friend to everyone on the department. The improvement in the department's atmosphere was apparent in contrast to that of the former management. The morale of the department seems higher than it has been in quite some time. All the officers are friendly and courteous and appear eager to assist in the many administrative tasks that has befallen you.

Several of the officers who have been close friends over the years have hinted to you about their promotion. Apparently they assume their friendship will carry a great deal of weight regarding promotions.

When you took the Chief's job, the thought of promoting your friends into these positions occurred to you. You know these officers well and knew they would be loyal to you. Now, you are looking at these same officers wondering how effective they would be as administrators. You realize that many of your friends in the department would be poor leaders.

Take John Cupp for instance. John has been Sergeant for seven years and is about the same age as you are. John has been a close friend for over eight years. He has recently been hinting about his promotion to Assistant Chief. You like John, but are aware of the characteristics that would render him an inadequate leader in that particular position.

Some of your other friends on the force are also hinting to you about being promoted to Lieutenant and Captain. Apparently everyone thinks they know who is going to be promoted. The officers have apparently accepted the idea that you will promote only individuals who have been your friends. This has not seriously affected the morale of the officers since everyone on the force considers you to be basically a "good guy."

Being promoted to Chief was a big break for your career and you want to do the best possible job. You are aware of several other officers in the department who have education and leadership qualities that surpass your friends' capabilities. If you were to make the department as effective and efficient as you could, you would have to promote only the individuals who were most qualified. You wonder what the negative effects would be if you promoted those officers who deserve it most.

Several of the officers are beginning to become disorganized and less structured in their duties. The officers still call you by your first name and are not as respectful as they should be to your new position. Some of the officers have even disobeyed minor directives and departmental policies. Even your best friend, John Cupp, has told the other officers that they can disregard orders from the previous administration concerning procedures.

"Look John, we can't tell the officers they can ignore departmental policy. You've already told them they can go on high speed chases, carry whatever handgun they want to, leave their assigned beats, and numerous other contradictions of policy. We must, for the time being, continue these policies and enforce them," you explain to Sergeant Cupp.

"Hey, wait a minute. We haven't done anything that you haven't done before you made Chief. You used to say all the time how screwed up those directives and policies were. Remember when you used to tell me what you would do if you were Chief? Well, here's your chance partner," Sergeant Cupp answers.

You remember your previous boasts all too well. Now life is different. It's time you made some tough decisions.

Based on what you have read, answer the following questions:

1. Describe the new Chief. What kind of person is he? What kind of Sergeant was he? Is he having a role conflict as the new Chief?

2. What should the Chief do at this point? Should he have performed differently from the first when he accepted the Chief's position? If so, how?

3. Can the Chief of Police in any sized department be "friends" with his subordinates?

Case 6

Over the Hill?

You are the Chief of Police for a medium-sized police department serving a city of 80,000 people. You are 61 years old and have served as Chief of Talbott for the past twenty-two years. You began your career as a patrolman in Talbott when you were 29. You have always loved law enforcement as a profession and are proud of your department's accomplishments over the past few decades. When you first began as Chief, you were overly ambitious and career-minded. The stresses of the job almost cost you your wife and children. In addition, you became an alcoholic. You overcame the alcoholism only a few years ago. But you also became more subdued in your job. You know that you have been somewhat lax in "running" the department. It really does not matter as much to you at this point since you are planning to retire next year. The kids are grown and have families of their own now. Your wife is looking forward to moving to Florida next year. You are tired. You feel as though you have paid your dues and it is time to get out and enjoy your retirement.

A few months ago the city council decided you needed a new Assistant Chief of Police that could replace you when you retired. They hired Richard Sykes from a large metropolitan police department. This created a great deal of anger and frustration for many officers in your department. A number of high-ranking officers in your department had applied for the job. You had even recommended Captain Wade for the job. The city council felt the department needed "new blood" and only seriously considered applicants from outside the department.

Your first impressions of Sykes were not good. He always gives examples of how they did things at Metro. He has a Master's degree in criminal justice and usually reminds you and the other officers of that fact. Sykes seems to have an enormous ego and is always trying to portray himself as an intelligent man by using a sophisticated vocabulary. You never had a formal education. You always considered yourself a simple man with a "common-sense" approach to law enforcement and leadership. You feel somewhat lost in trying to understand the "new methods" of law enforcement technology. Computers, PPBS budgets, grants management, statistics, criminal profiles, models and simulations are all foreign languages to you. Sykes is familiar with all these things. You have on occasion even felt a little jealous of Sykes.

Sykes came into your department and began making changes at once. His directives and policy changes seem to cause more frustration and problems than relief. He is always in the limelight, making press releases, appearing on local television and radio. He does not consult with you on much of anything. You have accepted that you are pretty much of a "figurehead" and not taken too seriously. After all, you will be retiring next year.

"Excuse me, Chief. May I speak with you?" Captain Wade asks, peering inside your office.

"Sure, Jim. Come on in. What's on your mind?" you respond.

"Well, Chief. It's about this new assistant chief. I'm having all kinds of problems with my officers in carrying out Sykes' orders," Wade replies.

"Can you give me an example?" you ask.

"Well, Sykes has this new directive on measuring police patrol productivity. It's really nothing more than a quota system on ticket-writing. Sykes wants all the officers to write a minimum of five tickets a day. He uses it as some sort of statistical analysis for productivity. The day-shift officers usually are able to write five tickets each but the other shifts are unable to make their "quota." I've talked with him about it but all he said was if I could find a better way to measure their productivity in numbers to let him know," Wade explains.

"Yes, I can see where that would cause some problems with the officers. If the public knew about this 'quota' system they'd be writing letters to the editor at the newspaper," you respond.

"That's not all he's been doing. His directives and orders are not going over well with the officers. I could give you a bunch of examples where he's just not working out," Wade adds.

"I'll talk with him about this and see what I can do," you state.

For the next few days you wonder about what Captain Wade told you. You were surprised and impressed that Wade came to you with the problems. The officers do not seem to confide in you anymore. Wade's visit to your office was refreshing and made you feel needed. His visit has prompted you to take a closer look at what is going on around your department. The officers have low morale. They do not seem to laugh and joke with one another like they used to. You are beginning to feel you have let the officers down with your laissez-faire attitude over the past few years. You decide it is time to have a real talk with Sykes.

"Richard, I'm concerned about some of these directives you've been handing down. The officers don't understand the reasons behind a lot of them and, frankly, neither do I. Morale is at the lowest point I've even seen in this department," you begin.

"Look, Chief, I was hired with the understanding that I would be Chief when you retire next year. I'm running the show as I see fit. I'm a professional. You haven't done anything around here in the past three years. That's why I was hired. You're on your way out. Why are you so worried about what goes on here?" Sykes responds.

"I'm still the Chief of Police in Talbott," you state, growing angry.

"In name only. Look, why don't you just make your time as easy as possible and retire. Retire early; why wait for next year? It's time for a change in this department. Education and professionalism are in. Good old boys are out. Well, I'm late for a golf date with the Mayor. I'll talk with you later if you like," Sykes adds with a grin, leaving the office.

Sykes' words burn in your mind and your heart. He is right in his accusations that you have not accomplished anything in over three years. You are just a "figurehead." You could easily ride out the problems, retire next year or earlier as Sykes said. Your wife really wants to go to Florida. On the other hand, you do not have to retire. It is not mandatory. You do have your dignity and could rally some local support. In fact, you could handle this job for several years to come. You are in good health since you kicked the drinking habit. You could pull in all the favors owed you and really straighten this department out, make it proud again. It would be a hard fight but you know you could win. On the other hand, everyone expects you to retire, including your wife. Maybe you are too old to stay on. It would be difficult to "start again" in Talbott or in Florida. You reach for the Maalox.

Based on what you have read, answer the following questions:

1. What would you do if you were the Chief?
2. How could the Chief gain respect, keep his dignity and still retire next year?
3. If the Chief decided to stay and "straighten things out" in his department, what tactics could he use?

Case 7
An Out-of-Shape Department

You are the Chief of a small-town police department. Your force of 21 officers is mainly composed of older men with a median age of 43. There is little turnover in your department and at present there are only two officers under age 30. Your town lies twenty miles from a large city. Most of the trouble your officers face comes from transients coming through your town. The primary disturbances are comprised of week end drunk calls and family fights. You took the job as Chief two years ago. You had previously worked for the District Attorney as an investigator and took the Chief's job as a career move. You like the idea of stepping up to a larger department as Chief but this town is nice and would not be a bad place in which to retire.

You are called to a meeting of the City Council to discuss your plans for the next fiscal year and to answer any questions about your proposed budget.

"Chief, we've looked over your budget proposal and we have a few comments to make. But, first we want to hear what you have to say," the Mayor begins.

"I'm only asking for a seven-percent pay raise for the men, some new equipment, a new cruiser and one more officer for the department. I hope your comments support that," you state with a nervous grin.

"Well, we can see the need for a new cruiser. The one I've seen around town looks as though it's gone through the ringer," the Mayor states.

"That's unit 8. It's got over 150 thousand miles on it," you advise.

Stretching back in his swivel chair, the Mayor continues, "we're concerned about the seven-percent pay raise and the hiring of an additional police officer. You know we're under a budget crunch. We've approved five-percent across the board for all city employees. Why do you need a seven-percent increase for your men?" the Mayor asks.

"They've done a good job all year and their pay scale is lower than the fire department's," you respond.

"What good job have they done?" a councilwoman asks, looking over her glasses at you from the end of the conference table.

"Well, I can bring in their activities reports so you can see for yourself if you want," you respond, not liking the tone of her voice.

"Activities? I haven't seen them do anything except cruise around town, write a couple of parking tickets and hang out at the hamburger joint," the councilwoman replies.

"That's right, Chief. I haven't seen any accomplishments from them. They're all overweight and out-of-shape. Why, just last month a teenager beat up one of your officers. Did they ever catch that kid?" another councilman asks.

"I have heard a lot of jokes about your officers, Chief," the Mayor adds. "I believe the kids call them 'McCops?'"

"Yeah. If they'd stop buying all those milkshakes at the hamburger joint, they might have enough money without the pay raise," another councilman adds. That comment brought a laugh from everyone but you.

Knowing your officers receive free meals at the hamburger joint, you decide not to respond to his comments.

"I know they're a little out-of-shape and need exercise. but they've been here a long time. We've got a state law requiring officers to meet minimum physical fitness but my officers are all 'grandfathered' in," you argue.

"Well, it's your problem, Chief. We approve a five-percent, cost-of-living raise. A new cruiser. No new employees and no new equipment for your department. I'm sorry, but that's all we can do. Furthermore, let me offer you a little friendly advise: I think the townspeople would be a lot happier with your officers if they saw them on the job more and at the table less," the Mayor states, the other council members nodding their heads in agreement.

Leaving City Hall, you think about what the council said. It is true your officers have little community respect and apparently have little respect for themselves. Morale is low due to the low pay. Most of your officers do little more than grumble about their working conditions. You remember reading a police article about developing a physical fitness training program for officers. Your officers would never go for something like that.

Based on what you have read, answer the following questions:

1. How could the Chief convince his officers to engage in physical fitness training?
2. What resources could the Chief use to begin such a program?
3. What are the advantages of providing physical fitness training for police officers? How might the officers in this town benefit? What are some ways such a program could affect the opinions of the townspeople?

Section VII
Selected Bibliography

Bergsman, I. (1976). "Police Unions," *Management Information Service Report*, 8:3-4.

Bopp, W.J., and P. Whisenand (1980). *Police Personnel Administration*, 2d ed. Boston: Allyn and Bacon.

Bowers, M.H. (1975). "Police Administrators and the Labor Relations Process," *The Police Chief*, 42(January).

Di Grazia, R.J. (1976). "Upgrading Police Leadership," *The Police Journal*, 49(July).

Federal Bureau of Investigation (1986). *Selected Readings in Law Enforcement Management*. Quantico, VA: Management Science Unit, FBI Academy.

Felkenes, G. (1977). *Effective Police Supervision*. San Jose, CA: Justice Systems Development, Inc.

Gaines, L.K., and T. Ricks (1978). *Managing the Police Organization: Selected Readings*. St. Paul, MN: West Publishing Co.

Hale, C.D. (1977). *Fundamentals of Police Administration*. Boston: Holbrook Press.

Lynch, R.G. (1978). *The Police Manager*, 2d ed. Boston: Holbrook Press.

More, H.W. (1979). *Effective Police Administration*. St. Paul, MN: West Publishing Co.

Schultz, D.O. (1979). *Modern Police Administration*. Houston, TX: Gulf Publishing Co.

Shanahan, D.T. (1978). *Patrol Administration*. Boston: Holbrook Press.

Sheehan, R., and G. Cordner (1988). *Introduction to Police Administration*. Cincinnati: Anderson Publishing Co.

Truitt, J. (1978). *Dynamics of Police Administration*. Cincinnati: Anderson Publishing Co.

Vanagunas, S., and J.F. Elliott (1980). *Administration of Police Organizations*. Boston: Allyn and Bacon.

Wilson, O.W., and R.C. McLaren (1977). *Police Administration*, 4th ed. New York: McGraw-Hill.

PILGRIM PRAYERS FOR
GRANDMOTHERS RAISING
GRANDCHILDREN

PILGRIM PRAYERS

for

GRANDMOTHERS RAISING GRANDCHILDREN

Linda H. Hollies

Foreword by Giraurd Chase Hollies

THE PILGRIM PRESS · CLEVELAND

DEDICATION

This work is dedicated to my awesome grandson: Giraurd Chase Hollies.

To the memories of my foremothers: Doretha Robinson Adams, Mom, who raised grandchildren Carlton and Michael Morris; Lucinda Robinson Weston, my grandmother, who raised grandchild Troy C. Brodie; Eunice Robinson Wade, my aunt, who raised my mom and me; Lula Smith, my childhood pastor's wife, who helped to raise us all; Louise Holloway, the church mother who modeled style and grace as she loved me.

To the memory of my beloved Sista Girlfriend: The Rev. Dr. Janet Hopkins, who was my "Diva partner"-in-ministry and "Let's do breakfast in bed this morning and skip the meetings!" roommate at conferences around the country.

To the educational nurturing of: Dr. Della Burt, my first African American college professor, who taught me to be a risk-taker; Mrs. Hortense House, my seventh-grade teacher, who took time to teach me culture, personally.

And to every brave, courageous, and keep-on-keeping-on grandparent in the world!

The Pilgrim Press, 700 Prospect Avenue, Cleveland, Ohio 44115-1100
pilgrimpress.com
© 2002 by Linda H. Hollies

All rights reserved. Published 2002

Printed in the United States of America on acid-free paper

07   06   05   04   03   02   5   4   3   2   1

Library of Congress Cataloging-in-Publication Data

Hollies, Linda H.
    Pilgrim prayers for grandmothers raising grandchildren / Linda H.
  Hollies ; foreword by Giraurd Chase Hollies.
        p.   cm.
     ISBN 0-8298-1490-6 (pbk. : alk. paper)
        1. Grandmothers—Prayer-books and devotions—English.
2. Child rearing—Prayer-books and devotions—English.   3. African
American women—Prayer-books and devotions—English.   I. Title.

BV4847.H545   2002
242'.6431—dc21

                                                        2002029074

CONTENTS

FOREWORD
Being Raised by My Grandparents

*B*eing raised by my grandparents means that these great people love me. It means I have been loved my entire life. They have always been supportive of me. It doesn't matter if it was right or wrong, they have always been there for me.

Although I really miss being with my mom, through thick or thin times we have always been there for each other. Like they say, "blood is thicker than water." I would never trade my family, not even for all the riches in the world. In our home we love each other, no matter what.

My grandmother created and sang a special song to me when I was young. I haven't ever forgotten that song. It told me that I was special. I love my grandparents. They love me. This is what makes us a family.

—Giraurd Chase Hollies

ACKNOWLEDGMENTS

*W*riting can be a solitary experience. Yet, there are individuals in my life whom I cannot do without. My husband, Charles H. Hollies, who takes better care of me than I often deserve, heads the list. My grandson, Giraurd Chase Hollies, is the joy of my life and my inspiration for the days to come. My children are my motivation for leaving what I have learned documented on paper. Gregory Raymond, Grelon Renard, Grian Eunyke and her children, Germal Chasad and Symphony, will allow me to live in the coming generations. My siblings push, promote, and support me; they are the essence of "family" at its best: sisters Jacqui Brodie-Davis and Bob; Riene Morris; Regina Pleasant and Arthur; and my brothers James Adams and Jeannette; Eddie Adams and Onnette; David Adams and Kim; and Robert Adams and Lisa.

I honor a group of sister-friends who nourish my soul: Barbara Jean Vinson; Rev. Vera Jo Edington; Alberta Petrosko; Rev. Daisy Thomas-Quinney; Rev. Dr. Eleanor Miller; Rev. Beverly Garvin; Rev. LaSaundra Dolberry; Rev. Louisa Martin; Rev. Harlene Harden; Rev. Joyce E. Wallace; Rev. Genevieve Brown; Rev. Michelle Cobb; Rev. Dr. Valerie Davis; Rev. Ida Easley; Rev. Carolyn Abrams; Rev. Dr. Linda Boston; Rev. Connie Wilkerson, and Rev. Carolyn Wilkins. Each of these women counsels, prays with and for, challenges, and loves me so that writing flows, preaching continues, and my spirit is continually renewed. I count each one of these women as blessings, gifts, and treasures in my life. Then, there are my brother-friends, whose love uplifts me and makes me more secure in my position in the family of God. Rev. Anthony Earl (and Bobbie); Rev. Dr. Michael Carson (and Katherine); Rev. Bernie Liggins (and Carolyn); Rev. Dr. Zawdie Abiade (and Nancy); our adopted son, Rev. Dr.

Dennis Robinson (and Darlene); and my friend, Eric Thornsen, accept me fully as they uphold my life and ministry in their gentle hands. Without them, my life would be so incomplete. But, because of them, I am more wholly alive in the body of Christ.

I take great personal liberty with scripture! I believe it was written for me. And I know it needs to have inclusive language so none of us are excluded. So I have attempted to be true to documenting the sources of every scriptural reference, using the New International Version for most of them. However, this version is not wholly inclusive in its language. Therefore, I pray you will be indulgent as you read your select version and find it does not say exactly what I have stated. It's what I saw and felt was intended.

INTRODUCTION

$\mathcal{M}$y "grand parenting" days came as a great surprise. Our daughter, Grian, was in college. She's a very bright, gifted, and talented young woman. With scholarship offers to the five states surrounding us, she chose a school in New Mexico. The summer after her freshman year, she announced that she didn't want to go back to college. In September, quite by accident, I discovered her pregnancy!

Imagine, if you can, going to the doctor's office for your annual physical. Everyone there knows and greets you by name. When the nurse is taking your blood pressure with easy chitchat, she asks, "And how did you feel about Grian's news? She said that you were going to kill her!" How would you inquire, "What news?" What would keep your blood pressure from skyrocketing? Would it have been easy to keep steady on the exam table? Well, I had to "play it off"! And I passed the physical!

When I left the doctors' office it was to the Church that I returned to talk with my spouse, Mista Chuck. I will never forget the pounding headache. I will never know how I made it back to my office without causing an accident. But Chuck and I talked about our choices. We made serious decisions. Then I called my nail technician and went to get my nails done! For a woman's gotta do what a woman's gotta do!

Our journey to being grandparents began that day. Years later, we have legal custody for the child of that pregnancy. We brought him home when he was three days old. Our whole life changed as we began to parent the second time around. The child is a Godsend. The prayers of many have surrounded us. When Giraurd was three months old, an entire conference of women encircled him as we offered him back to the loving care of God. I baptized him into the Church, with family, friends, and members agreeing to be part of his caring community. The Church has never let us down! And the prayers of the righteous keep us strong in our faith, anchored in our labors, and joyful in our spirits.

My prayer is that these short encounters will speak to your heart and allow you to know that you are not alone. I pray that the scriptures refresh you on the days when you feel as if "it's simply not worth it!" And I hope that the prayers will encourage you to keep on keeping on as you journey another day. For we are pilgrims and we do not journey alone! A great host is traveling with us. God is for us. Jesus is with us. The Holy Spirit is in us. All of heaven's angels are on our side! Our faithful prayers will see us through.

Shalom, Dear Ones!

—Sista Linda

NIFTY FIFTY?

$\mathcal{I}$ truly had decided that there was one of two ways to turn fifty. Either I had to celebrate it in grand style or enter it with depression. I chose to celebrate! It was a grand occasion with a harpist entertaining guests who arrived. There was a sit-down dinner with a strolling violinist. Instead of "stuff and things" I asked folks to donate money for a scholarship fund to assist an eighth-grade student of a single parent to prepare for high school. A video camera captured friends from school and current and former congregation members, who talked about me being "nifty fifty!"

My sister Riene spent the night to help me prepare for Sunday and church. Early Monday morning, we were sitting in my bedroom, watching Oprah and opening up cards and gifts, when my back door opened. It was my daughter, Grian, and grandson, Giraurd. They had been conspicuously absent from the party. Grian walked up to my sister and handed her the baby. She threw four pampers and one undershirt on the foot of my bed. She said to my sister, "Auntie, I'm going to New York. There is no room on this trip for a baby." With these brief comments, she turned and walked out of the house.

I was speechless. The baby was crawling up the bed toward me and I opened my arms to receive him. He was my "birthday present"! My sister sat there, watching, listening, and hoping she didn't have to keep the baby! And she prayed!

We went shopping. We went through potty training. We found a day care center. We bought the "stuff and things" little boys need. We adjusted our lives. And for almost ten years we have been engaged in parenting the second time around! Chuck cannot fully retire. We don't live a wild, jet-set life. We go on family trips. We attend school programs. We check homework. We provide discipline. For we don't have the luxury of grandparenting and "spoiling" Giraurd. We are his parents!

There is an adjustment that must occur internally when you have felt that parenting days were finished. There is an emotional shifting that must take place when cooking, grocery shopping, and meal planning have stopped being a primary consideration. There is a major spiritual engagement that takes place when a child is put into your care that you did not plan for and birth. Prayer is essential!

Pray continually; in all things give thanks!
—1 THESSALONIANS 5:17–18

Great Parent, you have given me much more than I can imagine. This child is not "the gift" I was expecting from you! And, yet, I know that even this awesome responsibility is part of your plan. How I wish I could see the whole picture. How I wish I had the capacity to comprehend your vision for this life now under my care. If ever I needed your guidance and care, it is now. If ever I needed your grace and your mercy, it is now. If ever I needed to be carried by your powerful hand, God, is it now. Thank you for being a "right now" God, always present to sustain and help. In the midst of this, another "new beginning," I am assured by your unfailing love. For this I truly do give you thanks. God, bless us indeed!

PRAYER FOCUS: Surprised "new" parents

2

New Directions!

*C*hildren who are unplanned have a great way of disrupting your daily schedule and routine. I do have a job, a career, and a profession. I have put a number of years of education and training into becoming the very best pastor I can become. So it was not easy to "blow off" my position and make the necessary arrangements to tend to a child. Think of all the many adjustments that are required when a child enters your life. Chuck was retired from over thirty-four years of work but had another full-time job too. Because Grian got pregnant while in college, we had continued to "underwrite" much of the expenses for her and Giraurd. There was no available child-care provider in our house! Yet, we had a child.

Professional child care is a major expense. Child-care providers must be screened, checked out, scrutinized, and verified because too many unfortunate incidents have occurred in too many centers. So I had to make the time, call around, and find out the information necessary to enroll Giraurd. It was a traumatic event to discover the weekly cost required. Whatever happened to the infamous two dollar per hour babysitting fee? There are rules, regulations, and parental requirement forms that eat up your time. And there is the obligatory PTA even in preschool!

There were no toys dropped off with Giraurd. His "education" required the correct toys for his age. We have spent many days in Toys R Us! Let's not even talk about potty training and diaper changing and wet beds when he made a "mistake." Try to imagine deep sleep when there is an infant lying between you and your spouse. Let me tell you how many different beds we considered before we settled on his. All the while, my job never slowed down. The people and their crises never slacked up. Being the pastor didn't get any easier because our life had changed drastically! We had to adjust and go! We had to seek a new direction.

Thank God for lay folks who have made local congregations aware that child care is necessary for night meetings. Giraurd became a "church baby." When church members saw either Chuck or me, people began to ask us, "Where is Giraurd?" He became a fixture in our home, our lives, our conversations, and our dreams. He was "ours." We had to change directions. And we did!

In all your ways acknowledge God, who will direct your path.
—PROVERBS 3:6

Director of My Life, lead me and guide me along this new path. There are so many things that I have forgotten about being responsible for a little one! I never thought there was so much that I didn't even know! My life is no longer my own. The days are too short for all that must be accomplished. The nights are too short for getting the rest and the energy to try and keep up with the next day's needs. I need you, oh, how I need you. Wait, I forgot! My spouse needs you too! We are both struggling simply to keep up the pace required. Direct our steps, we pray.

PRAYER FOCUS: Older adults with young children

3

LOST DREAMS

I remember distinctly the day that I decided to get pregnant with my daughter, Grian! My youngest son, Grelon, was seven. I went into the boy's room to lay out his clothes for school the next morning. As he watched me, he said, "Mom, I'm a big boy. I can choose my own clothes." The words cut me to the quick. Was I no longer needed as a mother by a seven-year-old son? I determined to have myself a daughter, a girl child who would want me to select pretty things for her. I went on a three-day fast! Was I desperate or not? I wanted a girl.

There are four sisters and four brothers in my family of origin and I am the oldest child. All of my siblings had boys. We had no girl babies. I wanted to break the cycle. I got pregnant. We all knew it would be a girl. For I had fasted. I had prayed. The girl clothes were picked up, smiled at, and even bought. The girl toys begin to make their way into my room. We were all getting ready to welcome a little girl into our family.

Grian Eunkye was born on my grandfather's birth date of 27 May. She was given a name that combined the first two letters of each of her brother's names, Gregory and Grelon. These letters were added to my middle name, Ann. Her middle name is for my grandmother Eunice. All of my children were given the letter "G" to remind them of the greatness that is within them! All of my children were named to indicate the unique and special qualities they possessed from before their beginnings. All of their names indicate that they have the "divine spark" within them that comes directly from God! All of my children were the products of my love and my dreams for their "good success"!

There is no way I can describe the love, the care, and the welcome that my daughter received from my family. I can tell you that my grandfather came outside and took her from me when we arrived from the hospital. I can tell you that my sister Jacqui continues to tell Grian that she did not walk until she was three because everyone fought to carry her! I can tell you that no other little girl was treated with more respect, dignity, and proper treatment than my daughter. She was certainly our little princess and we all tried to "give her the world."

Grian took piano, dance, and drama and excelled in all she did. Grian was an outstanding student, winning scholarship offers to the top five Midwest colleges. I preached for Grian's Baccalaureate, never knowing I was giving a word of prophecy to her. For I asked the young graduates to consider the poem, "Pussy Cat, Pussy Cat, Where Have You Been?" I talked about all the little cat could have seen while on a trip abroad. But the little cat's aim was too low. She only saw a mouse, under the queen's throne. The pussycat, and my daughter, went into a big wide world with low aspirations, low vision, and low achievement in mind. My daughter simply wanted to get far, far away from home. She went to the University of New Mexico. She came home, after the first year. She was pregnant. It was the death of many dreams.

As surely as the Lord lives, I can only tell you what the Lord tells me. —1 KINGS 22:14

Great God, high and exalted, you give us dreams and make us dreamers. It is the divine spark within us that seeks new ways, new vistas, and new worlds to explore. Thank you for the awesome opportunity to go out and do things our way! In doing them our way, too often we fall short. We experience the death of our dreams. We are pained as dreams die, unfulfilled and unrealized. Yet, you have a way of providing other dreams. You have a way of lifting our sights, picking us up, and turning us in ways that will lead to new life, greater vision, and higher heights. Keep us dreaming, we pray. Give us bigger dreams, in the name of your Son!

PRAYER FOCUS: Those whose dreams have died

4

DEATH, SOMETIMES A SWEET RELEASE!

*T*he young woman was "unidentified." She had been found in a ditch, badly beaten, bruised, and dead. Her clothing was in disarray but no evidence warranted saying she had been raped. The news was bad. The news was typical. The news was commonplace—that is, until I discovered that her father was a pastor in town. We had spoken about our daughters only a few weeks prior. We were both raising grandchildren. They were the offspring of our daughters. We sat in prayerful consideration of each other's testimony.

Her name is not needed. She could be anyone's daughter. She is dead. She lived too short a life. She died too soon. Yet, her death brought her release from the evil that had ensnared her and kept her bound. She was the product of a "good" family. Her parents have a strong relationship. Her father is a kind, compassionate man. Her mother is a strong and hurting woman. They took their daughter's three children to allow her the time and space to "find herself" and to give the children an opportunity for stability. Now, their daughter is dead. Explanations to the children are in order. But how do you explain to a child that death is sometimes a sweet release?

Like many of our daughters, this young woman became a victim of "the fast life." She decided that the God of her parents was not large enough to suit her purposes. She went on a search for a god of her own. Drugs, sex, and all the kinfolk of these evils became her constant companions. She got pregnant. She had the babies. She went back to the haunting lifestyle of "yesterday." Her parents kept the children. She kept having them and bringing them "home."

When a group of pastors met for breakfast, I was seated next to a father who was raising grandchildren. One of his good friends began to extol the many ways this dad was providing excellent care to a young black boy. This certainly caught my attention. We began to share and exchange stories. When I asked him how he came to have a "young boy" at his age, looking at his years of wisdom, we laughed. His reply to me was, "My daughter is fast." You need to know that "fast" is a catch-all term in the black community. "Fast" can mean anything from trying to play adult to doing the wild things young women will to do in every community. So, I asked for clarity. Being blunt, I inquired, "Is she on drugs? My daughter is." He replied, "Yes." We discovered we had something in common. It was a painful commonality. We agreed to pray for one another. The prayers continue, even more today than then.

Be gracious to me, O Lord, for I am in distress; my eye is wasted from grief. —PSALM 31:9

Gracious God, holder of every good and perfect gift, we come before you in prayer. Our hearts are heavy. Our grief is overwhelming. Our distress is great. Our despair is constant. We have multiple questions, but no answers. We have great pain and need your comfort. Life is so uncertain. Death is so confusing. Let the lessons we learn from our grief teach us how to love those of us left behind better, more fully, and with even greater intentionality. Be our vision, our hope, and our abiding Source of Strength, we pray.

PRAYER FOCUS: The bereaved

5

NOW WHAT?

*S*he is beautiful and striking. She is delightful and refreshing. She is wonderful and generous. She has raised her children and those of her dead sister. She met and married a man from this community. He was nice, good looking, a committed Christian and single, with a daughter who lived with her mom. She came expecting a new life, new hope, new joy, and new beginnings. Life has thrown this newly married couple a curve. And today she is asking God, "Now what?"

She is middle-aged. She came to be a new bride. She came seeking to learn the community and make it her home. They were settling into being a couple. They were attending his church. She was seeking to find a beautician, a nail tech, and a Sista's Book Club. Life was moving. She was keeping up. The stepdaughter came to visit and they checked each other out. One weekend, the mom dropped the young woman off and the visit was pleasant. Sunday night as the child was packing up to return home, the phone rang. It was "Mom." She asked to speak to the girl's father.

"I'm not coming to pick Sherry up. I've decided that you and your new wife can raise her!" But the new wife didn't ask for this. The new wife never expected this. The new wife didn't want to raise another child. "God, now what?" she cried. She began to seek prayer from girlfriends "back home." She began to seek counsel from others she had met in her new environment. What do you do when an eleven-year-old is dropped off and left like a mailed package? You find ways to cope. You discover new ways to pray.

Dannielle had come to visit our congregation because she had read several of my books. She became a part of our Boot Camp for

Warrior Women group. She needed to discover the strategies for doing spiritual warfare with this new situation that was forcing her to rethink her decision to marry and to move from family and familiar surroundings. She told the story. She sought counsel and prayer.

We met at the nail shop one Wednesday. We began a conversation that soon included others, about the notion that the world we live in is messed up. For we know how to deal with the "disappearing father" acts, which are fairly common. What is surprising, shocking, and amazing is how many mothers are "giving" their children away! Who can explain to a young girl that her mother doesn't want her anymore? How do you say to a girl that her mom is not coming to take her home? How do you say, with conviction, "You're welcome to stay with us" when so many perplexing and disturbing thoughts are flitting, racing, and bumping up against each other in your own mind? Who is to fill this huge, ugly gaping wound that will remain with this young woman all the days of her life? Who has the answers? Where does the help come from? When the heavens are silent . . . now what?

> May the Lord give strength to the people and bless all the people with peace. —PSALM 29:11

Mystery we call God, speak. We listen, expectantly, anxiously. Answer now!! Please.

PRAYER FOCUS: Parents of "dropped off" children

6

NEW CAR? COLLEGE?

$\mathcal{I}$t was time for a new car. Can I share with you how long I have waited for the moment in my career when I felt secure enough to go and purchase "the car of my dreams"? You know "the car." The one that is really out of your price range today, but . . . you go and look at it, drool over it, pat it, and wish! Several of my friends had "the car." I was lustful with envy. Whenever I rode in one, my head seemed to elevate and the thought kept running through my mind, "Soon!"

My books were doing fairly well on the national market. My publicity agent (God!!!) had me traveling, preaching, and lecturing on the circuit. So I felt the time was ripe to go and purchase "the car." I wish I could describe for you the delicious feelings that had me trying to decide model, size, color, trim, accessories, and whether new or used. It was an awesome feeling to know that in a few days the time would come when I could drive "the car" off the lot and park it in my driveway. I was geeked, as the kids would say. "Soon!"

Seemingly from nowhere a thought begin to bounce around in my head. "You have a child to prepare for college. You are now responsible for a child's future." Car? College? It was time to make a choice. Yes! I chose to call an investment broker and talk about how to get Giraurd some money put aside for college. It was a deep moment. It was a despairing time. It was a period of depression. For I had to realize and deal with the reality that I was back where I had been almost twenty-five years prior, wondering how to get three children through college. "Here we go again!"

Somewhere in the back of my mind, I had always believed that my daughter would get her life straightened out, that she would come to reclaim her child, and Chuck and I would be off the hook! Sounded like a good plan to me. It was my trip over the rainbow! For as I told this lie to one of my good friends, she responded: "Linda, you and Chuck are Giraud's parents. If you gave him back to Grian, he would feel abandoned!" Talk about shock therapy! Talk about reality snatching me back from my short visit with Toto to Oz!

Provisions had to be made for Giraurd's future. "The car" had to wait. It was praying time again. For the promise has already been given: "I know the plans I have for you, plans for your welfare and not for evil, to give you a future and a hope" (Jer. 29:11). I claimed this precious promise for me, Chuck, and Giraurd. God has already promised to provide!

> I am not able to carry all this people alone, the burden is too heavy for me. —NUMBERS 11:14

Carrying and Promising God, here I am again in need of your blessed assurance. I cannot carry all this burden alone. It is too heavy for me. I have plans for my life. I have plans for my future. Those plans included "the car." We have already sacrificed and made provision for our children's educations. Now, here I am again with my dreams on hold! It's not fair. It makes me angry. You know how much I wanted "the car"! Yet, you have reminded me of our obligations to this little one. So, you take away my grief and anger. Help!

PRAYER FOCUS: Parents with resentments

7

N E W   M A T H ?

*W*e were on our way to the airport. It was after Sunday worship and all my "official" duties were complete. I was going off to teach, somewhere. It would be a time to rest! It would be a short getaway from the responsibilities of home. There would be no cleaning up after others. I wouldn't have to shop for, plan, or prepare meals. I was ready to go! Giraurd was in the back seat, strapped in, singing to himself. He began to sing about numbers. He had several of them out of sequence. It was teaching time, again.

All math is new math for me! Math has never been one of my strong suits. So, to have to reengage numbers causes difficulty for this "mom." Yet math, spelling, checking homework, and helping with assignments are all part of the parenting routine. We got Giraurd through preschool and the first six grades. Now, we have tutoring help for the new math, for these new concepts are foreign to me and my "older" spouse. It's about learning how to do things differently.

Different is about change. Change is about adjustment. Adjustment is about rearranging. And rearranging is about learning new things, including new math! It's not easy. It causes you to stretch. It's a major challenge. And it costs you, big time. You would be shocked at how much learning centers charge to tutor! (It's worse than the cost for preschool care!) Chuck and I are yet in the learning, growing stages. For even with the tutoring centers, we have to check homework!

We are teachers. We are learners. We are both at the same time. We thought we were on the other side of learning. A new child brings about a new education for all concerned. This interruption in our lives is a new form of ministry. It's outreach at its highest form! Jesus specialized in the ministry of interruptions. Often he was on his way somewhere when someone asked him to stop and do something else. Is not this the way of life for those of us learning "new math"?

> Behold, I will do a new thing. Now it shall spring forth. Shall you not know it? I will make a road in the wilderness, and rivers in the desert! —ISAIAH 43:19

Amazing Teacher, instruct me in the ways I should go! When I think I have learned all there is to know, you teach me something new. When I feel that the challenges are too great and the hurdles are too high, you stretch me even more. When change comes into my life like a whirlwind, be the steadying force beneath my wings. I can't still this raging storm, but I'm asking you to teach me how to ride these new waves! I'm holding on for dear life!

PRAYER FOCUS: New teachers and new students

CREATING NEW SONGS

Giraurd is special to his Grandma.
Giraurd is special to his Grandpa.
Giraurd is special to his uncles and his Mom.
Because God made Giraurd special!

I made up and sang this "new song" to our three-year-old grandson, who wondered about the whereabouts of his mom and dad. I made up and sang this "new song" to our three-year-old grandson, who had been conceived by a young woman, out of wedlock and while a college student. I made up and sang this "new song" to encourage his heart, to embolden his spirit, and to put fresh courage into his mind for the days ahead. I made up and sang this "new song" to help Chuck and me remember why this little boy was indeed in our life. He's special to God!

Being special is so necessary for little black boys. Being special is so necessary for little black girls. Being special is so necessary for any children who are deprived of the love and nurture of their parents. Being special helps to ease the pain of abandonment. Being special is part of the fabric that must be stitched well to help them hold themselves together in the days ahead. All of us need to know that we are special. For being "special" means we really matter to God.

Being raised by other than our parents is a heavy psychological blow to the self-esteem. Being raised by other than our parents brings a serious barrage of questions as to the reasons why we are not "worth" the love, care, and attention of the ones who conceived and bore us into the world. Being raised by other than our parents provides the possibilities for mean things to be said, which can further damage fragile and tender emotions. When you are being raised by those other than your biological parents it is essential that the reinforcements are there to say that "you are so very special. You matter more than the average child!"

The average child comes into the world. A special child comes into your heart. The average child is born. A special child is received. The average child is cared for. A special child is cared about. The average child receives love. A special child gets love and tenderness! Isn't it wonderful to be "special"?

Giraurd grew up with this new song ringing in his ears. It continues to be our favorite chorus on down days and significant occasions. He remembers that his Grand (not Grandmother!) created this song just for him. He is of an age where he's beginning to realize the unique position he holds not only within our home, but within our hearts. For he knows that he is special. He understands that our love for him is special. He recognizes that because of our love for his mother, he is doubly special in our family. This is Giraurd's new song. It is a song of praise unto our God, who created this little boy, special!

> God lifted me out of the horrible pit . . . and put a new song in
> my mouth. —PSALM 40:2–3

Creator of New Songs, let the melody within my heart take flight. For too long I have been humming the dirges of discontentment. I have wailed the tunes of sadness and despair. My troubles have taken me down into the pit of desolation. I have settled into the throes of moaning and groaning. Yet, I hear you singing through the trees. The birds sing unto you early in the morning. The passing waters whisper your name in praise. God, my throat is dry. I need a new song!

PRAYER FOCUS: Those without a song

BE CAREFUL! THIEVES ARE NEAR!

I remember my Big Mama, Lessie Bell King. She was a round, wonderful, and beautiful soul. She had six children of her own. She "took in" her own sister, Hat. And she received the four sons of another sister and the only child of yet another! She believed in the art of family. My dad was that last child. He grew up in this huge and dysfunctional family where there were two "mothers" and an alcoholic father. There were good times, fun times, happy family times spent at Big Mama's house. Making a pallet on the floor became an enjoyable exercise for us as children. We grew up believing that we were some of the most favored people in all the world. It's only in retrospect that I can see how terribly poor we were and how it was not "usual and normal" for a family to be that big and extended!

One of the "four sons of another sister" began to date and have children early. His oldest daughter was named for Big Mama. What a ploy that worked to win her heart. We called the little redheaded girl Plooky. I don't know where it came from or how it stuck. But today, over fifty years old, she's still Plooky! Big Mama's oldest daughter, Annie, kept the child most of the time. After awhile it became apparent that the mother was not coming to take Plooky home. So, she became part of the family circle. She stayed until she was almost twelve.

The phone rang one day and it was Big Mama calling a family meeting. My parents got us all together and off we went to see what had Big Mama in tears. Plooky's "mother" had come and "taken her home"! Now, ain't that a stitch? For twelve years, home had been Big Mama's house. The school knew Big Mama and Annie. The church knew Big Mama and Annie. Plooky knew Big Mama and Annie. But her "mother" had come to take her home.

Big Mama was a born-again Christian, a devout woman of God. That day, at the family meeting, Big Mama talked about doing bodily harm to Plooky's "mother." The boys in the family were dispatched to bring Plooky back "home" and to give her "mother" a warning not to darken Big Mama's doorstep ever again. There were no "official" adoption papers. There were no formal foster care arrangements. Plooky had been dropped off years earlier. Big Mama wanted her child home. Plooky came home. She lived there until after high-school graduation. Her "mother" lives with the reality that birth doesn't give you ownership! Love is the cost of motherhood. The "thief" learned her lesson. Plooky always had a home. The lesson for us is to get the legal paperwork done!

Why even the hairs of your head are numbered. Fear not; you are of more value than many sparrows. —LUKE 12:7

Watching and numbering God, we bring to your attention our fears about those who will steal our love. We don't think that there is enough love to go around. We tend to believe we need to hoard the love that we receive. Let us be the Big Mamas of the world who intuitively know that there is more than enough love to go around! Her heart just kept stretching to include "one more." Give us open hearts. Let your love so encompass us until we can overflow into the lives of others. Teach us how to "fear not"! It sounds so easy. You know how difficult this command is to follow. Fear is rooted in lack. Love is grounded in love. Increase my love quotient!

PRAYER FOCUS: Those in need of love and acceptance

10

CLEARING OUT

*W*hen a child moves into space that has been occupied by other things it requires cleaning out and making room. I really don't believe in guest rooms. They seem to attract "stuff and things." Empty rooms always draw adult children! Objects that are not quite fashionable enough for the living room or the family room tend to park themselves in guest rooms. My habit has been to make an office out of what may be referred to as the spare room.

When Giraurd came to live with us, it simply made common sense to decide that his bedroom would be the spare room, the guest room. But this decision required our clearing out "stuff" for which we discovered we had no space or good purpose for retaining. They were simply things we kept around for the sake of memory. Now we had a living, breathing human being who needed his own space to reflect him and his unique personality. It was clearing out time.

Throwing away "stuff and things" requires sorting. Getting rid of useful "junk" mandates recalling where it came from, what its original purpose and function was, and honestly figuring out, "Why am I holding onto this?" Clearing out "stuff and things" will be both a cathartic and emotional cleansing period. Clearing out "stuff and things" will bring memories and times of reflection to your heart. Clearing out "stuff and things" will allow both smiles and tears as you recall the significant occasions for purchasing, receiving, and taking in articles that may be useful but not necessary. Sorting and clearing out the old is the only way to prepare and make ready for the new.

Clearing out often means passing on. When I clean out something that has value, meaning, and significance to me, I think of loved ones who might have asked about or looked at the piece with longing eyes. It allows me to appreciate the individual who gave it to me or the occasion that warranted my purchasing it and the dear one who will receive it with gratitude from me today, not when I'm dead and gone. So I can pass along some "stuff and things" that I might have wanted to use as heirlooms, treasures, and historical markers, today, right now, while I'm alive and can see the joy my gift brings to another. Clearing out can be a good thing!

We made space for Giraurd. The new space became his. We filled it with "little boy" stuff and things. It was a happy place for its new occupant. All we had to do was clear it out.

Where is the way to the dwelling of light . . . ? —Job 38:19

Space-Making God, thank you for making space for me! In the days of my wanderings, in the times of my roamings, you continually reserved a space for me to return "home." Thank you.

PRAYER FOCUS: Those who need to clear space in their lives

11

LIVING FAITH

*B*eing a grandparent and parenting the second time around is not a new phenomenon. As Paul the apostle writes to his son in ministry, Timothy, "I thank God, whom I serve with a clear conscience . . . As I remember your tears, I long night and day to see you, that I may be filled with joy. I am reminded of your sincere faith, a faith that dwelt first in your grandmother Lois and your mother Eunice and now, I am sure, dwells in you. Therefore, I remind you to rekindle the gift of God that is within you . . ." (2 Timothy 1:3–6) Grandmother Lois and mother Eunice were instrumental in being the "faith bearers" and role models for one of the greatest pastors of the emerging Church of Jesus Christ.

Parenting the second time around is not something one does without great fear, tremendous guilt, and awesome anger! The Kalamazoo Community College is one of the institutions of higher learning that makes available resources to the growing number of grandparents raising children. Rev. Melodye was the director of the outreach program there when I was invited to speak to the group. I went looking for a primarily African American group of folks my age. Was I ever shocked to discover the huge crowd of primarily Anglo people, many of whom were great-grandparents parenting again! It was a mind-boggling experience.

Kalamazoo Community College is now one of many places where this growing group of confused families can turn for answers to the growing body of questions that seem to multiply more rapidly than technology. The first resource extended is a support group to share the anger, dismay, and concern. The second valuable resource is a respite service that provides a time out from the stress of dealing with hurting and perplexed children, youth, and young adults. The third source of assistance is the pulling together of a body of information that can provide answers, people to call, and places to go for additional help with the problems that arise. There are enough grand- and great-grandparents taking over the responsibilities for children again, that easily a new voting bloc may emerge to impact the systems required to be in place for effective support.

Family systems are changing. The word "family" means a multitude of differing compositions of people living together. We don't hear anything about Pastor Timothy's father or grandfather. However, we come to know and appreciate that his "family" included a mother and grandmother who had faith in the bountiful resources and unfailing grace of God. The Wise Sage era continues! Thanks be unto God!

A faith that dwelt first in your grandmother Lois and your mother Eunice . . . —2 TIMOTHY 1:5

Grandmother God, rock us in the cradle of your bosom.
Grandmother God, hold us close in the security of your arms.
Grandmother God, allow us to rest in the ample space of your lap.
Grandmother God, whisper the soothing comfort that we need into our ears.

Grandmother God, rekindle our hope, renew our faith, and bless our efforts as we learn to parent all over again. Let it be more than sufficient! We do it simply because of our faith. Make it stronger still, we pray.

PRAYER FOCUS: Grandparents parenting the second and third time around

NEW TRADITIONS

*W*e were in the White Mountains of Arizona on vacation. It was a lovely, warm summer day. We decided to get out and take a nice leisurely walk. As we stepped out of the condo a little black puppy ran up to four-year-old Giraurd. We don't know where he came from. We don't know to whom he belonged. But he was a cute animal. The dog tried to attach himself to Giraurd. We walked toward the gate and the dog followed. We kept looking for someone to call the dog, come and retrieve the dog. But the dog continued to walk along side of us, playing with Giraurd's little hands.

There are no sidewalks in the area surrounding the condos. The roads are fairly rustic and rocky. There was no convenient way to walk with a dog along the road. So Chuck and I tried to get the dog to turn around, run back to wherever he had come from, or simply remain within the gated area. But the dog wanted to walk with us. "Shoo!" didn't turn the dog around. "Go back!" was not obeyed. "Get!" shouted in a loud voice did not deter the dog. So, as we approached the point of leaving the fenced area, which did not have a gate, Chuck picked up a rock and threw it at the dog.

Chuck did not hit the dog. Chuck did not aim for the dog. Chuck was not trying to hurt the dog. Chuck did not want that puppy to get hurt. He picked up a rock and gently "chucked" it to turn the dog around. It did the trick! The puppy ran away from us back toward the condos. Giraurd had a fit! "Granddad, why did you throw a rock at the puppy?" The walk stopped as we tried to console a hurt and crying little boy. The walk had to wait as we both made unsuccessful attempts to explain our concern for the dog's safety. Giraurd just didn't get it! The questions, accusations, and talk about being mean continued for the duration of the walk.

Thankfully, when we returned to the condo the puppy was nowhere to be found. We thought the matter was settled.

That night we went out to dinner at a "nice" restaurant. It required shirt, tie, and shoes. There was soft music playing and the ambiance was that of low lights and quiet conversations. We were the only African Americans in the restaurant. Giraurd was the only child. We were treated royally and the wait staff made a fuss over the "baby." When the drinks and appetizers were placed in front of us, Chuck bowed his head to offer grace. Giraurd stopped him. "Granddaddy, can I say the prayer?" "Of course, Little Guy. You offer grace." We bowed our heads but Giraurd did not. He climbed down out of the highchair. He walked around the table. He laid his tiny hand on his grandfather's head and he told God about Grandfather throwing a rock at the dog! He asked God to forgive Grandfather. He prayed for the dog. The whole restaurant stopped and listened to the prayer of this child. There were huge smiles. There was no laughter!

That night began a new tradition in our family. Giraurd always offers the grace at our table. We trust his heart. We trust his God. We trust his honest faith that God hears and answers prayer. He's not had to "lay hands" on his grandfather again. We have no further incidents to report of Chuck throwing a rock at any dog!

Give ear to my voice, O Lord, when I call to you. —PSALM 141:1

Creator of little boys and puppies, we do call upon you for their safety and protection. How wonderful to see the love between children and their pets. It is a matter of trust. It is a matter of them being in relationship with each other, caring for each other. This so symbolizes the community of which we are a part. We need each other. We need to be cared for and to care about each other. Help us to ensure that no violence comes to either little boys or the puppies to which they become so quickly attached. Bless us all and help us to refrain from ever throwing any type of rocks! In the name of the Rock of Ages, we pray. Amen.

PRAYER FOCUS: Children and the animals who befriend them

CALLING FOR HELP—
IT DOES TAKE A VILLAGE

*P*arenting cannot be mastered alone! It is even a biblical fact that the whole village is necessary for the birthing and rearing of a child. The story of the Exodus of the people of God begins with Moses giving credit, honor, and mention of the five different types of "mothers" who worked together to ensure his birth.

The Pharoah had decided that all boy infants of the Jews were to be killed by the midwives who assisted. Shiprah and Puah were two midwives who decided not to follow orders. With quiet resistance they worked for life. Jocabed, Moses' birth mother, decided that she would have her baby and then hide him from the eyes of those seeking his destruction. She made him a little cradle, able to sit in water, and put him in the river for safety. She worked for life. Miriam, Moses' big sister, was sent to stand as guard for the little cradle upon the water. She worked for life. So when the Pharoah's daughter came with her maids to bathe, they discovered the cradle, but Miriam was there with a believable story.

"You have found a baby. Let me go and find some Jewish woman who has recently had a baby who can nurse him for you." Babies are cute. Babies are a treasure to be discovered. And babies need the milk of human kindness to survive! The Pharoah's daughter worked for life as she sent Miriam off to discover some woman who would be willing to help her! Lo and behold, Miriam found Jocabed, Moses' birth mother! God worked it so that she had the opportunity to nurse and to love her own son!

It took five women to get Moses to the place where he would become the Deliverer of God's Chosen People. It is the prime example of how community is expected to play its part in the life of each and every child. We are not "single" parents unless we choose to remain alone. We must look to the surrounding community. And the community must look for us!

At baptism and with dedications, Christian congregations take the responsibility to help raise children that they did not birth. With ordination, pastors covenant to look out for and teach the children. With required public education, teachers become part of the local communities that impact and affect the lives of our children. Doctors, nurses, and community health workers are part of our parenting team. For it does take a village to raise every child.

The key issue is asking for the help that we need. When people ask "What can I do to help?" give them truthful answers. "I need a day away or even a weekend for myself." Looking for childcare providers is difficult. For you are forced to screen them carefully. Yet, getting away for renewal and respite is also mandatory for quality mental health. So, as I was questioning, "Who can care for Giraurd?" a single woman's name came to mind. I called her and was shocked at her more than willing response!

Connie had been the single mother of a physically challenged son, Rusty, who had died the year before my appointment to her congregation. She was an active participant in the church and a lovely sister friend. When I called to inquire whether keeping Giraurd was a possibility or not she laughed and said, "Why, yes! I need a child in my life! He will give me reason to go out and do fun things!" They had a ball! Going to video arcades is fun. Ordering pizza is fun. Watching Disney movies is fun. Hanging out at malls is fun. But the child is the excuse you need as an adult! It was a match made in heaven! For both Connie, the adult, and Giraurd, the child, are members of the same village.

> Let no one despise your youth, but be an example to believers
> in word, in conduct, in love, in spirit, in faith, in purity.
> —1 TIMOTHY 4:12

God of youth and age, we come with our grateful thanks for what we offer each other. It is of your beneficence that we find ourselves in the village at the same time, needing each other. Thank you for the many and multiple nurturing communities that come together and make up this global village. Thank you for the opportunities that we have to complement each other with our individual gifts. Help us to reach out to each other, to appreciate each other, and to provoke each other to more stimulating growth. For we ask in the name of the Holy One, born as a child among us. May it be so now and always, we pray.

PRAYER FOCUS: Those who need and want a child in their lives today

U N P A C K I N G   T H E   D A Y

*I*t happens five days a week during the school year. It is the inevitable homework! After a day of work, meetings, shopping, juggling the other items that force themselves onto our already full plates, the time arrives when we are called upon to either assist with or to check homework. It can be both a bane and a blessing. For this time of sitting close, talking quietly, and sharing school business also provides the time to help children unpack their day.

I remember Mama. It was during my time of wrestling with algebra problems. She'd never had algebra. She didn't know how to approach the computations. But she would sit close to me. She would encourage me. And her presence helped me to think and recall what the instructor had taught. It was "our" time. It was memory-making time. It was precious time carved out for just her and me. The "problems" of algebra could easily shift to the other "problems" in my life. This was a time when I could unload the serious issues facing a young woman dealing with complex, competing, and challenging worlds. Mama is dead, but the sweet memories of her sitting with me linger.

Homework is not my favorite event. But sitting and talking with Giraurd, listening and learning what is important to him, is both fun and necessary for both of us. I am in the very same position as my Mama when it comes to being efficient in "new math"! But I am also my Mama in that I can be an encourager, a cheerleader, and a reminder that "the teacher said. . . ."

Children need that period when they become the center of an adult's attention for a short period of time. They need to know that someone is listening and paying attention to what concerns them, regardless of how petty it may sound. For this is a time of stretching ideas, playing with different concepts, and expanding the world of possibilities. It's not simply doing homework. It's a time of unpacking the baggage that they carry. As they unpack it and look at it, they do it within the loving confines of someone who cares and is willing to hear them, challenge them, and help them to see different options, in love. And you thought homework was simply another chore!

Without counsel, the people will fail. —PROVERBS 11:14

Wonderful Counselor, we approach you with awe. For it is by your love that we have been given those who have listened to us and stretched our thinking. Now it is our turn to share this time of grace with others. Give us listening hearts and gentle spirits. Anoint our ears to be keen enough to hear what is not said. Still our tongues of sharp and too-quick answers. Prompt us to speak slowly and with the wisdom that only you provide. Help us to see this precious time as a prime opportunity to pass on what we have learned and what we wished we had learned! Be present to us as we are present to these in our care. For we pray in the name of the Christ.

PRAYER FOCUS: Teachers, principals, aides, and others who teach

NEW RULES

*P*arenting is a two-way street! You teach the children, and the children teach you. We had gone to a Disney movie. The main character had a dog that was very protective of both him and his little sister. The movie's bully had made a bad move at the town carnival and snatched the big teddy bear from the small girl's arms. As the bully ran away, the main character had yelled to the dog, "Get that weenie!" And the attack was on. Needless to say, the teddy bear was returned to the little girl. The movie ended and life went on.

At our house, the evening meal is conversation time. Everybody is expected to share and pass along information that the family needs to know. As we were eating, Giraurd told us of an experience at school. It seems that he and another boy had caps that were identical. The other child had misplaced his cap. In order to replace it, he had snatched Giraurd's off his head while they were lining up for dismissal. Without thinking about it, I replied, "Giraurd, you should have gotten his weenie!"

Giraurd's response was quiet and thoughtful. He replied, "Grand, that would have been inappropriate!" The table went quiet. Chuck quickly turned away as laughter was choked and tears began. I had to reply, "Giraurd, you are correct. That would have been very inappropriate." For we had been spending time discussing appropriate and inappropriate behaviors, a major topic at school where "zero tolerance" had been instituted concerning violence. My statement to Giraurd, if taken and acted upon, would have caused him to be expelled! Thank God, he had learned the lessons of what was appropriate conduct as the rules changed.

Rules change all the time. The world we live in is fluid. Things happen quickly. Life is moving at a faster pace than ever before. What was "normal" yesterday, might not be tomorrow. The only constant in life is God's word. God's word remains, "Do unto others as you would have them do unto you." It's called the Golden Rule. I gave Giraurd the bronze rule that is "Do in others before they do you in!" But Giraurd taught me that inappropriate behavior is never correct.

You shall love your neighbor as you love yourself. On these laws hang all the laws and the Prophets. —MATTHEW 22:39

God of the Golden Rule, thank you for children who remind us of your constancy. Thank you for teaching and teachable moments that come into our life, often with laughter and much surprise. Thank you for the opportunities to learn better how to be your examples on earth. Thank you for little children who show us that we really don't have it all together like we pretend! Thank you for amazing grace. Thank you for divine love. We receive it with gratitude in the name of Christ.

PRAYER FOCUS: That we may live the Golden Rule

NEW HOPE, ANOTHER CHANCE

*T*hey had all the money any family would want. They were millionaires who had earned their money the old fashioned way, with work. They were people who knew the meaning of the word family. Their parents had begun a family business and they had married young, finished college, and entered the work force with Mom and Dad. They were good Christian folks. They believed in being active, even evangelical, with their faith. All of their four children were raised in the local church. One of them strayed and went another way.

The daughter is beautiful. She has everything going for her, all types of opportunities. For whatever reason, that woman felt unworthy. She turned to a wild group and became addicted to drugs. Drugs have no respect of person! Drugs don't care about the "good" family name. Drugs are not particular about where your family attends worship. Drugs enjoys the fact that money is plentiful and available. Drugs took the daughter down. Drugs took a mother away from her three children. Money cannot buy an escape from pain, misery, and heartache.

The grandparents took custody of their three grandchildren. The great-grandparents were willing to assist with child care and relinquish duties at the business as the grandchildren became a priority. Providing them with a stable existence was paramount. They had seen too much, experienced far too much drama, and gone to too many "far countries" while with their mom. It meant enrolling them in school, starting them in scouts, taking them to sport activities, and going back to PTAs. They had to return to Sunday school and become active with the church youth group all over again. At church functions, these grandparents found themselves sitting with the young families who had children. For their friends didn't like all that noise!

They have raised another set of children. Their other children chipped in to babysit and allow them respite time away. It was a continuing family affair. At the funeral of their great-grandmother, the children gave honor and praise for the loving second chance at life they have been given.

Those three children grew up and graduated from high school. They each went away to college. They are settling down in lives of their own choosing. They all stayed away from the snare of drugs. They are the source of much love and hope to their grandparents. They provided them with many opportunities to see their previous child-rearing "mistakes" and correct them, the second time around. The birth mother is more like an aunt. After a number of treatment centers and many attempts at sobriety, she's doing better these days. The three children are grateful she's yet alive. They give all the credit to Mom and Dad—their grandparents!

Whatever you do to the least of these, you do it unto me.
—MATTHEW 25:40

Generous Opportunity Provider, we approach you with reverence and awe. It is a good thing to know that you provide grace and mercy every time we have needs. The prevalence of drugs within our communities is so demonic. Our children are snared seemingly without thought of their "tomorrows." Drugs are the only demons who have come and snatched mothers away from their own off-spring! We plead the saving blood of Jesus Christ over our addicted children and especially their offspring. Beneficent One, hear our prayers in the name of Christ.

PRAYER FOCUS: Children of the addicted and their caregivers

WIDENING THE CIRCLE

*H*is name is Wayne. He is a cute little boy, filled with laughter and mischief. He lives with his grandparents. He is the son of their son. He keeps them young, energetic, and involved. They were all members of our local congregation.

Her name is Tiffany. She is a beautiful girl, shy but extremely bright. She lives with her grandparents. She is the daughter of their son. She keeps them young, energetic, and involved.
They were all members of our local congregation.

It was the week before Mother's Day. Giraurd's kindergarten class was making cards for their moms. Giraurd wanted to make two, one for his mother and one for me. He was only allowed one. At the dinner table, he complained, "Grand, I wish I had come from your stomach. Then, you would really be my mom." I listened to his pain. I hurt with him. My response came, slowly, but accurately. "You did come from my stomach. For I carried your mommy here and you came from her." That satisfied him. It caused me to think of the other children in our congregation who were dealing with the very same issue. I had to preach to them and for them on Mother's Day.

That particular sermon focused on our belonging to God, the Great Mother who birthed the whole wide world! I talked about the first parents, who were charged with the responsibility of bringing forth other human beings into existence and how we are all related. I talked about how Jesus had to be born in the very same fashion as us, after being carried in his mother's womb, and about how Jesus gave birth to the Church, as he died on Calvary, and left us the broken body and shed blood to make us all one forevermore. As the Caribbeans say, "All a we is one."

It was a sermon to encourage grandchildren living with doubts in their minds. It was a sermon to encourage grandparents who fully understood their place and role in the lives of another generation. It was a sermon especially for Giraurd, Wayne, and Tiffany on Mother's Day as they tried to sort out just who was to be "loved" especially. It's a difficult question. Yet, just like Jesus, they love us all! That's mighty good news!

> But what can I do this day to these my [children] or to their children whom they have borne? —GENESIS 31:43

Womb of Being, it is in you that we live and move and have our being. We come from your generous existence and abide in you our whole life long. We need you. Oh, how we need you. For the questions of these children perplex us, confound us, and leave us searching for wisdom and speech. What can we do but look to you for answers? Thank you for providing what these children need through us. Thank you for loving us enough to trust us with these precious souls who need our understanding and nurture. Continue to speak to our spirits the words of life. Breathe upon us and give us counsel when words escape us. Fill us with your loving Holy Spirit until we can love them as you love us. Help us to sincerely believe and know that we are all one with you. Be glorified in all that we say and do as we role model for these children whom our children have borne. We pray in faith, through the name of the Holy One. It is so!

PRAYER FOCUS: The children of all our children

ABUNDANCE, NOT LACK

*W*e have never received one red penny of state support for Giraurd! It's not that we didn't try to get the state to recognize him as their "ward." But it was "assumed" that since he was our flesh and blood, living in our home, that we were totally responsible for his care. I remember once deciding to leave him at the local police station as abandoned. Of course, I couldn't do it. He trusted us. He needed us. He was ours. And God has never failed to assist us in more than meeting our needs. Giraurd is included in our every consideration. As a matter of fact, we have been more abundantly blessed since Giraurd has come into our lives. For God specializes in abundance. God gets no glory out of our being stuck in the "land of lack"!

This is not to say that grandparents ought not seek every possible means of assistance that is due them and the children in their care. This is not to say that the parents who birthed these children ought not be held responsible to provide, either. But God specializes in the law of reciprocity. "Give and it shall be given back to you, good measure, pressed down, shaken together, and running over will be put into your bosom. For with the same measure that you use, it will be measured back to you" (Luke 6:38). Mista Chuck and I decided to try it. We found God's Word to be more than true!

When we care for God's little ones, we are actually lending to God! God is indebted to us! The story is told that when Columbus was commissioned by Queen Isabella to get ready and sail the ocean blue looking for new lands to conquer, he was in business for himself. It is said that he questioned the queen, "But, what about my business, your Majesty?" The answer is quite notable. "Columbus, if you take care of my business, I will most certainly take care of yours!" The word of a mere human being sent Columbus on a life-changing adventure. The words of the queen guaranteed that the business of Columbus would not fail, would not go bankrupt, and would prosper while he was away! This is the very same promise that the God of the universe makes to those of us charged with tending to grandchildren! As we take care of God's "business," God will take care of us. It's a promise!

> Observe and obey all these words which I command you, that it
> may go well with you and your children after you forever, when
> you do what is good and right in the sight of God.
> —DEUTERONOMY 12:28

Promise Maker, we look to you in every time of need. We anticipate your law of reciprocity to work on our behalf. There are times when it appears that we are like the widow of Zerepath and the meal in our barrel is almost gone! Yet, we remember your promises. And we remind you of your trustworthy words. We are doing the very best we can. We wait on you to honor every promise made. Thank you for always being a promise-keeping God. For we pray in the name of the Promised One, Jesus the Christ.

PRAYER FOCUS: Those with both stretched budgets and straining faith

G U A R D   Y O U R   H E A R T

I am afraid of bugs! I hate flies and mosquitoes with a passion. One of the many part-time positions Chuck has had since his retirement was as a certified pest inspector. It's been a helpful "career" with a little one in the house who has no respect of place for food, crumbs, or partially eaten candy bars! As hard as we try to keep watch there are times when Giraurd's behaviors escape our notice.

For many years we got away with eating out, but with a young child in the house, it is essential that you cook every now and then to ensure proper nutritious meals and the taking of essential vitamins. So, we eat breakfast and dinner together most days. At breakfast I put Giraurd's vitamin pills in front of him. I admit that he's most likely overmedicated! For at our house we take additional vitamin C to ward off colds. So there were four tablets that he saw before him every morning. Of course, I believed he was taking them, as they did disappear.

I never shall forget the day that we were eating dinner at the breakfast nook. I was watching the sunset over the lake outside the window, when I noticed a parade! It was a parade of black ants crawling inside the window! I freaked! Chuck jumped up and so did Giraurd. Mista Chuck went to get his inspector's flashlight to discover where these obnoxious creatures were coming from and why they had decided to invade our kitchen area. "Ants only go where there is food!" declared the Inspector.

The parade continued in the window, along the edge and right behind the television set upon the counter. Believe me, there was a careful inspection made that day. When Mista Chuck moved the television, the culprits were discovered. There were many sweet vitamin pills and a couple of candy wrappers stashed behind the television. Now, how could they possibly have gotten there? Giraurd certainly had no idea! Both of the adults were well aware of how the "sweet things" made it to this unsuspected little corner.

There is another place that needs a careful inspection, my friend. It is the corners of our hearts. For "sweet little things" like resentment, anger, and unforgiveness can hide there, undetected until an outburst happens that we cannot explain. This job of parenting a second time is difficult! We are not as young, energetic, or patient as we used to be! Things that we were able to put up with now get on our reserve nerve. So it's not strange that we "stuff" issues and try to keep peace, especially with our wayward children who go on and continue living their lives while we sacrifice over and over again. You don't have to talk about it. And you certainly don't have to deal with your feelings. However, the "ants" will then show up.

Find someone to talk to who is going through a similar experience. Our experience is so common that we could start a club and be surprised at how many members would sign up! If you need to, just ask at the principal's office for the name of another grandparent who is raising a child. But the truth is that most of us have someone in our inner circle that is in our situation, especially within our local congregations. It's like attending an AlAnon meeting. You don't participate because you are crazy, but you attend to hear others validate your reality and help you certify that you are not crazy!

> Now the purpose of the commandment is love from a pure
> heart, from a good conscience, and from sincere faith, from
> which some have strayed . . . —1 TIMOTHY 1:5

Inspector of Hearts, turn the floodlight of heaven into every corner of my heart. Let me see what you see there. Help me to be honest as I search with you for all the little "sweet things" that I have stored and are now being infested by ants of resentment, anger, and unforgiveness. Root out everything that is not like you. Give me wisdom and courage to talk about my feelings. Let me feel them. Let me acknowledge them. Let me deal with them. Then, help me to let them go. Teach me how to guard my heart! Thank you for the pesticide of the Holy Spirit. I receive your clean sweep with gratitude, for it is in the name of the Light of Glory that I pray.

PRAYER FOCUS: The "ants" in our heart

You Are the Light

$\mathcal{T}$he carnival came to town! Eleven-year-old Giraurd took his grandparents for a ride! Although it was truly "small town" stuff, there was a giant Ferris wheel, swinging in the wind. Ferris wheels speak to me about our lives. We get on with birth. The climb begins as we age, begin school, go to college, get married, and have children. It reaches the top, wildly going back and forth somewhere around middle age as we continue to try and figure out how the ride will end. And on the other side of the top is a slow descent to the bottom where we exit in death. There is no detour on the Ferris wheel. I have never seen one that stopped and allowed us to go backwards. It's always on, up, and down. It's the cycle of life.

What delights me is the reality that the Ferris wheel keeps going. Folks get on. Folks get off. And the wheel keeps going round and round. So it makes no difference where you are today, the wheel is moving. If you hold on, your position will change. The faith step is to hold on. Some of us get stuck with various types of tragedy on the ride. The traumas of our life can impact us with such force that we may become discouraged, distressed, and even depressed as the wheel moves so slowly. But where you are today is not "the end." Don't put a period where God has put a comma in your life. The Wheel of Life's operator has not forgotten that you are waiting for "up."

And don't be deceived—everybody has their time in "down"! One of the ways that the enemy of our souls defeats us is to have us think and feel that others are better off than we are. Some folks know how to put on a happy face and talk with such positive conviction that we are deceived into believing that they have an inside track with God. But the same wheel that takes us up is the very same one that brings us down. There is biblical record to show that even Jesus had to go on the "ride," with emotional highs and lows. "Who do men say that I am?" he asked the disciples. "Could you not pray with me, one hour?" he asked on the night of his betrayal. But he stayed on the wheel! For he was the Light of the World. Now, it's our turn to shine.

Don't let your feelings sidetrack you about the ride you're on today. Emotions are not facts. Emotions are feelings that try to make us believe they are facts! But the truth is that you can shine despite your feelings. It's a matter of attitude with gratitude. As the AA/NA circles would say, "Fake it until you make it." Now, you can better understand why so many folks keep those smiles plastered on their faces! Giraud calls it a "cheesy smile." It's the one that does not come directly from the inside, but it can work its way down. For lights have to shine! And even "down" Ferris wheels eventually move up! Hold on and shine forth!

You are the light! You can't argue with the fact. You can't ignore the reality. You can't walk away from your responsibility to shine! For you were born to twinkle on the Ferris wheel of life in order that others could see how you do it and try to imitate your style! I know that there are times when the "twinkle" in you feels dim. I can understand that the day comes when it feels as if there is no wattage left for even flickering. But the word of God has already decreed it. You are the light.

Shine today. Move at your pace. Strut your stuff. Make your mark. Share your vision. Work your plan. Establish new goals. Review old ones. Dream. See visions. Keep on believing that the ride is moving you toward your grand destiny. This day is simply another day for you to make God look good! We serve an awesome God. We serve a God who will burst forth from behind clouds, peek up at us in new bulbs, show off as new sprouts and twigs, cover us in the brightness of snow, rain down on us the brilliance of colored leaves, and twinkle at night as both moon and stars. No less is expected from me and you. We simply need to take deep breaths and keep shining as the wheel moves us again.

Today, let's make a covenant. We will not whine one time today. We will bite our tongues and not complain. We will hold our mouths shut and not permit one negative comment to escape our lips. We won't have a crisis. We will not participate in drama. And we will not criticize. We will simply be determined to let the world see how brightly and how brilliantly we can shine! Remember, God is anticipating your very best this day, for you are the light! That's serious word!

I have made you a light for the Gentiles, that you may bring salvation to the ends of the earth. —ACTS 13:47

Light of the World, shine forth in me. The world has taught me not to shine brightly. The world has told me not to bring attention to myself. The world has said that I need to stay in my place, a background position, and applaud as others shine. Yet you come and call me light! You dare me to illumine every place that I am. You challenge me to go against all that the world has said about me. Tell you what—if you shine through me, I'll shine. Whenever. Wherever. For whomever. Shine through me, Light of the World, I pray in the name of the One who dispels gloom.

PRAYER FOCUS: Those who have lost their twinkle

RINGING THOSE BELLS

$\mathcal{B}$o Derek has nothing on Cherri! She is beautiful. She is gifted. She is talented. She is vivacious. She leads the bell choir at her local congregation. She had "Bo Derek's hairstyle" when I arrived as pastor. So I began to teasingly call her "Bo."

Cherri is one of God's most bubbly and effervescent people. Her creativity sets her apart from the average individual. She's married and her spouse is in the bell choir also. She's always early to worship on Sunday and stays late to ensure that all things are put away. Except for passing and smiling in the halls on our ways to worship, I would have not spent too much time with her. But one day she called the office. We had to talk.

Her son wanted to put his wedding date on the church calendar. He was her oldest child who was in the military. She and her husband were legal guardians of his three lovely daughters. Of course I'd seen the little girls, in pretty dresses being lead to or picked up from Sunday school classes. I assumed Cherri and Jack were some of the many grandparents who babysit on the weekends. It's not uncommon. But once again, "the story" was repeated.

In the midst of Cherri and Jack trying to adjust to the "empty nest," in a time period when they were learning how to live without others in their home, in a new situation where the opportunity for Cherri to lead the bell choir had come along and it felt like something she'd always wanted to do, her former daughter-in-law had decided she'd had enough! With their son stationed abroad, Cherri and Jack began parenting for the second time around.

How do you simply decide that "mothering" is not for you when you have given birth to three little girls? There was no readily available "reason" for the former daughter-in-law wanting out. She was not a drug addict. She claimed there was no one else in her life. She didn't leave the area or quit her job. Being a single parent was simply too much for her! So she packed up the girls and brought them to Cherri and Jack.

There has to be some special course called "Explanations" that we need to take. For I have no easy way to explain to little children that their mother finds them disposable! When you can use the excuse of drugs, abuse, or something "tangible" it makes it easier to talk about. But when kids are simply dropped off like the day's trash, or discarded like something bought at a bad sale, what do you tell them? Or do you behave like Cherri and keep right on ringing those bells?

Cherri makes every day a holiday for the girls! She and Jack act as if the girls are their special guests. They keep photos of the girls' parents in their rooms and throughout the house, as they have been all of their lives. They talk about what they know of the parents' whereabouts. They keep the hope alive, that the mother will come or call soon. It's what they all need to do to in order to survive the pain. Of course, the son calls frequently. The mother is yet continuing on hiatus! Thankfully, Cherri and Jack have included the girls in their ministry of ringing those bells!

Make a joyful noise to God, all the earth! —PSALM 66:1

Divine Parent who never tosses one of us out, we approach you with reverence and many questions. You made each one of us so unique, so majestic, so individual, and so filled with creativity—it's difficult to imagine. How did you conceive of blood vessels, brain cells, chromosomes, and regenerating tissues? Where did the idea come from to fill us with wonder, to endow us with potential, and to leave your universe's care in our feeble hands? How did you select who would be able to conceive and birth children and who would grieve due to their inability? How do you feel when innocent children are walked out on? How does your heart deal with their pain of abandonment and rejection? We need to hear from you. For we are having a real hard time with this matter of disposable children. Speak to our hurting hearts, we plead in the name of the Child you sent to die.

PRAYER FOCUS: The "disposable" children

You Can Kill Every Giant!

*O*nce upon a time there lived a wicked giant. (They seem to be everywhere!) The wicked giant lived in a castle perched high above the sea cliff. From this vantage point the giant could observe all the creatures that lived below. The giant was not only wicked, but very evil, enjoying the torture of lesser creatures as well as the kill. Every creature in the forest was afraid of this evil giant who tormented them just for the sport of it. One day an assembly was held and the creatures decided that desperate measures called for desperate actions. Something had to be done about the wicked, evil giant.

Elephants have always been big. Elephants have always had great size and large trunks. So during the meeting the elephant volunteered to go up the cliff and slay the wicked, evil giant. All the other animals agreed that this was a good idea. Off and up the cliff the huge elephant began to lumber. The giant saw the elephant approach. At just the right time, the wicked giant went rushing out, grabbed the elephant and flung that large body into the sea. With a great splash of water, and the death of their hopes, all the creatures became much more terrified.

At the next meeting, a lion volunteered. Lions are creatures that can make others cower. Lions have a roar that can make you shake in your boots. Lions look like winners. So the group cheered the lion on as another ascent up the cliffs began. But the lion met the same deadly fate as the elephant! The lion was crushed and thrown into the waters of the sea by a laughing, wicked giant. Talk about despair being generated among the little creatures of the forest. You can just imagine the panic and the anxiety created with the devastating turn of events. The creatures began to talk of their own approaching deaths. They began to say farewell to each other. They begin to plan for their own fateful ends.

In the midst of the talk of death, a tiny voice was heard. "I can kill the wicked, evil giant!" As all the creatures, great and small, begin to look to discover where this little, tiny voice was coming from, a termite crawled from beneath a log. The larger animals begin to laugh and make fun of this little bug. "Did you see what happened to the elephant and the lion? Little creature, you don't stand a chance." The noise of their laughter was great. When they had finished making fun of the termite, one asked, "Just what is your plan of attack, Little One"? The little insect replied, "Just be patient. Wait and see."

Off toward the castle went the termite. This tiny creature was unseen by the wicked giant. There was no obvious motion. There was no seeming activity in the forest. Yet the termite crawled up the cliff and into the castle. As termites are programmed to do, this one began to chew one of the massive timber beams that upheld the castle. Without fanfare, noise, or loud announcement, the termite kept busy doing its job. The giant was deceived into thinking that the quiet in the forest below was that of fear, while all the time, the lull was one of hushed expectation. The creatures were waiting.

One morning, just before the break of dawn, there was a great noise in the forest. As the central timber in the castle gave away, the home of the giant suddenly collapsed toward the sea, where the wicked, evil giant met his death and the water covered all that had held the forest captive in fear. Victory belonged to the tiny termite that had simply been doing what God had purposed in eternity for her to do! She did her job with patience and diligence. She ate slowly and with relish. She accomplished what the huge elephant and powerful lion could not. For within her was all she needed to achieve great things. And within you and me there is more than enough to work out our divine destiny that includes this second parenting act!

God provides each of us with the inner resources to make it through the difficult and, yes, even the scary times of our lives. For the giants are always there. Those people and things that would torture us needlessly can be found in every place we go. There will always be someone to mock us, laugh at us, and make every attempt to have us cower down and withdraw in fear. But within us is a reservoir of strength that calls us to work on, parent on, and live on, in faith, with diligence. Within us is that still, small voice that calls us to move at our own pace and do what God has purposed, before the Creation, that we were born to do. Like the termite, we simply must remain focused and on purpose. Yes, you can kill the giants!

> The jar of flour was not used up and the jug of oil did not run
> dry, in keeping with the word of the Lord, spoken by Elijah.
>
> —1 Kings 17:16

Termite and Giant Maker, we come before you. For we feel so small and insignificant. The giants are everywhere! We tremble at their sight. We cower at their size. We want to crawl under cover and hide. We have been taught that the giants always win. Thank you for a story about a faithful and persistent little termite that simply did what you created her to do before the foundation of the world. This day we pray for "termite ability"! We want to keep on doing what we've been created to do. Help us, we pray, in the name of the Giant Slayer.

PRAYER FOCUS: Those who are wrestling with what appears to be a giant

CAN YOU SEE THE SIGNS?

I missed the first clue. We have brown sugar for the oatmeal and the end of the bag seemed to have had a baby biting on it. I thought that was odd since we don't have a baby. I opened the bag, dumped the contents into our container and went about my business. I missed the second clue. It was time to make dinner and I pulled out a cooking bag and the contents were spilling out of what I supposed was a busted bag. Wondered how that had happened but didn't give it too much thought. A couple of days later I reached under the cupboard to pull out a skillet. I got the message loud and clear! The mice had left me unmistakable signs! The mystery was over. The clues came together. I threw the skillet in the sink. I called Mista Chuck on his car phone. I went and got in the middle of my bed!

We live close to water. We have much nature to appreciate. We have many little critters running around. But I surely never thought any would dare to come inside my dwelling and make itself at home! So, I wasn't looking for signs of dirty little "visitors" to invade my space. I didn't put the clues together even though I knew that all the conditions were prime attractions. I simply went about my business as usual. Until the unmistakable signs were in my face and there was no doubt as to the answer to this puzzle, I was clueless! Yet, there were signs all around me.

We have to be alert to see the signs. We have to be conscious about our surroundings. We have to be cognizant of the reality of our lives. For the signs are everywhere. The clues are always before us. And the signs have great lessons to teach us if we are aware. One of my favorite books is one about two smart mice who live in a maze with two very dumb "little people" who are the same size. *Who Moved My Cheese?* is a little book with a huge message about reading the signs around us. Dr. Spencer Johnson is the author of this "must read" book for those who, like me, can miss the little signs until it is late in the game!

Mice are smart whether we like them or not. They are so tiny that they can get into places other critters cannot. They move swiftly. They are flexible and try to stay out of sight. They know how to be elusive until you set the right type cheese on the bait! The whole book is about Sniff and Scurry, mice who have moved into a major cheese source and live with the two little people. When the cheese supply runs out, the little people begin to debate and pontificate as to who is responsible for moving the cheese, who is going to bring in a new supply of cheese, and who will answer the question, "who moved my cheese?" The little mice in the book are only conscientious about finding a new source of cheese in order to survive. They leave the "thinkers" to argue and linger in a dying state while they go in search of new life. They read the signs of the time. They get the clues. They move on to new sources of cheese.

The book focuses on the little people and their dilemma. It's a worthy read, especially for those of us who missed many of the signs with our adult children. Watch out, there are some signs in your life that need to be interpreted today! There are signs everywhere! Crisis is a sign. Sadness is a sign. Depression is a major sign. Frequent anger is a sign. Restlessness is a sign. Lethargy is a sign. The inability to make decisions is a sign. Don't let your "skillet" get full of mouse droppings before you stop and read the signs! All of these signs are "unknown tongues." We can't always read, understand, and figure out the messages being sent. But the power of the Holy Spirit interprets unknown tongues and makes them plain. We have to be willing to stop, look, see, and then ask God, "What's up?"

Today or tomorrow will be a good time to take a chill pill, to rest, relax, recreate, and allow yourself some breathing space to check out the meaning of the signs of the time. For the reality is that the handwriting is already on the walls and we don't want to read the unmistakable print! But God will not allow us to wander around in the proverbial dark.

God wants us to always be in the know. God wants our steps to be ordered well. God wants us to take the journey to our divine destiny. So the signs are everywhere. I'm praying that this day, you will open your spiritual eyes. Read the handwriting on those walls!

> Therefore, the Lord will give you a sign. The virgin will be with child and will give birth to a son, and will call him Immanuel.
>
> —ISAIAH 7:14

Way Maker, I'm seeking new cheese. My name is truly "Little-people" and I have sat waiting to see what others would do on my behalf. Have I ever been disappointed! You are Jehovah-Jireh, my provider. All that I need you have. At least make me a Mighty Mouse, so that I will sniff out the blessings that are everywhere and then scurry to do your will. Open my eyes. Let me interpret the signs I have refused to see. I thank you for what has been revealed to my sightless eyes! You have made some things so plain, until there was no escape. No longer will I live in denial that the handwriting is on the walls for me. In the name of the One Who Points the Way, I pray.

PRAYER FOCUS: Those who refuse to read the handwriting on the walls

C A L L E D   T O   D E C I D E

*T*here comes a time in every life when we must decide between choices. It is the way of life that decisions must be made. For no decision is really just a decision that will allow others to choose for you! The day has arrived when you can't sit on the sidelines, you can't remain on the bench, and you can't stay in limbo between two opinions. There is no room for "maybe" or "perhaps." There is not any wiggle room for a place of ease and comfort. With certainty, everyone of us parenting again has arrived face to face, at a time when voicing our choice with a clear voice of "yes" or "no" is mandated. We are role modeling for another generation. So, when it comes to God, we are forced to choose.

There is no other method for being on God's side. This is not some easy, dilly-dallying, "any ole way you want to come" routine. Just being born into America, the land of the free and the home of the slave, where "In God we trust" is stamped on our coins and bills, does not make any of us a Christian. To be Christian, we are forced to select God from among all the other options that claim to offer us salvation. To be Christian, we are mandated to voice our choice in the community and then to live out our choice on a daily basis. Yes! We have to choose God every day, for little ones are watching.

The way we live and talk tells the world that we have chosen God. The way we act and treat others says whether or not we have voted "Yes" for God. The way we do our job, perform our task, and interact with others says much about our selection of God and God's path for daily living. God is not some inner, solitary, hidden force that we salute with lip service on Sunday morning only! God is not some "big guy" way off in the sky that we pause to pay homage to with our quiet hour one day a week! God is not a cosmic bellhop, whom we call whenever trouble is on the horizon, tip, and then send away! The God who made heaven and earth demands total allegiance, total submission, and a total life of saying "Yes, Lord"!

We are faced with a confrontation that comes to trouble folks who wanted to interpret God's laws to fit their lifestyles. "Did God really say?" is not just the question the devil asked Eve in the Garden of Eden. This question is asked a million times a day as we wrestle with our consciences, disregard the Holy Spirit's nudging, and go our way, living our lives and telling the world that we are "God followers." It's time to choose!

If God is God, let us be aware that the Word means what it says, and says what it means. This means shacking up has got to stop! This means lying, even for "peace's sake," must come to a quick halt. This means that recreational drugs will take you to hell. This means that your cursing and swearing, using God's name in vain, must come to an end! This means that your taking time off from worship and skipping daily devotion is completely out of order. This means that no sex outside of marriage means no sex outside of marriage. And it means that if sex in the marriage ain't all that great, tough! Work on it! But tipping and slipping won't cut it! For today is about choosing whom you will serve! Serving God with lip service is not allowed!

We cannot turn God's words around to suit us. We cannot fix the situations in our lives by living with loose standards, low morals, and declining values. The only way to turn our lives around is to face the Word of God, heads up, and do the right thing! We can do it. For the Holy Spirit has been given to help us do all that is required. We can do it. For the Greater One lives on the inside. We can do it. For we can do all things through Christ who is our strength, and provides for us both the ability and the will to do what is required. We can do it. We simply need to choose God!

Granny used to say, "God don't like ugly." And our living ragged lives is too ugly for God to bless. It's no secret that God demands holy living. We have to choose to live holy, to be different, and not to fall into line with the status quo. Status quo living got Israel into serious trouble with God. God backed away from them. God's favor was withdrawn from them. God's blessings and provisions were withheld from them. They were taken into captivity. They became servants and slaves to foreign powers. Their nation was split. There was a separation of the Twelve Tribes of Israel that continues even today. Some made the wrong decision!

We need the favor of God in our lives. We need the divine benediction of God upon our lives. We need the provisions of God for our lives. We need God's face, shining among us. We need the blessings of God spread throughout our world, and especially upon our nation, our community, and the youth in our homes. And God wants to give it all to us!

The promise of Jeremiah 29:11 declares, "I know the plans I have for you, says the Lord. Plans for peace, and not of evil to give you a future with hope." We and those we are responsible for can have all that God has when we choose to live holy! This is a day for personal choice. This is a day for a new decision. Yes! This is election day! This is a day for voting, with our lives to live for God. Go ahead, choose.

Elijah went before the people and said, 'How long will you waver between two opinions? If the Lord is God, follow, but if Baal is God, follow. —1 KINGS 18:2

God, thank you for being. God, forgive me for not casting a serious vote for you before. God bless me to make the right choice this day and everyday. For I long to follow you. You, alone, are more than enough for me. In the name of Jesus, the Christ, I pray.

PRAYER FOCUS: Those who need to make a serious election of God

SERVICE WITH ATTITUDE

*L*et me be quick to point out that I have not forgotten that we have been the "mules of the earth" for centuries! Let me help you understand that I have not been struck with mental retardation or even "some timers" disease. You know "some timers." It's the first cousin of Alzheimer's, where you forget something, "sometimes." But our current situation is a reminder that slavery days and servanthood are not over.

Yes! We have come a long way, Baby. Yes! Affirmative action is a necessary legislative measure for assisting us in moving on up. And, yes, the mention of slavery, cotton, and tobacco fields with gunny sacks and singing dark-skinned folks will yet make the hair rise on the backs of our necks. However, there is something else to be said about slavery, servanthood, and service with the proper attitude, especially to those living in our homes.

There is an interesting story found in 1 Kings, chapter 12. It is the sad tale of the separation of the twelve tribes of Israel after the death of Solomon, the wisest man in the world. One of his sons, Rehoboam, was seeking counsel as to how to lead the people of God. Wise counsel came forth from the elders to this young leader. "If you will be a servant to these people and serve them and give them a favorable answer, they will always be your servants." The key words are "If you will serve!" Once more God is saying to us, be a servant with attitude!

Serve as if you already own the world and can afford to be generous! Serve as if you already know that as a child of the Most Sovereign God you have more than you will ever need. Serve as if you are willing to do more than anyone else in your circumstances.

Serve as if serving brings you pleasure, joy, and gratitude. Serve as if stepping up to the plate and doing business is what you were purposed to do before the foundation of the world. For "if we serve" these children in our control and serve them with a flamboyant attitude, others will become our servants and give us the assistance that we need!

We are called to serve. And we are called to do it willingly and without being forced. We are called to not ask the opinions of others who think we are being foolish, looking silly, and acting in a degrading manner taking care of children in our "golden" years. The question upon our lips as we get into the business of this day can be "Please tell me how I can serve you better."

Isn't this what we want from the folks who take our money after rendering their service? We find them giving us opinion polls, mailing us questionnaires, and calling us on the phone to seek our input as how to keep us coming back and spending more money with them! Service with an attitude of thanksgiving renders multiple benefits. Service with an attitude of "whatever my hands are finding to do, I'm doing it as unto the Lord" brings God's smile upon us and God's favors seeking us!

To be authentic, real, and whole, we need to learn how to serve others better. For we are born into community. Community means helping each other to exist, to survive, and to thrive. Community becomes real as we serve each other. Did you watch the last episode of the Australian *Survivor* series? It was another competition between sixteen people to be voted the most fit of the fit. Know that I'm proud to announce that a woman, a forty-two-year-old teacher, a specialist with youth, won the final round. She had developed her individuality to such an extent that she had a sense of wholeness that prevented her from being voted off by the "tribe." For when you learn how to serve with attitude, the "tribe" understands that they need you in order to survive!

"The tribe has spoken. You must go." These are the phrases used each week to extinguish the flame of every contestant down the line. Tina got the required final four votes to win the million dollars. When you and I learn how to serve our grandchildren with a godly attitude, we will not only win eternal life on the other side, but an overflowing abundance of favor, blessings, and goodwill on this side too.

For the leader of our "tribe" is Jesus. He is the ultimate survivor. For the "tribe" told him that they had spoken and it was time for him to be voted off the game of life. They didn't simply banish him, but hung him to a cruel cross. He died. But he rose again, the supreme victor over sin, death, and hell! As we serve, taking "low" as Granny used to call it, we rise too! I am a slave to Jesus Christ. And I glory in this fact. I believe in good service. Which means we need to learn how to be even better servants! Word!

> If you will be a servant to these people and serve them and give them a favorable answer, they will always be your servants.
> —1 KINGS 12:7

Sovereign God, thank you for the plainness of your living Word. Give me more of a servant's heart that I may be pleasing to you. I felt that I was being overworked. I thought I was being made a fool of again. It seemed as if I was doing more than my part already. Yet you call me to serve better, for I am actually serving you. Great God, you are worthy of more than I can ever do. As I serve these children who belong to you, let me remember with a smile and a servant's heart. You take care of my payment plan. I know your generosity. I thank you in the name of the Gift of Gifts!

PRAYER FOCUS: Those who miss the mark of flamboyant service

BEEN TO THE WAILING WALL

*T*he January 2001 issue of *Time* magazine featured a very poignant portrait of the Pope standing before the Wailing Wall. This pilgrimage had been a dream of the Patriarch of the Roman Catholic Church. This Mecca called him to leave the secure beauty of the Vatican and go the the Holy City of Jerusalem. A photographer snapped his picture, standing alone, before the Wailing Wall.

I'm sure that it was for security reasons that the Pope stood before this massive stone structure in isolation. For the Wailing Wall is a symbol of community. At this wall of wailing, people have gathered down through the centuries. And yet in the picture, Pope John stands there, alone, reading from his prayer book. To stand before the Wailing Wall with a prayer book seems a bit ridiculous to this right-brain female. For a wall for wailing says that I am invited to come and weep and cry with the millions who have stood in this sacred spot through the years. There are many days during our pilgrimage of parenting, again, that we find that we need a wailing wall.

The Wailing Wall is a prayer spot. Contrary to popular belief, wailing is a form of prayer. To wail is to pray without words. To wail is to allow the anguish of your soul to be released. To wail is to pray from your belly. To wail is to move past the restrictions of simple articulation into the mystery of being with God in your hurt, your pain, and your sorrow. God has been found at the Wailing Wall. The reality is that people meet a nurturing, caring, and crying God at the Wailing Wall. God expects us, during this season of our life, to cry and, yes, even to wail.

We are called to remember that we are only creatures of dust. We must often recall, afresh, our need of God. It was the sure posture of Jesus, who came to die in order that we might wear his divinity. As he journeyed through our humanity he allowed himself to feel our every emotion. He felt pain. He was acquainted with grief and disappointment. The Bible records that he cried and even wailed. So it is right, proper, and appropriate that we expect a time for us to cry, to grieve, to lament, and to wail over our emotional hurts. Thank God for a season to allow our tears to so touch God that a way is made for us. Yes, when life presents you with a brick wall, stand there and wail until God comes through! "For it is not by power. It is not by might. But it is by the power of the Holy Spirit, says the Lord" (Zech. 4:6).

In the course of human events there comes a time when all you can do is cry! God honors our tears. For our God is the maestro of the music of our wails. God catches the perfect pitch of our screams of anguish. God conducts a symphony with the differing screeches of our pain. The angels bow down in amazement as God stops to listen to our brokenhearted cries. The cherubim and seraphim don't know what to make of the Almighty, the Ancient of Days, the Creator of the Universe who ceases activity to capture our tears and put them in a bottle! In Psalm 56:8, David tells us plainly that he spent time at his own wailing wall and God answered his prayers of tears and brought him comfort and relief.

Sometimes our meaningless words, seeking the Holy Spirit's presence that sustains us, cannot be articulated. Often we find ourselves bereft of adequate expression for our particular type of pain. There comes the time when life just cuts up so badly that speech is snatched from us! It's at that time when the Holy Spirit will give us the both the power and the ability to wail!

I am a living witness that no prayer book can sum up my life's hurts, pains, and sorrows. I am a living witness that life has presented me with some difficult questions that have challenged me to my very core. I can testify that God has many bottles of my tears on hold. Yet, I have found the answer. I have learned to wail my prayers. It's all right. God knows our every need.

Likewise, the Spirit helps us in our weakness; for we do not know how to pray as we ought. But the Spirit makes intercession for us with sighs too deep for words. —ROMANS 8:26

Tear Receiver, I try so diligently to be adult! It is shameful for me to admit how often I want to cry and to wail. But pride says that I can do this by myself. Ego tells me that I ought be able to handle this role with ease and expertise! So, when the burdens overload me, I simply seek to discover other ways to squelch my tears. Thank you for permission to cry and to wail before you. Thank you for the role model of Jesus who shows us that adults can cry and you wipe their tears. I am aware of your awaiting me, in my stony silence and when I show up at the Wailing Wall. Thank you for the tears that can wash away the grime from my soul. I pray in the name of the Weeping Savior.

PRAYER FOCUS: Those who need to weep, moan, and wail

J O Y   I N   L I F E

*J*oy's life has not been easy. Her relationship with her mother is next to unbelievable. An only child, Joy now feels that her mother suffered from some form of mental illness. Given the name Joy, her life was anything but joy filled. Her mom would lock her outside during snow storms without a coat and laugh as she watched the child shiver in the cold. She wouldn't feed her as the mother herself ate. She woke Joy in the morning by beating her with an iron cord. With strange, bizarre, and evil behaviors, she never gave any indication of love. Joy grew up wondering what was wrong with her.

Joy married a man just like dear old mom. He was both emotionally absent and abusive. Rapidly having children, they all grew up together. She worked all types of jobs at home in order to raise her children properly and keep her family together. Along the journey she put herself through school. She wanted to teach. She needed to reach out to other unloved children. She needed them to reach out to her! Her biological children begin to act out due to the "frosty" atmosphere in their home. Joy's love, alone, was not good enough. It never is for any of us! Two of the boys ran afoul of the law, and one began to serve time in prison. Two of the boys are great achievers. Her only daughter is a Hollywood model. However, the marriage failed. Today, Joy is raising her imprisoned child's son and the little boy's half-sister.

The little boy's father was in jail. The older half-sister's father was absent, on drugs. Their mother was dying of cancer and addicted to drugs. It was not a pretty picture. The dying mother decided to become pregnant again. She was in denial about her certain death. The children begin to grow excited about the reunification of their family, not knowing that the mother's parental rights had been taken by the courts. Joy wondered about the impending birth. The little boy cried and had nightmares. The older girl begin acting out, both at home and at school.

Joy was teaching full time and working as an associate pastor at a thriving church. She was running back and forth to two different schools and juggling her own finances to care for the additional two mouths who had arrived without state subsidy. For almost a full year, Joy wrestled with finances alone, jeopardizing her home's mortgage and her credit record. When the state foster parent license came through, so did the monetary award.

The children wanted more contact with their pregnant mother, who was growing weaker and weaker. It was a period of great trial. The sacrifice was tremendous. Finances were extremely tight. Questions were always present. Joy kept praying, working, and juggling. All the balls stayed in the air. It was an experience of sheer grace.

A baby boy was born, whom the mother was never allowed to see. He was immediately put into a foster home. Three weeks later, the mother died. The children were distraught. Joy hauled them up and down the highways as they were part of the family grieving process. The little boy had to be affirmed that his father was yet alive. His father's sentence will be complete by the end of another year, but his parental rights may have been lost. The saga continues as the pain of rejection and abandonment batters both of those children's souls. Both of them are angry and hurt. The young woman, no longer a little girl, is filled with rage. Her acting out grows more and more wicked. Joy keeps praying and juggling. She is a real saint. Keep Joy and the children in your prayers.

Hear, O heavens, and give ear, O earth! For God has spoken: I have nourished and brought up children. —ISAIAH 1:2

Keeper of Children, our hearts grieve over the varied and sundry circumstances that children must face. We give you loving thanks for those with hearts big enough, wide enough, and charitable enough to reach out and take in those both with and without blood ties. You have adopted us and brought us into your royal and regal family. Help us to be so inclusive that those in our homes always know a warm welcome and gentle acceptance. Teach us how to reach the deep hurt within these little souls. Give us the wisdom to see beyond the acting out and feel the pain that is behind the behaviors. As you so often gather us to your bosom and provide comfort, help us do the very same. We pray in the name of the One who said, "Let the little children come unto me."

PRAYER FOCUS: Hurting little ones

28

You Can Do It!

*T*his is the day that the Lord has made and you can rejoice, be glad in it, and make it a great day! You can do it! For a "can do" spirit belongs to the people of God. Regardless of what is going on, in spite of how things appear, and no matter what seems to be the gruesome outcome, you can make it! I know that it feels many days as if you just can't make it through one more day! The challenges are overwhelming. The tasks are nonstop. And, the energy drain is awful. But you can do it! Take a deep, relaxing breath and hold on.

If I've never shared any valuable information with you before, listen up to this essential "411." This storehouse of wisdom will save you many headaches, heartaches, and lost energy in the days ahead. This is a piece of bought wisdom. This is a lesson I've had to learn the hard way while parenting this second time around. This is coming straight to you from my personal collection of hard knocks. So let me share with you a little "somin, somin" I've discovered in the past few days.

God wants us to know that every test, including this one, is only another step to our divine destiny. There is a bigger plan than what we can see with our natural eyes. There is a larger picture than what we can behold and see today. We are on a journey, following the Chief Shepherd. And there is One who knows the way we are to take! This is particularly important for those of us who are wrestling with whether or not we "need" to give up on a child that is acting out, cutting up, and challenging our last, good nerve. Listen up and prepare to be blessed with some sage advice.

We are sheep. But we are sheep who belong to God! As members of God's sheep fold, we always appear to be at the mercy of the big, bad roaring lions (especially those in little people clothing!). Lions are physically larger than sheep. Lions have fiercer voices than sheep. Lions are bold, courageous, and forward, while sheep are usually timid, afraid, and withdrawn. Yet God has named us sheep. Jesus named himself the Good Shepherd. So lions don't stand a chance against us! Wake up and smell the stench of the foolishness that we fall for too often. We get stumped and stuck by the roar of one with no teeth! Whatever problem you are wrestling with today is simply a toothless, roaring lion. Sound can and often does frighten us. But sound cannot destroy us!

As a sheep we need to know the pattern of lions. Like sheep, lions usually run together. While sheep are called a herd, a group of lions is called a pride. When the lions scope out a flock of sheep, the plan is that the pride will circle behind the them and lie down in the grass. They pretend they are harmless and nonaggressive. The females of the pride are the most savage, destructive killers. The males have the loudest roars. So the male with the biggest roar will go in front of the helpless flock and stand up and roar! Now, if the herd of little sheep turn around and run from the roar, what happens? They run smack dab into the rest of the pride!

The God we serve has a reputation of dealing with lions. Remember that Brother Daniel was put into a den of lions and God froze their mouths shut. Daniel slept with the pride of lions. "Stand still and see the salvation of the Lord," says Brother David in Psalm 42:10 as he remembered killing a lion who had come to destroy a member of his sheep fold. The lesson for this day is that lions are supposed to roar. A growing kid is supposed to act a fool! But sheep are not supposed to turn around in the midst of the noise and run backwards into destruction. Stand still; the Good Shepherd is on the scene. The Good Shepherd did not take a vacation, go on holiday, or run off to leave us alone! The Good Shepherd hears the sound of the furious, noisy roaring. The lion is in for a big surprise! In fact, so are we!

We have a divine purpose. We were created with a divine design. We are not left alone to fight the lion by ourselves. Remember, noise and fury cannot and will not defeat you! Stand still. For heaven's sake don't turn around to run away! For the danger is already behind you! (Did you get this? Did this compute for you? The worst is behind you, not in front of you!) This allows us to stand boldly on the alert for the Good Shepherd to show up and show out, despite the loud roar of the Toothless One!

God does not look good as we run away to be destroyed. Or as we throw up our hands in discouragement because we are going through a rough period with the children in our care! Finish what has been assigned to your hands this day. Don't let the noise, the sound, and the roar of a toothless lion scare, defeat, or depress you. In John 10, Jesus has already promised, "I lay down my life for my sheep and no one will take them out of my hand." This is good news as we engage all the noise of this day. This is good news as we engage the challenges before us. This is good news to encourage our hearts and invigorate our spirits as we move on up a little higher. This is good news as we determine this day to be a living testimony that dumb-looking sheep are wiser than big, bad roaring lions, regardless of the suit, dress, or play clothes that they are hiding within!

Stay focused. Stand still. For standing firm today is enough victory! Finish what you have started. You can do it! God's got your back! And that's good enough!

> However, I consider my life worth nothing to me, if only I may fin-
> ish the race and complete the task the Lord Jesus has given me—
> the task of testifying to the gospel of God's grace. —Acts 20:24

God of Timid Sheep and Roaring Lions, we come for your courage and wisdom. Our adversary, called by Jesus the prince of this world, is on a rampage and wreaking havoc on the hearts, minds, and spirits of our youth. We get tired. We get disgusted. We get fed up. It seems easier to give these children to others and rid ourselves of their troubled and pain-filled beings. Yet, we remember that you have never given up on us! We have played the fool. We have worked hard not to live up to our potential. We have wasted both time and talents. But your compassion waited on us to see your light. The noise that we hear is loud. Our human feelings say, "Walk away." Yet we hear you plead, "One more chance might make the difference!" Restore us. Strengthen our resolve to do your will and not our own, we pray in the name of the One who protects sheep and tames roaring lions.

Prayer focus: Those facing the roaring lions

GREAT GRACE

*I*t happened at Marriott's World Convention Center in Orlando, Florida. Chuck and I had taken Giraurd to Disney World. Isn't this every grandparent's dream for the grandchildren? We had tried to find all of the wonderful side trips that would excite, stimulate, and be fun for a "little guy." Of course, this included all the video arcade "stuff," which seems to draw boys of all ages. The arcades are not cheap. We had given him all we were willing to put into those baby slot machines, for which he had received little in return. Sales people know how to put the arcades where the most traffic passes by. This one was on the way to the swimming pool.

It was another day. The instructions to Giraurd were "Keep your eyes peeled on the pool. We are not stopping at the video arcade today." As a matter of fact, I had him by the shoulders, trying to steer his neck straight ahead! My goal was "no temptation!" We were walking down this long, beautifully apportioned hallway, and I nodded my head (you know the old southern style hello that Granny usta give) toward the shoe shine man, who was standing there awaiting business. We were wearing sandals, so he knew that we were not potential customers. As we passed him by, walking quickly to reach the pool just outside the door, he ran up and grabbed Giraurd by the shoulder.

The mother lion in me arose! But before I could act a fool, or even make a comment, he said to Giraurd, "Hold out both of your hands." Giraurd held up one small hand. The man replied, "I said hold out both of your hands." When Giraurd held up both hands, in cup style, the shoe shine man filled them to overflowing with arcade tokens! Talk about an awesome gift of grace and mercy for a little boy.

That man had just been waiting for an opportunity, not to make money, not to receive, but to serve God by serving someone else. I will never forget this act of grace and mercy. I will never forget the shoe shine man from Florida. He taught me several lessons that day. He taught me the art of being a blessing to little ones. Giraurd wasn't a potential customer. Giraurd wasn't a man who had the ability to be a big tipper. Giraurd didn't look like someone with wealth, status, or position. Yet, Giraurd was the recipient of bountiful blessings from a man who understood the need for grace and mercy.

The shoe shine man didn't give us his card so that we would write him up as "employee of the month." He didn't even wait around for us to finish picking up the coins that had fallen to the floor. His was an act of grace and mercy to a little boy with no means of repaying him, and he turned around and went back to doing business as usual. I learned again that day that those we tend to overlook, discount, and diminish are sources of blessings. If only we would open our eyes, our hearts, and both of our hands!

Parenting for another turn is evidence that you already know this gift of being grace and mercy to others. Without a doubt you have a generous spirit. However, those within our care need that "both-hands-filled-often" blessing that only we can provide. Sometimes it comes in a long hug, big kiss, and whispered "I love you so much." At other times it might be a day where you get away together on a "date." Perhaps it might be as simple as renting a video and sharing a bag of popcorn.

Giraurd and I spend some special days off from school at the local bookstore. We go and find books and magazines we like to read and peruse. Then we order and share a sandwich. Finally I enjoy my hot tea and he gets a favorite drink, and we look at our tall displays and laugh together. Many days we don't purchase anything of significance, maybe a sale item or a card, but the time spent sharing the hours "fills up both of our hands!" Memory making is always a grand gift of God's grace and mercy! Try it.

You'll like it. And you'll be remembered as being as kind as the shoe shine man!

> For even Jesus did not come to be served, but to serve and to give his life as a ransom for many. —MARK 10:45

Cup Filling God, thank you for the making of memories. Thank you for those who come along and just decide to bless us with goodness and with undeserved grace. They act on your behalf. They act in your stead. They act at your prompting. Give me the heart of the shoe shine man! Allow me to be as spontaneous. Help me to be as generous. Make me as loving to these I know as that man was to a child he didn't know. Forgive me for too often neglecting to do small kindnesses for those around me and reserving my great acts of charity for those away from my home! In the name of the One whose every impulse was grace filled and merciful, I pray.

PRAYER FOCUS: Shoe shine men and women

AN AMAZING MOM CONTEST

$\mathcal{M}$y biological sister, Jacquie Brodie-Davis, entered the following letter in a Tom Joyner radio show contest. It details the amazing ability that so many of us have who continue to enlarge our hearts to allow others room inside. The story needs to be shared. For it provides another model of parenting for us.

Jacquie wrote:

I know two Amazing Moms for the Thursday Morning Mom's Contest. I raised one son, Troy Cameron, who recently married Kristie and made me "Granny J" with my new grandson, Troy, Jr. Raising Troy was certainly a challenge. But my sister Reine, also a grandmother, has a best friend, Theresa, who is the mother of one son. I write to tell you Theresa's story. It has truly touched me.

For the past eight years, Theresa has been both aunt and mom to thirteen of her nieces and nephews. Theresa's sister, Willa, had four children. One of her sons was killed in 1989. Willa accepted responsibility for her nine grandchildren. This dynamic duo needed a plan. Willa, having the job with a better salary, became the "sole bread winner" and Teresa managed the household responsibilities and child rearing. In April of 1996, another of Willa's sons needed family to come to his rescue, and four more grandchildren were lovingly taken into their home.

When their church mother, Mrs. Mollie Walker, stepped into eternity at the age of one hundred, part of the family listed in her obituary were "her girls." These girls were Theresa, Willa, and Riene, who are all fifty-plus. None of them are related to Mother Walker by biology. But these women, who had known her all of their lives, stepped in to care for her as she outlived all of her biological kin. Each one gave of her time, her money, and especially her love to one in need. For over fifteen years, "the girls" cleaned her home, shopped, and spent the nights with her, for Mother Walker became blind and wanted to remain in her home. They cooked all of her meals and Theresa delivered them and fed Mother Walker three times daily, even during the last two years of her life when she was confined to a nursing home and refused to eat the facility's food.

These women certainly epitomize the unique dedication of true unsung "Sheroes"! The list could go on and on for the many ways they need to share the monetary gift. Theresa's birth son needs financial assistance to continue his college education. Their family van needs rear-end repairs and they want to take all of the cousins to visit another one who is developing his skills at a Job Corp Center far away.

My prayer is that the love of God, the peace and harmony of Christ, and the power of the Holy Spirit all be involved in the selection of these two sisters, who more than deserve the title and monetary reward of Amazing Moms.

And Jesus said, "Whatever you have done for the least of these, my little ones, you have done it unto me." —MATTHEW 25:40

God of all, to you we raise these our petitions for those who change their lives, rearrange their agendas, totally shift their priorities, and dismiss their personal schedules to reach out and enfold your "little ones"! We are so aware that the most vulnerable people in the whole wide world are the children and the elders. Thank you for loving the "little ones" through those with big hearts, generous spirits, and tender mercy. We join with Jacquie and bless the

names, the lives, and the continuing ministry of both Theresa and
Willa. We pray for their family. We certainly do pray for their
strength in you, Dear God. Wrap your arms around each one of
them. Speak peace to their weary bodies. Touch their spirits with
the rain of refreshing. Allow the Holy Spirit to shower them with
the words that say, "Well done, good and faithful servants." You
promised that their children would rise up and called them blessed.
We join in the name calling of these very special moms who open
their hearts, their homes, and their pocketbooks, time and time
again. Be glorified in the life of every child, we pray. Let them bless
these, their mothers, in return. Plant in each of them a great spirit
of gratitude for the multiple sacrifices made by these sisters. You
take note of dying flowers and birds, so we know these women are
recorded in your book of saints. Thank you for the witness of their
lives. Please open every financial door of opportunity for them and
others in like situations whose names we will never know. We ask
all these blessings in the name of the One who himself came as a
"little one" and is now our Christ. Amen.

PRAYER FOCUS: Moms sharing the roles

DANCING IN THE SPIRIT!

$\mathcal{H}$ow do you describe ministry in motion? What words can detail a poem floating through the air? When have you ever seen lyrics twirling, notes swirling, cords dipping, and music floating right in front of your eyes? It's called liturgical dance. It's praise to God, offered through a body moving to the words of a song. At its best, the dancer's name is Mishaela.

Mishaela Parks is the adopted daughter of another grandmother who is an artist in ministry. Rev. LaSaundra is truly an urban minister. For she takes the message of love to the streets and will bring those in the streets into her home! She's a beautiful woman with some of the most strangely colored eyes I've ever seen. She looks at you directly and sees what you do not say! She sings, plays keyboard, writes music, leads praise and worship, teaches, preaches, and opens her heart to receive the people of God. She is anointed. She flows in the power of the Holy Spirit. She is what she claims, one who reaches out to the needy in the urban area.

LaSaundra's three children are now adults, out on their own. She has a delightful granddaughter by her daughter, Ebony, a single mom. So Rev. Grandma is available! Some years ago, one of her friends' daughters had a baby. That infant was named Mishaela. Things happen. Mishaela was given into the care of the state authorities. The urban minister wasn't having that!

The state officials told her all sorts of troubling things about Mishaela's behavioral issues, her acting out, and claimed that the future for her was "questionable." The Reverend didn't listen to them. She took the child home as a foster child. She began to sing to the little girl. She danced with the little girl in her arms. She took Mishaela everywhere she went to minister. That little girl calmed down. The issues of behavior became less and less. The grades of that little girl began to climb. Soon she began to sing. Then she discovered dance.

Mishaela's dance ministry is pure joy. Her dance begins on the inside and works its way to the outside. She dances with her mind. She dances with her spirit. She dances from her heart. She is sheer poetry in motion. In the city of San Diego, she is already a liturgical "star." She is soft spoken and petite. She is gentle and gracious. She is well mannered and well behaved. She is gifted and talented. She ministers to all ages. She draws children and is now involved in the training of the smaller and younger children, who are a part of Perpetual Praise, a liturgical dance troupe, sponsored by Rev. LaSaundra's ministry, the Gathering Place.

We don't know who made the "misdiagnosis" of Mishaela. We do know that Rev. LaSaundra invested and continues to invest in this young woman who is a wonder to the Church.

Our foreparents used to tell us that we needed to "Hear Melindy Sing." But I'm a living witness that you haven't had a real praise experience until you see Mishaela dance!

> Now as the ark of the Lord came into the city of David, Michal, Saul's daughter, looked through a window and saw King David dancing before the Lord . . . —2 SAMUAL 6:16

Creator of Holy Movement, that awesome woman named Wisdom says in Proverbs 8 that she danced at your making of the universe and its inhabitants! David, the king, danced before your altar as the Ark of Covenant was brought back home, until his pants fell down! These were the origins of dancing in praise to your glory in the earth. The beauty, the majesty, the awesome scenes that unfold before us cause our heart to skip, our tongues to sing, our arms to lift in praise, and our feet to dance! Thank you for the ministry of motion, movement, and mobility that assists us in giving you worthy and worshipful praise. And when we age and cannot make the moves due to bodily restrictions and limitations, help us to know that you receive the dance we do in our spirits! We pray in the name of the One who died and rose so that we might have the abundant life that makes us dance!

PRAYER FOCUS: Those without a dance in their spirit

EVERY MONDAY

$\mathcal{W}$e sat next to each other at the book sales area of a convention for women. She looked innocent enough. She was selling books of poems. She asked me if I would like to hear one that she'd written. Of course, I agreed to a personal reading. The poem rocked me. I bought the book. For the poem reminded me of why I'm in Giraurd's life and why he's in mine! Every Monday morning, as I send him off for another week of school, I'm grateful for the privilege we both have.

Rebera Elliott Foston, M.D., is a physician with a masters degree in public health, who specializes in adolescent care. She is also a preacher, teacher, workshop leader, and national consultant. She cares about our children. I offer you her poem in order that you might be encouraged to continue the often difficult task before us. It's worth it. Think of it every Monday morning.

> For as long as I can remember
> I have always wanted to teach
> I thought with patience and love
> Some children I would reach.
> At first I had so much joy
> teaching kids that were not that smart
> knowing I was helping some child
> get off to the right start.
> But, I can't do this much longer
> No one warned me I could feel this way
> But, you should hear what I have to hear

Lord, every Monday.
One child told me how he got a big bruise
Another one hadn't slept
One hadn't eaten all weekend
While another just sat and wept.
One child's hair hadn't been combed
Another had really bad breath
One seemed wired on something
While another seemed bored to death.
One child smelled of cheap alcohol
Another one smelled of weed.
One just wanted to talk about sex
While another, on himself, he peed.
One child came in very late
and to me, he looked the worst
but then I remembered, he's always like that
the Monday, after the "first."
I don't know how much more of this
I can actually stand
When my own life is in shambles
Shoot, I don't even have a man!
But, if I give up people will talk
and I know exactly what they will say
"She called herself a teacher,
she was just in it for the pay."
But, they don't see what I see
or know about the things I pray
and they don't walk into my "preschool" class
Lord, every Monday!

(Rebera Elliott Foston, *In God's Time* [Gary, Ind.: Foston Adolescent
Workshop, 1996], 14. Used by permission.)

And God has made everything beautiful in its time!
—ECCLESIASTES 3:11

Time Maker God, we approach you in awe. We stand before your timelessness aware of our finite state. You carved time out of eternity. One day time will cease, as eternity rolls on, and you will require of us an account of our allotted time. Help us to be faithful with these precious few moments on the scale of eternity. Help us to be conscious of the fact that we are only investing miniseconds into the lives of these who face every Monday morning! Bless both students and teachers, we pray in the name of Jesus Christ.

PRAYER FOCUS: Those who face school every Monday

Is It Time for a New Rinse?

$\mathcal{H}$e is a busy bishop. He has pastors, congregations, and an entire Annual Conference waiting for him. He has a schedule that is crazy. He has to be on the go like the Energizer Bunny! He is a writer with a monthly deadline. He has reports to make. He sits on national and international boards. He is accountable to the Council of Bishops. He is in demand as a preacher across the country. He has a wife and adult children. It's time for him to think about slowing down. He's been in this rat race for over thirty years. Yet, in the midst of all the things on his "to do" list, he must find time each month to go and have the gray rinsed from his hair! He and his wife have adopted their grandson. They don't want him to be afraid that gray hair equals approaching death! So he keeps a date to have the gray rinsed from his hair. It's a necessary and standard appointment. Their daughter was in college when she got pregnant. Like many of us, they stepped up to the plate and accepted responsibility for her infant. The daughter returned to school. They adapted their life around the baby.

Woodie has been gray for many years. He began to gray in his late twenties. It helped him to "look" wiser and more mature. For he was on the fast track to the international spotlight in the denomination. The gray was almost a trademark of the years of service as pastor, preacher, leader, mediator, and activist. He talks relatively slowly. He smiles nonstop. He is extremely soft-spoken. And he is dearly loved and adored. He openly shared the new baby with audiences around the country. It was taken as a given. It was no big deal. Both he and his wife were known for their big hearts and generous spirits. So the "normal and usual" questions began to be asked about the new child in the family.

The first meeting that he walked into with all-black hair will never be forgotten! It was shocking. It was surreal. At first you couldn't actually put your finger on what was wrong, different, unusual about Woodie. But it was so very obvious that something had changed. Being the open man he is, he addressed the "new" Woodie in his opening remarks.

He and his wife had decided to adopt the baby. They were not willing to be simply grandparents. They made the choice to become parents for the little boy they never had. They reasoned that little boys need youthful, playful, strong, assertive father figures to emulate. They didn't need the worry and concern that "Granddad" or "Grandmother" would soon be leaving them in death. So the gray hair had to go! It made sense to those of us who listened. Woodie keeps that standard appointment to make his son feel more secure. That's a good thing! It's the manly thing to do!

But the very hairs of your head are all numbered . . .

—LUKE 12:7

Wisdom of the Universe, we approach you with humble gratitude for the hairs upon our head. And, as you have chosen us, aging, balding, and graying, to care for babies and the young, we pause to thank you for rinse, dye, tints, wigs, extensions, falls, and pieces, which help us to feel better about ourselves and give a measure of security to these who look to us for care. This day we bless the barbers and beauticians that hook us up! Accept our thanks in the name of Jesus Christ.

PRAYER FOCUS: Barbers and beauticians

WISDOM IS A LITTLE GIRL

*E*very one of us needs to have a copy of the movie *Mulan*! We had to go and take Giraurd to see it when it was the new Disney release. I sat down, prepared to eat my popcorn and take a quick snooze, until I heard the voice of Mushu, the wannabe dragon, who sounded suspiciously like Eddie Murphy. Did I ever wake up! The movie tells the story of a young Chinese girl who is expected to be loyal to her family traditions, get married, have a child, and be a good wife to the man selected by the marriage maker. But the best laid plans go astray.

When the Emperor decrees that a man from each family must serve in the Imperial Army to fight off the invasions of the mighty Hun warriors, her crippled father must return to active duty. Although Mulan knows that the consequences of impersonating a man for any reason are dire, she decides to enter the army in her father's place. She prays before the ancestral altar, and Mushu the "wannabe" is dispatched as a guardian spirit to provide her with wisdom.

Mulan goes off to war. The story is wonderful. This movie is a "must see" for every little girl in our homes! For this movie teaches us and the little girls we are responsible for the lessons of courage, honor, and love. The heroine of the movie turns out to be even wiser than Mushu (although that character was hugely funny!).

The young woman is not Christian. Yet in her tradition she shows others the power of family love; she instills in them honor and respect for the Elders, and she shows them how to seek the guidance of Wisdom in every endeavor. She is part of a wonderful family, although she is an only child and a mere girl! She is a rebel spirit and her father loves her in spite of her nonconforming ways.

For she does not please the matchmaker, who personifies tradition and the Chinese Way. Mulan's grandmother lives with them and is a stitch with her witty and uncensored remarks. She loves and accepts Mulan and provides her with much wisdom.

Many might feel that Mulan is foolish in risking her life by impersonating a man and entering the army. Many might conclude that she put the lives of "worthy men" at risk when she could not measure up to their physical strength. But wisdom provided her with ways to get around "manly strength." For what macho brawn cannot do, the wisdom of the Ancient of Days teaches her to accomplish.

This is the same type of wisdom our little girls (and big girls) need today! This is the very same wisdom that led Harriet Tubman to lead slaves to freedom in Canada as a female Moses. It was this same wisdom that called Isabella Bumpry to change her name to Sojourner Truth and demand the right to vote for people of color. This is the same wisdom that led Mary McCloud Bethune to begin an educational institution on a garbage dump and Mary Church Terrill to enlist the powers that be to begin the NAACP. Wisdom has led many women to do the seemingly insane and win despite their "femaleness." And Wisdom ain't through yet!

Who knows what secret wisdom lies within the very soul of the little girl in your home? Who can predict her destiny? Who can determine what role God has destined her to play in the future? No one who looked at Mulan or any of the above-named women could see greatness within them. Yet it was there all the time. This is the day when you need to hug that little girl and look deeply into her eyes. Perhaps she'll share a secret or two with you!

Wisdom is more precious than rubies and nothing you desire can compare with her. —PROVERBS 8:11

Wisdom of the Ages, we come with gratitude and with praise. How like you to pour wisdom into us, finite human beings. How like you to share with us the secrets of the universe, hidden from the naked eye, but planted deeply within our spirits. How like you to be so loving that you shared wisdom with both males and females, as you created, in the beginning! Thank you for being an equal opportunity God! Help us to look as closely at the little girls in our homes as your divine vessels of honor as we do the little boy children. Help us to teach them to expect great things of themselves. Thank you for the gracious gift of divine Wisdom, a free gift to all who ask. And, by the way, God, I'm asking for more for myself! In the name of the Christ, I pray.

PRAYER FOCUS: Little girls

W H A T   A R E   Y O U   L O O K I N G   F O R ?

*T*his is a true story! There is no stretching of the truth involved. There is no need for the use of your imagination. This is a true story! Anyone of us over the age of thirteen has had this real life experience. It's part of growing up. It's the cycle of adult formation. It's the process required of each one of us as we seek for someone to love. We all do it. We swear we won't, but we do anyway. This true story reveals that a woman, a sister, was in the dark, in a graveyard, looking for a man!

You know what it feels like to be in the dark. You know how it feels to be lost in a relationship. Especially with those we have already raised and watch go out into the world on their own. You know how it feels to believe that all hope is gone; the future is dim and there is no sunshine for tomorrow! For the children that we have raised have the ability to make their own decisions. And they, like us, make choices that others do not like! We have all been there! It's part of the life cycle. We love. We lose love. We feel adrift, torn apart, left behind with a sinking pit in our stomach. At that particular time you feel that love has bid you a fond farewell.

It's drama at its best. "Good-bye, cruel world!" In our growing up years, we live soap opera lives. There is no need for us to video-tape "all my children, searching for tomorrow" without discovering "the guiding light," when too many of the characters we allow in our life should win academy awards for their stellar performances!

This story is for my sisters. After viewing the movie entitled *The Brothers,* I feel they need to listen up too! For the Holy Scriptures reveals a story about a group of women going on a hunt for a dead body! This is a resurrection story. Without a limo service, without a motor bus, and without male escorts, this group of sisters were on their way to the cemetery in the dark, without a clue of whom they were looking for, before the break of dawn. And, like too many sistas, they were carrying their stuff with them to take care of a dead man. It's serious business. It's a sista habit we need to break!

Easter is truly about the business of our getting up, moving on, doing differently, and starting all over, fresh and new! We cannot move into this new relationship with grandchildren, doing the same "dead" things over and over again. We cannot reraise our children. But we can take a different route of parenting with these "new" children left in our charge. We don't have the privilege of being their grandparents and spoiling them. We didn't get a "manual" with the first set of children and on-the-job training is not always effective. We can go and take refresher courses called "Effective Parenting." Our county and state institutions offer all sorts of helpful aids to make our parenting skills stronger.

Come on, be honest, how many times have you stood waiting at the window, watching the cars, counting the stop lights, waiting for your significant other or older children to come home? How many times have you dialed the car phone, the cell phone, and the pager trying to hunt down someone who's lost, on a dead-end street called "Nowhere"? How many times have you gotten in your car, used your gas, expended your energy to search for someone unworthy of your time, only to be hurt, dis'ed, and insulted when you discovered where their tired behind had been all the time?

These sisters had no great expectations. They were on their way to do what women usually did, minister to both babies and dead men! Jewish women had little social value unless they were mothers. So they took care of the babies they birthed. Then when anyone died in the community, the women were the "official" mourners, who also did the embalming with oils and spices. The women were in the dark about new life. They did not even know how they were going to roll the stone away from the door of the tomb, being the fragile females that they were. But they were on their way to do their duty. They were filled with sorrow. They were in the dark. They had to be afraid. You know we don't do cemeteries before high noon! We have serious issues with graveyards. But these sisters were there.

The stone was rolled away! The grave was empty. The dead man had gotten up! Resurrection had occurred! Easter had happened! And the sisters were challenged by God's messenger's, "Why do you look for the living among the dead?" (Luke 24:5–6) What a question for us to ponder and reflect upon.

We can't keep doing the "same ole, same ole" after resurrection! The "stone" blinders have been removed. The "stone" excuses are gone. The "stone" reasons are lame. It's time for change. New life has come. Why are you seeking life among dead things? What makes you think that something good is coming your way out of the graveyard? Jesus was not there!

Thank God for the women who pressed on in the dark to discover the empty tomb! Thank God for the sisters who, in their blindness, continued to forge ahead. But, when the word of new life reached them, out of the cemetery they went to tell the good news! Thank God they passed the word that Jesus rose as he had promised. Jesus Christ was a promise keeper. I pray you come out of that place of dead things. The stone has already been rolled away. The promise is that new life is already awaiting you! Now, look at that little child again! This is our new life story!

I pray a blessed resurrection in your spirit indeed! I pray that the Christ of Easter enlarges your borders and gets you out of graveyards, wherever they may be. I pray God's mighty hand protects you as you spring to new life. And I pray you are never a "dead thing" for anyone else! It's time for you and me to discover new ways in order that we might tell new stories!

Why are you looking for living among the dead? —LUKE 24:5–6

God of the new, this business about learning new ways to parent scares me. Yet, I know that I allowed too many things to slip past me the first time around. Now I'm older and wiser. And, God, you know that I'm also more tired and certainly often weary. New ideas, different concepts, additional theories, and patterns might make sense. But, why me? Why now? Okay, I'm whining. I'm complaining, but at least I'm entertaining the idea that there might be something else I can learn in this new parenting time. Don't make me have to search too hard or too long. Help me to discover a place where new knowledge can be obtained while I can have fun, relax, and be with others who understand this journey, the second time around. Maybe it's time for something new. For, God, I certainly don't want to be a "dead thing," in the way of these I'm modeling for today. Bless me as I, like those women, see the stone rolled away and find the new life that is in store. Thanks be to the Risen Savior. Amen.

PRAYER FOCUS: Those choosing to stay with dead things

IT'S ALL ABOUT THE SEASONS

*O*ne of the great mysteries of God is the way the seasons roll around and change. They come without fanfare. They come without too much disturbance. They don't need grand announcements. They don't wait for our individual invitations. The seasons just change. It makes no difference what your favorite season is, the other seasons are coming and they must be endured. For God designed creation with four different and distinct seasons.

Nora knows about changing seasons. Born in Alabama, part of a huge family with eighteen children, she entered life in the season of winter poverty. It was a hard and difficult life. Her parents were farmers who lived on the outskirts of town. She and her siblings were laughed at, looked down upon, and talked about due to their family size and for being the least of the least. Nora says her memories of that season are filled with unhappy reminders of those who looked like her making fun of her. She was in a hurry to leave the South.

Her older siblings moved to the Midwest and sent for their younger sister. She moved and married and soon began her own family that included four children. When they thought that the spring season had finally brought flowers into their life, she and her husband were surprised with the news of twins at midlife! She had begun working toward her life's dream of being a nurse. She was in college. She was living her dream. Then, pregnancy and starting over. School became a thing of the past.

The twins were born and were healthy. The older children were able to help with their care. She was working and back in college.

Surely, the summer of life was smiling upon her. She had found and claimed Jesus as Lord and Savior. She was busy everywhere. She was living the life she dreamed. And then one day her finger began to swell. After months and months of doctors, hospitals, and clinics, the diagnosis came of a debilitating disease. Nora had sarcoid that had attacked her lungs and bones. She had to go on disability. Once again the season of her life was changing. Without notice. Without warning. Without fanfare she was pushed into a changing environment.

Prayer became her friend. Seeking understanding. Longing for answers. Pleading for direction. Nora prayed. It was a good thing. For her twins were growing and doing well. It was one of the older daughters who began acting out. She seemed to change before her family's eyes. It was the story of drugs and drugs' misuse of our families. Prayer was the only solace. The downward slide began.

A child was born to Nora's daughter. A mother on drugs doesn't really have the capacity to care. The grandparents took that little boy home. Nine years later, another little boy was born. The grandparents brought him home from the hospital. They were granted legal guardianship of both boys. They are the parents. The mother continues her spirals. The grandparents wonder what season will approach them next. Where is their summer? Is this their fall? Sometimes is seems like winter is just around the corner. But there are two little boys dependent upon them. There is a daughter, "out there" who needs love, compassion, and understanding. When will their season allow them to enjoy the life they so richly deserve?

The questions haunt Nora even as she sees peeks of summer sun upon their horizon. She and her spouse have been blessed with a big fifteen-room house, which accommodates them all with room to spare. Nora loves to entertain and there is a garden growing out back. Her husband enjoys the big yard. The boys have a nice and safe environment in which to live, grow, and play. God is the miracle worker who smiles upon them in every season. Nora says, "My seasons continue to change. I never know what one is coming next. But, I know who controls the seasons. And that's good enough for me."

She lives as if she means it! There's a constant smile upon her face, even when her heart is breaking. She and her husband fast and pray together. For they are jointly involved in this parenting, the second time around. It is their season of "wait and hope in God's goodness."

> To everything there is a season, a time for everything under heaven. —ECCLESIASTES 3:1

Season Maker, we come and we wait and hope for the season of sunshine. Yet, in the deep, cold, and dreary season of winter, the yearning within us is there, alive and burning. We nest, we settle down, we draw closer to you and each other, but we long for signs of the Son/Sun! We understand the need for the earth to die, to rest, to replenish. We recognize your wisdom in this season of hunkering down and pulling within. Yet we pine for summer. For summer is the season of your smile. Summer is the season of refreshment. Summer is the season when your creation puts on its best face. When will our summer come? When it comes will it be all that we dream? Or will it be a summer of scorching heat and no gentle rains? Will the summer produce our vision of play or will its reality bring drought and lack of bountiful harvest in the fall? God, you know best. We wait. We hope. Bless us in this season. Let us find your grace wherever we happen to be today. We pray in the name of Christ.

PRAYER FOCUS: Those waiting on a new season

LET THE MUSIC NEVER STOP

$\mathcal{R}$onnie is an accomplished musician. Ronnie is a sought-after minister of music. Ronnie is a woman who loves to share the word of God in song. Like many of us she was raised in the church and learned first to play piano by ear as she sat through rehearsal after rehearsal as a child. Music lessons in both school and with private instructors brought Ronnie to a level of professionalism that is enhanced through her spiritual gifts of encouraging the people of God and her abiding faith in God. Music has helped her to make it through many long nights.

Pretty, outgoing, and often in the spotlight, she married a man from her youth. They had a child. But the husband refused to grow up, and the marriage ended in divorce. Ronnie raised her son alone. She worked to ensure that he had what he needed. She worked to make sure that he never felt deprived. He was a smart child. He never gave his mother reason to doubt that his future would be secure. After high school, he went to a historical, black college. His mother continued working, ministering music and giving private lessons to allow him his college years.

Having a boy, Ronnie often felt safe. Of course they had the talks about sex, protection, and "the birds and the bees." Their relationship was fairly open and comfortable. Ronnie was counting the years until his graduation. Then life would be easier, she comforted herself. She was the provider. "Soon, this will be over, and then I can . . ." she imagined. Nothing could get in the way of his and her emancipation! She hummed. She sang. She played. The melodies pushed her forward.

It was his last year of college. She had driven with him to help him unpack his apartment. He was going to live off campus and get a taste of adult freedom. She had flown home, happy as a lark. The last year! "Freedom is coming," was her theme song, until the phone call came and the music stopped. "Mom, this girl is pregnant. She claims that I'm the father."

Ronnie was hurt. Ronnie was shocked. Ronnie was angry. "Didn't I teach you about protection?" But Ronnie had no idea what the lack of protection would mean for both her and her son. For the girl's parents were not having any part of a pregnancy! They forbade her to come home. They had sacrificed too much for her to go to school, only to return with another mouth to feed. They would not relent. They did not recant. The baby was born. The mother left the infant in the hospital. When her son called, Ronnie went to pick up her granddaughter!

Babies come to earth still singing the angelic tunes of their pre-existence. Ronnie heard the melody. She begin to hum again. The music returned to her soul. She learned new tunes and added sharper pitches and more melodious concerts to soothe her own soul and to bring security to a new addition to her life. She and the baby attended the graduation. All three of them returned to Ronnie's home. They have lived together now for over eight years. It's a sound of beautiful music.

Ronnie continues to work. She continues to minister music. She continues to attend rehearsal after rehearsal. She has someone new to accompany her these days. The music continues. It's a new harmony. It's weaving together a third generation song.

The women had come out of all the cities, singing and dancing . . . with tambourines, with joy and with music . . . so the women sang as they danced . . . —1 SAMUEL 18:6–7

Music Maker, we approach you with hushed awe as we hear the songs of the rain and snow, the birds and hooting owls, the rustling leaves and flowing rivers, the calling animals and the rumble of thunder. There is music everywhere! It is all produced to offer honor and majesty to your created order. We thank you that there is no day, no time, no place where the cords of your harmony cannot be experienced. From the great rushing falls to the tinkling sleet there are rhythm and perfect pitch, which exalt your wondrous name. The beating of our hearts is a tune that calls all of nature to attention. The pulsating blood in our veins courses with careful measure. The music of your glory cannot be escaped. Thank you for the gift of music. It calms our soul. It lifts our spirits. It stills our fears. It lulls our anxiety. It brings peace into our lives. Always give us a song. The tune may change. The beat may differ. But we need a song from you to make it through. You are our music. Place your notes of love within our hearts and let the song continue. We pray in the name of Perfect Pitch!

PRAYER FOCUS: For a new, God-given song

CAB IS NOT A CAR!

*H*onestly, I don't know if his name is Calab or Calip. We have always known him as Cab. He was adopted into our family when he was less than ten years old by our Aunt Barbara and Uncle Clint. He had been in the foster care system for most of his life. Of course there is a story about why. We all have stories about how we have become who we are today. I just know that my aunt and uncle had three daughters and one son, Clinton, Jr. My aunt was a social worker and the issue about whether or not black children ought be raised by white families had become a prominent discussion. The next thing we knew, there was a new cousin. We were told, "His name is Cab." It's over thirty years later and Cab is yet his name—the only first name that I know.

My uncle Clint was always my hero. He was my first "boyfriend." He stayed single for many years and went to Korea. We wrote back and forth to each other. When he returned from duty and got married, I traveled to Detroit for his marriage to Barbara Ruth. She was a member of the Nation of Islam. It was my first introduction to this "new" religion. For gifts they received huge bags of rice, beans, dried peas, and "unusual" food stuff because they don't eat pork. I went to "judge" whether or not this strange woman was worthy of my uncle. We became good friends. She was more than worthy! Since I was my uncle's adopted "daughter," she simply accepted me as a "lil sister" since we were relatively close in age. I remember the many good times when as a youth I "lived large" in Motown!

Barbara Ruth came from a large family. She had been raised by an aunt and uncle. The family dynamics and "good reasons" were never explained to me. They didn't need to be! Family is family is family. So, when they decided to adopt Cab it didn't seem strange. It seemed par for the course. They were both extremely generous and kind people. Cab was included as family, even though we all knew the horror stories of the labels that came attached to him from the state. Labels like "behavioral problem," and "attitude" and "dyslexic." Barbara quit her job and became a stay-at-home mother. And Cab adjusted well until his teen years.

Cab was not the "intellectual" that the other children were. He was a hands-on, tear-it-down and fix-it-up fellow. He didn't use the socially acceptable "standard" English, but continued to sound "ghetto," thinking it was cool. He began to act out in school. He was suspended and even expelled. We finally all celebrated his high-school graduation. But he wouldn't have anything to do with college. He was ready to get out and do his own thing. He wanted to prove himself. He wanted to "find himself." So he got an apartment and a job as a mechanic's helper.

The other children went on to institutions of higher learning. They remained at home. Cab would stop by on Sundays to see how folks were getting along. But he wouldn't stay long. Trouble seemed to follow Cab. My aunt and uncle were always there for him. He came to every family function. He became the family comedian, telling funny tales. He got a girl pregnant. The little boy looks just like him. But Cab refused to marry her. Now the little boy comes to family functions. We call him "cousin" too. He's family. So is his mother.

Four years ago, Cab's mom got sick with cancer. Cab was one of the most faithful of the children who came by to see what errands needed to be done. He cried harder than anyone else when Barbara died. He knew whom he had lost. Two years later, his dad got sick with cancer. Cab, again, was one of the most faithful children and came by to see what help could be rendered. He was the last one to leave the casket at Clint's funeral.

Cab just stood there. He looked long. He looked diligently. He looked hard. He called the other children to come back and to stand there, as they all looked at Dad for the final time. Cab knew whom he had lost. Cab has a little boy. Cab has four adopted siblings. Cab has a broken heart. For the folks who took him in, loved him, helped him, nurtured him, and stuck by him are gone. No! No! Cab is not a car. Cab is a man who knows the meaning of love and of loss.

> Be gracious to me, God, for I am in distress; my eye wastes away from grief, my soul and body also. For my life is spent with sorrow, and my years with sighing . . . —PSALM 31:9–10

God who knows the sorrow of a broken heart, we stand before death, and we are lost. Whether that death is the result of illness or the aging process, we are numb when death comes and snatches our loved ones away. Thank you for the gift of precious memories. Thank you for those who will dare invest themselves in the lives of those not born of their biological bloodlines. Thank you for the various reasons you provide for open hearts, open doors, and the opening of others' lives. Thank you for the gift of loving parents, regardless of how we came to them. Let the love we have received be shared with other needy souls. We pray in the name of One who adopted us into this royal family. Amen.

PRAYER FOCUS: Those who have lost their parents

IF IT WASN'T FOR ME

*I*f you search long enough, dig deep enough, read about, and look intensely enough, you'll find all sorts of women's truth hidden away in scripture. There is something to uplift and encourage women of all ages. We don't hear their stories often enough. We don't have a whole lot of information provided about them. But what the "forefathers" allowed into the canon gives some clues as to the importance of their lives.

As I sat in the car, on the way to another conference for women, having a "head" conversation with biblical women, a young slave girl jumped up, demanding that I hear her voice. I was busy writing about adults who were "serious sistas" when Ms. Mouth wouldn't shut up or go away. She said she been silent and unnamed too long. She claimed that she has been invisible, like too many domestics. But she was insistent that I tell her story and bring her to life. "You, the womanist. Will you also relegate me to the continent of the unheard?" I really had no further choice in the matter. She was telling the real truth.

It is not known who collected the history that is recorded in the two legends recorded in the Books of Kings. Scholars have attributed these stories to Jeremiah. The people of God had wandered off into idolatry and corruption, again. They found themselves embroiled in many wars that they lost. Their people were captured.

One of their most vicious enemies was the army of Aram. With their constant raids upon Israel, one little girl was captured and made a servant to the wife of Naaman, an Aramean army commander. Like most of the women and girls in scripture, Lil' Sista is unnamed. We are not given any physical description or genealogical background. It is enough to know that she became a domestic. The work is hard. The time is big. The duties are repetitive. The results are unappreciated. And the workers are all invisible!

I've been reading a series by Barbara Neely, an African American woman who has made an art of writing about being a domestic. Her protagonist, Blanche White, is a hoot. Girlfriend is forty-two, single, adopted mother of two, sassy, determined, sharp, and intelligent. Blanche appears first in *Blanche on the Lam*. She returns in *Blanche and the Talented Tenth*. The final sequel is *Blanche Cleans Up*. Blanche knows her business. She sizes up a house and its owners in short order. She can assess personalities from food preference, bedroom decor, and bathroom habits. She has a keen sense of perception and can unearth what many would prefer to leave buried. For as a domestic worker, Blanche sees her employees in the raw. She gave me much insight into our young sister who was serving Mrs. Commander.

Young, without family, in a foreign land, uneducated and a domestic employee, this child had a right to be real angry. "House workers" are not thought to be very intelligent, nor looked to for the value of their wisdom. Our Lil' Sista was just a child. Yet she seemed to have made a place for herself in the home where she was forced to live. She made such an impact that the storyteller records her work ethic. "She served" (2 Kings 5:2). She understood the value of making herself necessary. She picked up the "domestic skills" of acute listening and storing information. She discovered a household secret. Her male enslaver was captive to the disease of leprosy.

In a few days he would personally come to discover the inner thought life and lonely feeling of Lil' Sista. How ironic. I would have said, "Goody, goody, gumdrops!" I would have thought this was his "just due." I would have been glad to see my enslaver get the punishment of a long and slow death sentence. I would have kept my mouth shut, done my job, and been waiting for the day he was forced out of his home and away from his family. It's a good thing for him that I wasn't Lil' Sista.

She teaches all of us a better way. For she's a young woman with a heart of forgiveness, a spirit of compassion, and an attitude of caring and sharing. This young woman takes a risk and goes to give information to the woman of the house that saves her husband's life. This young woman had been taught about God in her home before slavery. She was stolen from her land. The lessons of love she brought in her heart.

Young. Enslaved. Exiled. Alone. A lowly, despised captive foreigner. An invisible domestic worker. This young woman saved a life. She saved a family. Her witness calls us to look beyond our own circumstances and to earnestly see into the hearts of those who are in our homes. Who knows what plan God has for the child that came to you in a special and unique way? This story is recorded to give us courage, inspiration, and motivation to look again at the gifts we too often overlook. She was a lifesaver. She simply wouldn't shut up!

Thus and thus said the girl who is from the land of Israel.

—2 KINGS 5:4

Speaking God, who talks to us through the mouths of the young, help us to look more closely and to listen more keenly to what the children are saying. Thank you for the gift of children who can see you so clearly. We pray in the name of Your Child. Amen.

PRAYER FOCUS: Talking children and listening adults

GRANDFATHERS NEEDED!

*I*t's all about choice! To be or not to be a father, for another time, demands a conscious decision. Grandfathers are not just born, they come about due to their personal acts of self-determination. A grandfather is not simply the individual who supplies the sperm that meets and matches the egg, which creates a new being. Often times, this is an incident of chance and not of choice. But a father is that male who chooses to be around, stay around, engage, role model, support, and encourage a little one into adulthood and beyond.

There are many male biological parents. There are too few honest-to-God fathers and grandfathers. I recognize that this paints a broad brush stroke across the male populace. However, the state of our runaway, wild, undisciplined, disrespectful, nonproductive youth is testimony enough to the reality of "too few fathers and grandfathers." There is something about a father that a mother cannot duplicate or replicate. There is something about a stick-around, stay-with-it male figure that impacts a life in ways I cannot articulate. The benefits of positive, consistent father and grandfather figures are evidenced through the enriched, rewarding, and productive lives of those who have been touched by real fathers. A real father, a real grandfather is a gift from God.

As we read Holy Scripture we discover many diverse father types. Some are strong, honest, and of good character. Others leave a bad taste in our mouth. Adam didn't have a biological father to role model for him. He was "born" and created an adult. So I wonder where he picked up his blaming, shaming qualities? Surely, he was not behaving like God! Yet Adam became a father and a role model for his sons. Cain picked up his father's worst traits—blaming and not taking responsibility for his actions. He even added physical murder to the list of sins. It was not a pretty picture. And it was all about choice. It's all about the consequences of the choices that we made. Too many fathers have made bad choices and their children suffer. Grandfathers are needed.

I salute Dock Wade, who stepped up. Dock never had a biological child. But he chose to be the father figure for my nine-year-old mother, who came from Mississippi to live with her aunt and uncle in the steel towns of the Midwest. Mom never knew her biological male parent. But as he "wandered" the earth, unmindful of his offspring, Dock and Eunice filled in the gap. That made him my grandfather and he was truly a "Grand Father" to me and my siblings. He was not related by blood to my mom; she was Eunice's sister's child. Yet, accepting her into his home, he raised her. He provided for her. He "gave her away" when she married in his home. She was his daughter.

Dock loved us. He provided for us. He stayed around. He worked after his retirement in order to assist his "daughter" with her eight children. She had a husband who worked. But his pay from the steel mills didn't provide the "extras." Uncle Dock and Aunt Eunice did! I'll never forget the morning we awoke to the sounds of playground equipment being placed in our back yard. That was unheard of in our neighborhood. But, we had a Grand Father! He played the numbers and, when he hit, our deep freezer got filled up. When he hit, Eunice was given money to "buy those kids something." When he hit, Christmas became better and we were in the Easter parade. When he hit, the back of his pickup truck would be filled with us and our friends, on our way for "treats and surprises"!

When he was eighty and Eunice was in her early seventies, they followed me off to college! They gave up their home and traveled with me to care for my children, their "great-grandchildren"! When I decided that I needed to finish college and make a decent living for my children, I followed my heart's dream, and my grandparents came along. We completed college! I graduated in May. Dock died in December of that same year. He had completed his role in our life. His memory is blessed. His life was dedicated to family. He showed his love toward me and my children and for that we will always be grateful.

Dock Wade is another name for dependability. Dock Wade is another name for accepting love. Dock Wade is another name for responsibility. Dock Wade is another name for grandfather. He taught my father about being a man. He taught my brothers about being a man. He taught me what to look for in a man! I salute grandfathers. I expect much from a grandfather. I anticipate that they will go the distance for the children in their care. Dock did. All real Grand Fathers do the same thing. For God knew that Grand Fathers would be needed!

> If you do what is right, sin is crouching at your door. It desires to have you. But you must master it. —GENESIS 4:7

Grand Father God, this is the name by which the Native Americans call you. I think that it's a regal concept when I remember my grandfather. Many don't have the gift of a "biological" grandfather. Yet, you have provided men of loving care, wisdom, and compassion all around us. They are present in the neighborhood. They are present in the church. Some are in the schools. Many are throughout our communities. Help children see Grand Fathers all around them, that they may know the genuine nurture and guidance of sage, wise counsel. Be glorified in the lives of those who step up to the plate and go the extra mile. Bless them, as they have blessed so many. We pray in the name of Love. Amen.

PRAYER FOCUS: The grandfathers and Grand Fathers who go the distance

C AUGHT U P S HORT ?

I really do consider myself to be somewhat of a fashion coordinator. When it comes to Mista Chuck and Giraurd, I have no doubt in my mind that no one can dress them more sharply than I! So it should come as no surprise that when Giraurd was in public school, I would lay out his clothes the night before. I recall one fall night laying out a wonderful little outfit with short sleeved shirt, slacks, and a lightweight jacket. Giraurd looked so cute.

When we got home that evening. Giraurd complained about being cold. I sent him upstairs to put on some long-sleeved pajamas. As we sat around the table eating dinner, he asked, "Grand, why did you send me to school with short sleeves on today?" "Grand" began to talk about the colors of his fashion wardrobe. Giraurd, being six, was not impressed with my color choice. As a matter of fact, colors meant nothing to him at that moment. For he pressed on. "I've been cold all day. It was rainy outside when we had recess. And my jacket didn't even have long sleeves. Grand, why did you let me get cold?"

I became defensive. "It was warm this morning. I didn't want you to get overheated." It was a logical explanation to me. But, Giraurd's answer was one of stunning fact. "Grand, didn't you watch the weather report last night? You have got to use your head!" As Mista Chuck tried to keep from that choking kind of laughter, all I could do was accept the very real fact that I had just been caught up short by a little child!

Talk about embarrassed! Believe me, I have been very careful since that occasion to be mindful of how I layer Giraurd for school. As a matter of fact, he's not in public school and has to wear a uniform, but the real deal is that they are layered also! Let me hurry to say that he yet finds my faults and lays out many of my deficits in the parenting area. And I can't argue with his logic. It's my responsibility to be the parent. It's his responsibility to need me to be the parent! He's a child. I cannot afford to be caught up short where he's concerned. He depends on me!

There are many occasions where we have been warned by God, reminded by God, and notified by God that we are not doing a sufficient job in the parenting area! Too often we refuse to change our inappropriate and offensive behavior. When the accusation is brought to our attention that there are severe consequences for our action, too often we want to cry "unfair." But God has provided us with ample notice that we are to train up the child in the way that they are to go. We cannot allow them to lead us down the yellow brick path while we foot the expenses for the trip!

There is no excuse for our children coming home with failing grades and bad conduct reports, for wreaking havoc in the neighborhood and acting unseemly in the church. We are the adults. Whether we were ready or not, we now have the serious responsibility of parenting again. And, it requires a hands-on approach! We have no excuses that will stand in the judgment. For we are the parents. The child is just that, a child who needs discipline and correction.

The handwriting is on the wall! The parents have already been numbered, weighed, and found short. That's why we have their children. Now, we have got to use our heads! (Giraurd's words of wisdom to me.) What they do might be cute today, but we have to stand before God for what values, morals, and spiritual nurture we provided or failed to provide. Didn't we get caught up short the last time we laughed at their little "cute" ways? What will it take to help us see that parenting the second time around demands more rigorous attention to the small details that we might have allowed to slide the first time around? This is serious business. God knows I don't want to be caught up short by God!

Mene. Mene. Tekel. Parsin. I have given you a number of days and you have not changed, straightened up, or decided to do the right thing! Count your days. Check your record. Recall how long you have gotten away . . . now, you have been weighed in my scales and found to be lacking! —DANIEL 5:26–27 (My very loose but literal translation)

Weighing, Watching God, HELP!

PRAYER FOCUS: Those not using their heads to parent

4 2

It's Always a Trip!

*M*y sister Riene is my surrogate "oldest child." I'm the oldest of eight siblings. Riene is my second sister. By the time she was born and nicknamed "Heavy Booty," I was old enough to be her chief care provider. She was a sweet and lovable child. She grew into a sweet and lovable woman. Yet Riene has always been a trip! She is brilliant. She is a poet, author, and public speaker. She is gracious, a cleaning and cooking genius, with a degree in culinary arts. And she talks like she was born in the deep, deep south. It takes her forever to tell you the main point of any story. She takes the long way. Any conversation with her is going to be lengthy. She has a granddaughter, Cierra, who is exactly like her. Together, they're a real trip!

Every year for the past several, we have been renting vans and taking Riene, her two granddaughters, Cierra and Ashante, and Giraurd on spring vacations across the country. Talk about some trips. Actually they can be fun. The children need to spend time together. Grand Mo, as Riene's grandkids call her, has a lot more patience with children than I have ever had. Cierra and Ashante are the daughters of Riene's oldest son and daughter-in-law, Carlton (Tony) and Lynne Morris. Tony is huge, massive, and tall. He is known as Big Mo. His petite wife is Ms. Mo. Their home is Morris Manor. Therefore, Riene is Grand Mo. I told you it was a trip!

Our first joint venture was to take all the children to visit the Mother Land of Mississippi. We have plenty of kinfolk there, as it's the birthplace of our grandparents and our mother. So we were going to visit the children's aunt, Agnes Robinson, a school teacher in Bay Springs. We met each other at a hotel with an indoor pool, which all the kids love, in Indianapolis, Indiana. Chuck's plan was that we'd drive for eight hours and spend the night at another hotel with an indoor pool in Memphis, Tennessee.

Who was going to sit where and by whom? How often did they get the chance to change seats? Who was messing with whom? When were we going to make a "pit stop"? Where were we going to eat lunch? When would we arrive at Aunt Agnes'? Chuck was driving. I was in the midst of trying to complete a manuscript that was due at the publisher upon our return, so I was "lost" in writing. Grand Mo was the one who had to answer questions, settle disputes, and keep order.

It was a trip! It was a worthy time of showing the children civil rights sites, sharing memories, and watching television news and documentaries come to life for them. It was a good trip having them go downstairs and prepare our breakfasts from the continental bar! It was a good trip having them able to swim indoors and enjoy the company of "the Cousins." It was a good trip having them be responsible for how they spent their allotted monies when we made the "pit stops" at convenience gas marts. It was a trip so delightful, as we looked at photo albums and shared with them the memories of our younger days at Aunt Agnes's. It was the trip that said we have to do it again. We have, and we continue our tradition of sharing quality time with the grandchildren and with each other.

When I talked to Riene recently, she said, "The girls are asking where is our next trip?" I knew what that meant. It's time to talk to Mista Chuck and get out the maps. It's time to plan the next trip! For family relationships are always worth the trip!

> Without ceasing, I make mention of you in my prayers, making request if, by some means, now at last I may find a way in the will of God to journey to you. For I long to see you . . .
> —ROMANS 1:10–11

Beginning and End of the Journey, how grateful we are for time to share in memory making with our families. Thank you for the ways that you connect us across the miles. Thank you for spouses, siblings, children, and grandchildren that make our many, various, and sundry journeys worthwhile. Thank you for the safety that you provide, the angels who go before us to make our way plain. Thank you for the means you provide that allow us times of refreshing, renewal, and recreation. Thank you for the different times and seasons that call us to pack up, get together, and head down the road, singing, laughing, fussing, arguing, whining, complaining, asking, being denied, eating, and being glad the second time for arriving at destinations! We thank you for living in a country where travel is an option. We appreciate the beauty that we see in all the places that we go. We ask your continued blessings as journeys to see loved ones continue. For we ask and receive these blessings in the name of the One who journeyed from heaven to earth, back again, and is going to journey to earth again, soon, and accompany us all home!

PRAYER FOCUS: Those on journeys and trips

THE NAME IS ZANNIE

She is affectionately known around our town as Rev. Z. Zannie Mitchell is an itinerant elder in the African Methodist Episcopal Church. She is a wife, a mother, a grandmother, and the adopted mother of two special needs young people. She is one of the most energetic people I have ever known. And, like her name, she is a completely crazy woman!

She's crazy about family. She took care of her ill mom at home until she died. She's crazy about her spouse of many years, Leroy. Three years ago, he begin to exhibit signs of Alzheimer's disease. When the doctor had him admitted to a nursing home, Zannie brought him back home to take care of him until he died. She has an adult daughter who has special needs. Zannie helps her with shopping and cleaning so that she can live on her own. Zannie has four other children and biological grandchildren to see about. Her home is a way station, filled with hospitality.

Rev. Z is crazy about her ministry and her church work. No one can be sick or hospitalized without her going to visit and to pray. She's known for carrying home-cooked food as well as the Communion elements along on visits. She's crazy about her community, especially the youth. When her denomination began the campaign for One Church, One Child, she jumped right on board. Approaching the upper end of midlife, with all of her children being adults, Rev. Z shocked us all by adopting two little children. They both have special needs. It's no wonder that she's crazy about praying. Her praying spot is at her kitchen window as she washes dinner dishes. She says that God meets her there. Isn't that crazy?

For years Zannie kept her hair a flaming red. It suited her personality. She's a woman who loves sharp clothes and practices the ministry of a pretty woman. She's a delightful, cheerful, and faith-filled woman of God. You can't whine, moan, or complain around Zannie. She won't tolerate it. You can't get away with the "poor me" syndrome. She won't put up with it. You can't feel sorry for yourself around Zannie. She won't play that game. She has gone through hell several times and keeps a smile on her face. She is loaded to the gills at present, but you will never hear a word of complaint from her mouth. She will offer to pray for you, provide counsel in your time of distress, and bring you joy when you're down. All the time she's dealing with the constantly demanding changes that these two teenagers bring into her life.

She's a grandmother who has willingly become a parent the second time around. She's in the PTA. She's at Sunday school. She's at Youth Group. She's at Easter and Christmas programs. She's at Youth Choir rehearsals. She's at Youth Ushers meetings. She's baking for the schools. She's shopping for school clothes and uniforms. She's keeping doctor and dentist appointments for the children. She's all the way involved in their lives. She's a positive influence, an excellent role model, and the paragon of a virtuous woman! I nominate her for Mother of the Century. She's Zannie. She's genuine. She's real!

> Who can find a virtuous woman? Her price is far above rubies . . . The heart of her husband safely trusts in her so he will have no lack . . . Her children rise up and call her blessed; give her the works of her hands and let her own works praise her in the gates. —Proverbs 31:10–31 (selected portions)

Nurturing God, let the "Zannies" of this world know their worth to you and others. Crown them with wisdom, compassion, love, and strength. Let the love they give be doubly multiplied as it returns, we pray in the name of the Risen Christ. Amen.

Prayer focus: The hands that rock the cradles of the world

44

SEEKING TREASURES?

*T*he holiday catalogs are coming fast and furious through the mail. Almost daily there is a new one to grab our attention and to capture our fancy and to cause us to want to pull the credit card out, charge it, and help out the slumping economy, while we put ourselves in further debt! The Nieman Marcus catalog seems to get more and more ridiculous by the year. The offering for "the man who has everything" is his own helicopter at the "mere" price of what it would take to feed three high schools for the next five years! If you are seeking treasures, hold on, they will certainly show up in some catalog!

As we approach the season of seeking treasures for our loved ones, it is a time to be reminded that love and time are the best gifts we can give one another. Martha Stewart took a survey the first week of the year, with a camera crew, of children in downtown New York. The question she asked was, "What did you get for Christmas?" The sad response was that almost 90 percent of the children could not remember.

For we give toys, trinkets, and junk to them all year long. They are trained and programmed to get "things" with their kids' meals at the fast food places. So toys, trinkets, and junk excite us! Children pretend on Christmas morning that they are thrilled, excited, happy, and pleased for us! Two or three days later, the stuff we bought is found on the floor, under the bed, or thrown in the closet—and the first credit card bill has not yet been printed or delivered!

Think about it. What did you get for Christmas last year? What did you give your significant others last year? Have you seen it lately? Is it paid for already? Are you yet paying the credit card interest on something that has been relegated to the back of the closet or the garage? The question has been asked in recent years, "Whose birthday is it anyway?" Why are we giving gifts to each other?

YES! I am guilty of being caught up in the gift buying, gift giving, and gift charging madness. I will not tell a lie! However, I am slowing down and pulling back and learning a different approach to this holy season. For the greatest gift is Love. And Love doesn't come wrapped in pretty paper and bows. Love was given unto us at Christmas. All the seeking that we do, all the exchanging of things we are involved in will not make up the difference if Love is absent!

Our mental programming has been done by a culture that seeks to tell us that we can buy and sell Love. Our social culture says that through a catalog we can make up for being absent, not giving proper attention, and not making time to reach out and touch others through the year. The children in our lives need us to be about ensuring that our relations are right with the Gift of Christmas and then sharing, spreading, and seeking to "gift" that Love to them and the others in our lives.

It is no surprise that my working in missions for such a long time has helped to change my priorities and my catalog shopping sprees. There are too many lonely, hungry, hurting people in the world for me to spend needless money trying to impress my family with "things" if I have not evidenced love to them during the year. We have put a limit on the number of things Giraud receives at Christmas. Chuck and I exchange pajamas, a lounging set, or robes to encourage our spending the full day in the house as family.

It is becoming easier for me to toss the catalogs in the garbage before I sit down and allow my fleshly lust for things to take its grip in my spirit. For I admit that I am tempted and will "go there" if I don't train my will not to even look! Our traditions have a stranglehold on us. It requires the power of the Holy Spirit to break this economic stronghold in our life.

Take a different look at the way your family honors Christ's love this year. Take some of that "stuff" back and have it credited to your account. Give out "coupons" for bowling dates during January. Give out "coupons" for the movies or babysitting for a couple or a single mom. Include some single person in your Holy Day festivities. Go, take the whole family, and serve at a mission or shelter. Love is active. It's not wrapped in tinsel and glitter. Love is wrapped up in you and me. This is good enough!

Seek first the Realm of God and right living, and all the other things will be given unto you as well. —MATTHEW 6:33

Giver of Every Good and Perfect Gift, hear the anxious desires of our hearts. It's not that we want to spend money, it's just the way we have been taught! Teach us new lessons. Old dogs can learn new tricks! It's been proven. And we are willing to learn. Write new agendas upon our hearts. Give us new scripts to live by as we come to see ourselves as gifts to the world! Thank you for the precious gift of your only begotten Son, in whose name we pray.

PRAYER FOCUS: Those who don't know they are the gift

L IVING FOR THE C HILD

I pray for each of us a Mary's Christmas! That time and space where the Christ is welcomed afresh and anew. I wish for each of us that excitement and anticipation of opening our treasures before him, for use in the days to come. I wish for us a Mary's Christmas, where the power of the Holy Spirit overshadows us and makes us pregnant with the new and "never been done that way before" experience! I wish for us a Mary's Christmas, where some "Elizabeth" will be there to help see us through the dismal days of trying to figure out what in the world is going on in our lives. I wish for us a Mary's Christmas, where her song of wonder and delight simply bursts forth from your lips as you reflect, recall, and remember that Jesus Christ was born to die for your sin.

By now, we have already done the Christmas thing. I pity the fool who waited until the last minute trying to "catch" a bargain. The official, legal holiday is about ready to be packed up, put away, stored, or trashed until we begin the cycle of "seek and find" again next year after Thanksgiving. Early in October when the J.C. Penney catalog arrives, we give Giraurd instructions to go through and mark and number his selections. Some years ago, we burst the mythical lie about some ancient white man delivering trinkets down our chimney. Giraurd is fully aware that if "Santa Penney's" doesn't have what he wants, it won't be under the tree.

Being a computer literate child, by the end of October, he has generated a computer list that provides us with page number, item number, item name, and price . Being the efficient "Grand" mother that I am, all of his stuff is ordered and put away before the "it's not in stock, may we back order it for you?" song begins. Wouldn't you know that by mid-December, Lil Brother will come with another, "really, really want" list? Sorry Giraurd! Wait until your birthday. Know that it will have changed again by then!

As parents, we have lived up to and surpassed the "legal, normal and customary" duties toward this child for Christmas. Much of the "stuff and things" that he orders will not be as exciting as he thought. Come "clean and toss day" in the spring, many of those items will be taken to the Goodwill. Wouldn't it be nice if when we took down the Christmas tree, put away the twinkling lights, and finished eating all the leftovers our obligations would be complete until the next holiday? It simply doesn't work that way. For all of our year is dedicated to living for the child.

The Christ Child came. The Christ Child now lives in each one of us called by his name. The Christ Child continues to seek hearts to serve as mangers and lives to model his transforming witness in their daily lives. The Christ Child's Advent calls us to live every day as Christmas! For there are too many folks yet declaring, "No room in this inn!" So, my friends, Christmas is not over for me or for you.

We live for the Christ Child who grew into a powerful, life-giving man of color. We live for the Christ Child who grew, went about doing good, and allowed the dominant culture to put him to death on Calvary's tree for our sin. We live for the Christ Child who rose with victory over sin, death, and hell from the grave to provide us salvation and at-one-ment with the Ancient of Days. We live for the Christ Child who sent the Holy Spirit to abide in us, work on us, work through us, and, sometimes, in spite of us, to make us aware of the Christ Child in every little child!

Each of us is a child of promise and hope. Each of us is a child of pregnant possibility. Each of us is a child born with a divine destiny. The child in each one of us continues to live. We must nurture, feed, protect, and build that child up on a consistent basis. For the Christ Child must be affirmed daily! We are forced to see the Child in those we are in relationship with. We must see the Child in those who need more than the "stuff and things" we purchase for them.

Thank God for the Wise Ones who came, living for the Child, bearing gifts of gold, frankincense, and myrrh. The gifts were not ordered through Penney's or over the internet, but were brought forth with care and symbolism that remain in our collective memories. Their gifts were their personal treasures. They were offered freely.

Gold was for recognition that the Child was a King. The Child was born to reign throughout eternity as the Sovereign. Because the Child was born into poverty among stinking animals and lived his life in a stinky environment, among stinky people who handed him over to the dominant culture to be crucified, the Wise Ones presented him with frankincense. This sweet smelling tree resin, from a sturdy balsam tree, signified the Child's coming to offer each of us release from stinky living. The myrrh, from a shrub, was a fragrant ingredient used for embalming. For the Child was born to die!

Every child comes to earth bearing the seal of the Child of God. Every child comes to earth with the Light within them. Every child deserves people who will see them and delight in them. Every child requires adoration, admiration, and praise of those adults responsible for their care. And every child is due the offering of the treasures of ourselves to them freely and lovingly. For every child is a different facet of the love and continued hope of God for this stinky world! Christmas means that God is yet in love with the child in you!

Revel in this fact. Delight in this gift. Bless the Child in you by enjoying this holy season. Covenant to make time to acknowledge and live for the Child throughout the coming year. And always remember that you are God's Beloved Child!

Lo, the star stood over the place where the young child was.
—MATTHEW 2:9

Parent of every child, we come to you with praise and adoration. Thank you for sending Jesus as a child. Thank you for the gift of making mere human beings serve as his earthly parents. Thank you for the gift of him having siblings. Thank you for all that he was taught by living in an earthly home and growing in stature, in wisdom, and in favor with those around him. Thank you that he grew up and made the decision to leave home and venture out in ministry. Thank you that he shared his love through teaching, healing, and feeding. Thank you that he loved little children and drew them unto himself. Thank you that he spent time with both men and women, loving them both the same. Thank you that he made a new family of the disciples. Thank you that he teaches us how to be interdependent upon each other. Thank you that he loved us enough to die for us. Thank you that he rose again as our example of new life in you. Thank you that he sits at your right hand, pleading for us and being our cheerleader in life. Thank you for another opportunity for us to say "Thanks" to Jesus in this precious season. Thank you that we can pray in his matchless name.

PRAYER FOCUS: The Child in each of us

AFTERWORD

*T*hanks for taking this journey of parenting again with me. Thanks for taking on the responsibility for child care again, with me. Thanks for passing up the opportunity to "rest and relax" while little children are in need of our love and care. For we prove to the world that there are serious numbers of us who are more than determined to keep on getting up. I know that God is in the blessing business and we are surely in line for multiple blessings. The Word declares, "Therefore, we do not lose heart . . . for our light affliction, which is but for a moment, is working for us a far more exceeding and eternal weight of glory, while we do not look at the things which are seen, but at the things which are not seen. For the things that are seen are temporary, but the things which are not seen are eternal" (1 Cor. 4:16–18).

Transitions are temporary. They come to pass. One day, too soon, these children will be grown and on their way. Childhood doesn't last. It's a fleeting and temporary season. They will look back at the sacrifices we have made on their behalf and bless us and our memories. So today, I am persuaded that we can buckle down, keep a stiff upper lip, move forward with faith and determination by affirming, "This will soon be over and then I can . . ."!

Go in peace, and the God of Israel grant your petition . . .
—1 SAMUEL 1:17

Shalom, Dear Ones! Giraurd, Mista Chuck, and I pray for you God's very best Shalom!